Victoria Thorn

W9-BWH-169

THE VULNERABLE CHILD

THE VULNERABLE CHILD

What Really Hurts America's Children and What We Can Do About It

Richard Weissbourd

Addison-Wesley Publishing Company
Reading, Massachusetts • Menlo Park, California • New York
Don Mills, Ontario • Wokingham, England • Amsterdam • Bonn
Sydney • Singapore • Tokyo •Madrid • San Juan
Paris • Seoul • Milan• Mexico City • Taipei

Many of the designations used by manufacturers and sellers to distinguish their products are claimed as trademarks. Where those designations appear in this book and Addison-Wesley was aware of a trademark claim, the designations have been printed in initial capital letters.

Library of Congress Cataloging-in-Publication Data

Weissbourd, Rick.
    The vulnerable child : what really hurts America's children
and what we can do about it / Richard Weissbourd.
        p. cm.
    Includes bibliographical references and index.
    ISBN 0-201-48395-5
    1. Child welfare—United States.   2. Problem children—United
States.   3. Problem families—United States.   4. Family policy—
United States. I. Title.
HV741.W32 1996
362.7'6'0973—dc20   95–36789
                                                                    CIP

Copyright © 1996 by Richard Weissbourd

All rights reserved. No part of this publication may be reproduced, stored in a retrieval system, or transmitted, in any form or by any means, electronic, mechanical, photocopying, recording, or otherwise, without the prior written permission of the publisher. Printed in the United States of America. Published simultaneously in Canada.

    Jacket design by Suzanne Heiser
    Text design by Wilson Graphics & Design (Kenneth J. Wilson)
    Set in 10-point New Century Schoolbook by Douglas and Gayle, Ltd.

    123456789–MA–9998979695
    First printing, November 1995

*To Avery,
and to our children
Jake, David, and Sophie*

CONTENTS

A NOTE ON METHODOLOGY

THE STORIES OF CHILDREN HERE ARE PRIMARILY based on interviews that I have conducted over the past ten years. In the late 1980s, I interviewed about one hundred children, mainly seventh and tenth graders in public schools, while working for the Casey Foundation's New Futures Project in Little Rock, Arkansas. I spent a good deal of time with a handful of these children. For this book I also interviewed children and/or professionals working with children in several other parts of the country: Danville, Arkansas; Boston and several towns in the Boston area; New Haven and Rogers, Connecticut; Chicago; New York; Baltimore; and Seattle. As I have noted in the citations, several descriptions of families and programs are based on interviews conducted by students at the Kennedy School of Government.

All of the stories here are based on the lives of actual children, but the names of the children have been changed to protect confidentiality. In many cases other identifying details, such as the names of neighborhoods or towns, have been changed as well. In some cases the names of parents, professionals, and agencies have also been changed to protect children's and families' anonymity.

ACKNOWLEDGMENTS

THIS BOOK RELIES ON THE EXPERIENCE OF MANY parents and children who were willing to disclose difficult details of their lives but requested anonymity. Special thanks to the family I have called the Morans, who excavated one painful memory after another, motivated by the simple wish that others might benefit from their experience.

This book began as a joint project with Mary Jo Bane. Although she moved to New York and then Washington, her influence on this project remains profound. Many of the ideas, especially in the first chapter, are hers, and her judgments about what this book should highlight and how it should be shaped have been keen and unerring. Even in her absence, I have held as a model her compassion for children and her great intellectual integrity.

Several students provided research help. Teresa Eckrich Sommer's excellent interviews and research skills helped launch this book. Lisa Hicks worked with me during the longest and most difficult stage of writing, and this book has benefited enormously from her great competence and intelligence. Patricia Savage very skillfully assisted me through the latter stages and was a pleasure to work with. Rosemarie Day provided valuable assistance early on, and Stephanie Fuerstner's unfailing good spirits and research skills mercifully kept the last stage of this book from dragging on. Amy Taylor both provided valuable research help and shared her wonderful intuitions about children.

Several friends contributed to this book. The ideas presented here are far stronger because of my ongoing conversations with a remarkable human being, Ron David, and many of the ideas evolved in a course we teach together at the Kennedy School of Government. Every writer should have a great friend and colleague like Martha Minow—constantly encouraging, constantly generous, constantly wise. Joseph Finder, too, has been remarkably supportive and generous, and has been a valuable guide in almost every aspect of writing and publishing a book. Tom Davey has a great book about American children in him, but in the meantime he encouraged and strengthened this one. Naomi Goldstein's great resourcefulness and judgment have helped move this book along from start to finish. Melissa Roderick understood and supported my research from the beginning, and has a gift for seeing children from many different angles and disciplines. Tom Joe and Cheryl Rogers provided helpful feedback on drafts; much more, my work is built on basic truths about social policy I learned while working for them fifteen years ago. Many other friends came through at key moments. Thanks especially to Paul Jargowsky, Jan Linowitz, Neal Michaels, Jesse Solomon, Virginia Knox, and Tom Kane. Thanks to Julie Wilson and Frank Hartmann for providing me with a home for writing this book, and thanks to the entire staff of New Futures for Little Rock Youth, for their kindness when I was away from home.

My parents and siblings have each given helpful feedback, and in no small measure this book has been influenced by my brother Bob's work in low-income urban communities and by my mother's wonderful work in the fields of early childhood and family support.

My agent, Doe Coover, has my great gratitude for keeping faith in me through thick and thin over many years, and for representing this book so adeptly. My fine editor William Patrick managed to be both calming and stubbornly insistent that I scrape away clichés and clutter.

Many other people facilitated the writing of this book. I thank Davis Ayres, Manual Batista, Deborah Belle, Fran Collins, Don Crary, Don Davies, Josh Dohan, Peggy DiCouri, John Donnelly, Robert Dorwart, Felton Earls, Richard Elmore, Ron Ferguson, Rob Fladger, Tom Flanagan, Dan Frank, Margaret Gallagher, Sid Gardner, Jack Geiger, Olivia Golden, Janet Gornick, William Harris, Gerald Hass, Toby Herr, Jody Heymann, Sally Jacobs, Christopher Jencks, Paul Johnston, David Kennedy, John Kyle, Sarah Lay, Melinda Leonard, Ruth Levy, Tom Loveless, James Mahfus, Ann Maillet, Kim Marshall, Will McMullen, Stephen Brion Meisels, Jacob Murray, Gil Noam, Ellen O'Brien, Ann Piehl, Ann Peretz, Harold Pollack, Betsy Pratt, Mary Quinn, Mamphela Ramphele, Beverly Rimer, Verdell Roberts, Harold Richman, Anna Rodriguez, Christine Roderick, Tom Roderick, Desiree Roderick, Dennis Rorie, Dan Rothstein, Luz Santana, Audrey Saxton, Lisbeth Schorr, Joyce Seltzer, Robert Slavin, Douglas Staiger, Cindy Taylor, Tram Tran,

Jane Waldfogel, Ron Walker, Gloria White-Hammond, Carl Willis, Alice Wolf, Peggy Wyoskus, Diane Zaccheo, Ed Zigler, and Barry Zuckerman.

As always, my most profound thanks go to my wife, Avery Rimer, who waded through innumerable drafts, who shared her great wisdom about children, who gracefully punctured my dumb ideas, who has an uncommon capacity to support and find gratification in the enthusiasms and accomplishments of other human beings. This book about children has deep roots in our life together and in the first, great years of our children's lives. I owe it to her and to them, every inch of the way.

PART I

So all that is in her will not bloom—
but in how many does it?

Tillie Olsen

1

WHAT EVER HAPPENED TO HUCKLEBERRY FINN?

MICHAEL MORAN WAS NINE YEARS OLD. Straight, thick brown hair fell over his forehead, and he had the beginnings of sideburns. When he walked his upper body pitched forward slightly, as if he were walking uphill. He was gangly, and he had an almost frightening amount of energy. Often he chattered, his delicate hands slightly fluttering or buried self-consciously in his pockets. He wore Kmart gym shoes and sweatpants and T-shirts emblazoned with comic-strip heroes. To his mother, Cora, and her friends he was an unusually trusting, extremely bright child. At age two he spelled Budweiser on a beer can. By age nine he seemed to have an adult understanding of the world. "He dazzled people," his mother recalls.

But to other children he was no wonder. Michael was awkward with them, an awkwardness that was complicated by a learning disability. Cora remembers watching the young faces screw up in disdain as Michael, feeling ill at ease, told stories that were too long or interrupted other children at the wrong time. By the time he was seven, for reasons he did not understand, he was tagged "nerd," "fag," and "bucky," a reference to his large front teeth.

It was 1986, and Michael had just moved with Cora and his younger brother, Joe, from a largely poor and working-class neighborhood in Malden, a town outside Boston, to Ferguson, a mostly middle-class Boston suburb. Michael had lived in Malden his entire childhood, staying in the same home even after his father, Bill, left the family. His parents' marriage had only lasted three years. When Michael was two, Cora discovered that Bill was having an affair. She kicked him out of the house, and he vanished for good. Cora managed to keep the house, but everything else seemed to slip out of her grasp. She tumbled onto welfare and found herself in a life she had never imagined, struggling to meet her children's simplest needs. She improvised. She used dish towels for diapers. Many days Michael and Joe went to sleep hungry. She found herself anxious and distracted or hovering around Michael and Joe, worried by minute signs of distress. About two years after the divorce she found a job, but she did not earn enough money to escape poverty.

Since his birth, it seemed to Cora, Michael had had to endure one trial after another. When she returned home from the hospital after delivery, she became profoundly depressed. She knew that these were the "new baby blues," that her hormones were turning against her, but it was weeks before she could stop crying all the time. Michael was colicky his first four months, and from two months to nine months he suffered from a stomach disorder that caused him to vomit with great force. Cora also questioned her own parenting. She was approaching motherhood, she chided herself, as if she were getting a Ph.D. She read voraciously: books would be for her children a kind of inoculation. But all this deference to the developmental experts at times made her mothering mechanical—she found herself going against her own instincts—and she still worried almost ceaselessly, calling her pediatrician at least four times a week.

Despite these problems, Michael's early years were not unhappy. Pictures of him at six months show a narrow, radiant face and a wide, heartbreaking smile. When Michael was not physically uncomfortable, Cora recalls, he was nearly always smiling, patting, laughing, bubbling, churning out new sounds. When he was one year old he seemed to have boundless energy and curiosity, and in the neighborhood he became a kind of ambassador, always finding ways to engage strangers. Yet after Bill vanished it seemed to Cora that Michael gradually became more guarded and unsure. By the time he entered nursery school he was unable to settle down and had difficulty finding his footing with other children. He was diagnosed as hyperactive.

To Michael, the new neighborhood seemed like another country entirely. In his old neighborhood, it had been hard to find a square foot of grass. Here he lived on top of a wooded hill, and nearby there was a community swimming pool. Yet his new apartment was cramped, and he found himself alternately excited about making new friends and terrified that he would again be tormented. Nearly every night for a week after the move he woke up in the middle of the night and sat in the living room, wondering how he should approach other children.

Within two weeks, he was being teased again. First one boy started tormenting him, then others, all part of the same clique, joined in. In addition to the usual names, he was called a grub and a "welly"—a reference to welfare—because he wore clothes from Kmart and came from Malden, which was perceived as a poor town. Growing up in Malden among other poor children, he had never thought of himself as poor.

When school started it seemed to Michael that his tormentors multiplied. Twice when his teacher left the room the teasing became so intense that he took refuge in a coat closet. One week he was stalked by three boys, who trailed him in the halls, hooting deliriously, insulting him, pushing him hard in the back. After school one day he found himself a kind of prisoner in the school building as these boys waited outside. When he did venture out he spotted three bicycle tires behind a tree and narrowly escaped an ambush.

The teasing broke down Michael's concentration in class. Back in Malden, he had spent most of his school day in a special education classroom, where he had worked hard to focus. Recognizing his progress, the Ferguson school system placed him in a regular classroom. Yet now, preoccupied with warding off insults, he found himself unable to follow simple instructions. Moreover, for the first few months of school his teacher, William Barkeley, did not even know that Michael had a learning disability; he had never seen Michael's school records. Michael felt as if he was "getting blasted" with information that he could not absorb. When Barkeley eventually called Cora Moran about Michael's difficulties, she could tell he was badly confused. "Michael seems like a bright boy," he said. "Why does he have so much trouble staying with his assignments?"

Every day Michael would report on his day to his mother in clear terms. "I hate school. The kids all tease me, and I don't want to go back." When Cora insisted he return, he felt that she, too, had turned against him.

Cora did not know how to help Michael defend himself or to whom to turn for help. She thought about talking to some of the parents of Michael's peers about the teasing, but she feared being branded in the neighborhood as a difficult parent with a problem child. After Barkeley told her that he did not know that Michael had been a special education student, she thought that she could diagnose at least part of the problem and that Barkeley and she could plot some solution. She also considered quitting her job so that she could be home for Michael after school. Soon after the move she had struggled hard to land a job. She hated being on welfare, and she felt that welfare was a scarlet letter in Ferguson. But sending Michael to her mother's house after school, where he watched television, was not going to be part of the solution, and Michael was now beseeching her to stay home. He told her flatly that he was near his breaking point. On a few occasions he even talked with distressing earnestness about wanting to end his life.

One day Cora received a call from Barkeley, who sounded at the end of his rope. Barkeley told her that Michael was under a desk and that all his coaxing could not bring him out. Michael's hands were over his ears, and he was screaming, "Go away." Michael recollects that around this time his real troubles began, troubles that would take years to resolve.

———————□———————

For decades Americans have been pelted with images of disadvantaged children. Though these images arise from many sources, they reflect common assumptions. Disadvantaged children, conventional wisdom has it, come from poor and broken homes. They are commonly neglected or abused, and they—or their parents—often abuse drugs. Most are African-American and live in ghetto neighborhoods. The future for these children is dark and virtually sealed: it is now widely assumed that most disadvantaged children are destined to fail in school, become parents too early, land in jail, neglect or abuse their own children, and drift in and out of employment or never take home a decent wage at all. Most will be poor their entire lives, and their children will be cemented into poverty. When Americans think about disadvantaged children, they do not think of Huck Finn, that quintessentially American boy, homeless, beaten, and abandoned though he was. For some Americans, disadvantaged children conjure up a nightmare image of pregnant, crack-addicted African-American girls, and marauding, Uzi-toting African-American boys.

Many of these images are rooted in certain truths—growing up poor can make childhood miserable and the climb into adulthood steep. The destructive repercussions of poverty and growing up in a single-parent family are felt every day by children like Michael and his brother, Joe. But most of these images provide only partial truths—and sometimes they mangle the truth entirely. For example, the great majority of poor children, like Michael and Joe, are not ghetto dwellers. Most poor children do not seriously abuse drugs or commit crimes. Large numbers of children prevail in the face of crushing poverty or despite the drug addictions of parents.

Moreover, these prevailing conceptions of disadvantage are far too narrowly drawn. Poverty hurts children such as Michael in a range of subtle ways that have nothing to do with neglect or abuse. And a good deal of evidence suggests that most vulnerable children are not poor. Although the national debate on improving children's prospects is now focused on poverty and single-parent families, poverty and single parenthood are only two of many hardships that undercut children. Whether parents are chronically stressed or depressed often more powerfully influences a child's fate than whether there are two parents in a home or whether a family is poor. Millions of children are hurt because they or their parents, like Cora Moran, are marooned in their communities. Many children are hurt because their parents, although they belong to communities, are scapegoated or play other negative roles. Many children are damaged, like Michael, by serious peer problems. Frequent residential mobility undermines large numbers of children as well. Perhaps most often, children are vulnerable because of a chain of interactions involving their own attributes and the attributes of their families, schools, and communities. Michael did not end up screaming under his desk simply because he had a peer problem. His peer problems were intricately tied to his learning disability, his temperament, his developmental stage, and his poverty; and his difficulties managing his peer problems were intricately tied to the demands on his mother and to the inability of his teacher and his school to deal with his troubles.

This book is about the true nature of childhood vulnerability. It shows how such concepts as the underclass badly distort the experience of poor children, African-American children, and vulnerable children. It reaches beyond the categories currently used to understand childhood vulnerability, categories that have brutally polarized Americans, such as race, the underclass, and single parenthood. It identifies instead the conditions that all children need in order to prosper and the circumstances that threaten these conditions.

To be protected from destruction all children, minimally, should live in environments that provide some order and meet their basic physical and material needs. All children should have a continuous relationship with a consistently attentive and caring adult who treats them as special—not as just another inhabitant of this world—who is able to stimulate and engage, who provides appropriate responsibilities and challenges, who passes on important social and moral expectations. Some strong friendships and the affirmation and affection of community adults are often critical to children, especially those who are deprived of the consistent presence of a parent or guardian. All children should have freedom from exploitation and discrimination in their communities, some sense of the justice of their world, and opportunities in school and in communities for constructive achievement. Many children also need special health, social, and educational services to deal with inherited and acquired ailments and disabilities. When children have these ingredients, they are likely to have trust in themselves and in the world, inner vitality and resourcefulness, and the capacity in adulthood for zestful play and for gratifying work and love even if they suffer hardships and abrasions.

Children who grow up without these ingredients are clearly not African-American children or underclass children or children in single-parent families only. Looking at children in terms of these ingredients forces policy makers and the public to widen their field of vision to encompass all poor children, including poor white children and children from diverse ethnic groups. Looking at children in this way forces policy makers and the public to see the many vulnerable children in this country who are not poor. Stresses on parents, limited opportunities for meaningful accomplishment, peer problems, the absence of adults in the community, and learning and other disabilities are among the pervasive problems that hurt children in every race and class.

These problems must be at the core of a nationwide agenda that unites Americans in improving the prospects of all children. Given the serious plight of ghetto children, we surely need to devote greater public resources to meeting their needs than to meeting those of other children. But developing an agenda for all children is good politics—it creates larger constituencies for children's programs—and it reflects reality. Children in jeopardy—dazed, distressed, uprooted children—are not *their* children. These children can be found on every patch of earth in the United States. They are *our* children.

Beyond identifying the general conditions that all children need in order to grow, this book identifies the many interacting factors that explain why an individual child is vulnerable. Those who care about children need to move beyond seeing individual children as bundles of risk factors or as victims or victimizers, abbreviations and stereotypes that reflect little about an individual child's life. In addition to creating environments that provide children with the basic conditions for healthy growth, policy makers and caregiving professionals need a more dynamic and complex model of childhood vulnerability to help them understand how an individual child interacts at different developmental stages with families, schools, and communities that have their own constellations of strengths and weaknesses. Looking at children in terms of these interactions also clearly shows that children are not typically doomed because of poverty or other risk factors at early ages. Nor can children be inoculated at early ages against all the various hardships that later stages of life can bring. Children commonly flourish in certain stages of development while struggling in others, and there are many pathways to both healthy and unhealthy adult life.

Finally, this book provides concrete strategies for improving the prospects of vulnerable children. Many Americans have become bitter and fatalistic about children in this country. Yet the irony is that as public confidence has plunged, it has become possible to identify the tools needed to turn around the lives of vulnerable children. A great deal is now known about how to meet the basic needs of all children, about how health-care agencies, schools, police forces, and other institutions can turn the negative interactions that undermine individual children into cycles of success, and about how communities can support children along the various pathways to gratifying adulthood.

Poverty:
Quiet Catastrophes

It would be perverse to suggest that the problems of gang violence and drugs among ghetto children are not extremely serious or that the number of such children is insignificant. It is equally perverse, however, for these children—paraded on talk shows, dissected in scores of conferences on the underclass, and subjects of so much voyeuristic fascination—to symbolize poor children in the United States and to dominate debates about solutions to poor children's problems. To understand childhood vulnerability, it is important to understand who poor children are and how poverty affects them.

Many Americans define poverty simply as living in a poor neighborhood or belonging to a mythologized underclass or "culture of poverty" that is populated with long-term welfare recipients who have lost their moral bearings. Strictly speaking, however, poverty means inadequate income, and families without sufficient means are extremely diverse. In 1993, 22 percent of all children under 18 lived in families with incomes below the federally established poverty line—which was then about $14,764 for a family of four. The conditions of children in these families vary in almost every conceivable respect: in the length of time they are poor, in the circumstances and quality of their families' lives, in the work patterns of their parents, in the circumstances of their communities, in the nature of their problems.

Rather than plotting monolithic solutions to the problems of poor children based on such notions as the underclass, we have to begin to see poor children as distinct individuals who have poverty in common, but who struggle in very different ways. For example, a child such as Michael Moran is *not* born into a poor family that belongs to a culture of poverty. He and other children tumble into poverty from many rungs of the economic ladder—and their parents are usually not long-term welfare recipients.

The great majority of poor children are only poor temporarily. Whereas about 8 percent of American children are poor for more than six years, more than 30 percent of children suffer poverty at some point in their lives. These bouts with poverty take their toll. Michael and Joe were jeopardized in their early years because Cora was suddenly dumped into poverty and humiliating welfare dependency, hampering her ability to parent effectively. In the last three decades, huge numbers of skilled workers laid off because of factory and farm closings, divorced middle-class mothers, and ousted professionals have suffered downward mobility, a sudden and severe loss of income, creating unfamiliar physical and emotional burdens for their children. Like Michael Moran, these children often must face the daily indignities of all kinds of overt and unspoken comparisons with better-off peers. "Poor children are scum," a high school student announced to me in Fall River, Massachusetts, well within earshot of a poor child. In Little Rock, graffiti on a school-bathroom wall reads: "I like myself because I'm not poor." Because of their parents' sudden poverty, some children are forced to move to new neighborhoods that lack good schools and accustomed amenities. Their parents, too—as Katherine Newman documents in her book *Falling from Grace*—are often reeling. Some parents go to great lengths to disguise their poverty and lack coping capacities and survival skills. Because downwardly mobile families often camouflage their poverty and poverty-related problems, such as malnutrition, these problems are often not detected by health-care providers and other professionals.

Concepts such as that of the underclass similarly obscure the particular problems of children whose parents work. There is a deeply held faith in the United States, virtually a covenant, that if you work you are not poor. Poor parents are seen as choosing or at least tolerating a life on the dole. Yet the truth is that large numbers of poor parents, like Cora Moran, move back and forth between work and welfare, and many poor parents stay in jobs that never allow them to clear the poverty line. About half of poor children live with a parent who works. These children, too, often suffer serious hardships. Poor mothers who work frequently have great difficulty productively filling the void that their absence creates for their children. Cora Moran vacillated between welfare and work because she knew that Michael needed close adult attention after school and she could not afford a good after-school program for him. Children of poor working parents are more likely to be deprived of other key ingredients of growth, including decent medical attention. They are six times more likely than welfare children to lack health-insurance coverage (welfare recipients are automatically eligible for Medicaid) and are twice as likely to lack a source of routine medical and dental care. Because Cora Moran did not receive dental coverage for her family when she worked, she was unable to have Michael's buck teeth fixed, even though other children teased him mercilessly about this defect. Katherine, a five-year-old girl described by Sylvia Ann Hewlett in her book *When the Bough Breaks*, fell frequently because her parents could not afford corrective shoes.

Poor children vary perhaps most widely in their living conditions, variations that are entirely obscured by the concept of the underclass. It is one thing to be a poor African-American teenager in a Boston ghetto who has few job opportunities and wrestles with a learning disability; it is quite another to be a poor child living in the hollows of eastern Kentucky and suffering from chronic hunger and untreated illness; or a newly arrived Cambodian girl in rural Arkansas who is resented in her community because her parents seem to be displacing local workers; or a white sixteen-year-old girl who has left her suburban home and now barely survives as a prostitute and drug pusher on the streets of Seattle; or Michael, ostracized in a middle-class suburban neighborhood. Only 17.5 percent of poor children live in a ghetto neighborhood; the remainder are distributed fairly evenly among urban stretches outside ghettos, in suburbs, and in nonmetropolitan areas. Nor do the majority of African-American children live in ghettos: only about 19 percent of African-American children reside in ghettos.

Perhaps most serious, the concept of the underclass makes no allowance for variation in the nature of the problems of poor children and forces attention away from problems that typically deprive poor children of basic needs. As serious as neglect and abuse, crime, gangs, and teen pregnancy are, these are not the most common problems afflicting poor children. Even in ghetto areas, the problems are more often quietly corrosive, devoid of the drama of gangs and serious abuse and far less threatening to mainstream Americans.

Consider the children in Mary Martinez's first-grade classroom in Lawrence, Massachusetts, a city of 60,000 about thirty miles north of Boston. In the last two decades, Lawrence, once powered by large textile and shoe-making industries, has been dragged into a muck of poverty and despair. In 1991, forty-five percent of Lawrence's children lived below the poverty line. A lucrative drug culture has sprung up, and crime is pervasive. The children in Martinez's class hail from a neighborhood that has been especially hard hit. Twenty-two of Martinez's 24 schoolchildren are poor.

One child in Martinez's classroom is suffering from a number of dramatic problems. Hector, an artistically talented child with an impish smile, often comes to school dirty and hungry and is a small cyclone of disruptive activity in class. He regularly hits other children and is sexually explicit and provocative—at times he upsets his classmates by jutting out his rear end. His teacher worries that he has been sexually abused. Another first-grade boy, Anthony, is also often visibly distracted and upset in class. He knows only a few phrases in English, but "freebase" is one of them. Mary Martinez has met his parents and is worried that they are selling drugs. She is especially concerned that this six-year-old boy has been enlisted in their drug business. Recently, he has shown her how to weigh cocaine.

Children such as Hector and Anthony operate like brushfires in a classroom, igniting other children and engulfing the energies of their teachers. They require constant vigilance: they are always in the center of their teachers' "radar screens." A larger number of children float in and out of Mary Martinez's screen. These children have quieter troubles that demand less of her, but that also choke their ability to learn. Several children are sometimes distracted because they are hungry. Almost half the children, she estimates, sometimes come to school upset or don't come at all because they don't have the right clothes. Sheila, a thin, pale, pretty child, does not have socks some days. Aaron comes to school in the winter without a coat, and another boy often wears the same dirty T-shirt for several days in a row. Some of Mary Martinez's students are disoriented and out of sorts in class because they have been shuffled between homes, between schools, and between neighborhoods too often, or because they have moved back and forth between Lawrence and the Dominican Republic two or three times during the year. Geographic mobility among poor children is extremely high. Although Mary Martinez has had a relatively constant class size of about twenty-two children, thirty-nine children have been in her class at some point this year. Not even the schoolroom can be counted on for sameness and stability in the lives of these children.

Some quieter difficulties become louder, of course, when children enter middle school and high school, and sex and drugs and gangs press upon their lives. But many of the troubles that older children face are also surprisingly quiet and banal when compared with the media-touted images that form the basis of current policy debates. Many older students from poor families drop out, for example, because of economic stresses and constraints on their parents: these children need to generate income for their families, or take care of a sick relative, or care for a younger sibling if their parents can't afford day care. A survey of high school students in Little Rock;

Savannah, Georgia; and Dayton, Ohio, found that about 20 percent of students in each city listed "staying home to take care of a family member or close friend" as the reason for missing days at school. In 1992, 12 percent of high school dropouts nationwide reported that they had to care for a family member and 11 percent said that they had to help financially support their families (these groups overlap, since respondents could answer yes to more than one question). Family responsibilities that are almost entirely unknown in affluent communities beset large numbers of poor children. Byron, an eighth grader in Boston, arrived at school late one day because he had to take his pregnant mother to the hospital. Many older children suffer just as younger children do—they come to school hungry, they experience various material hardships, they ricochet between homes.

Poverty creates other quiet problems, too. For various reasons, poor children such as Michael Moran are more likely to suffer a wide array of health problems, including obesity, asthma, malnutrition, and physical disabilities. Hearing and vision problems beset many poor children and the principal of a Boston school reports "an almost one-to-one correspondence between kids with vision problems and kids who are failing." There is evidence that early hearing and vision problems are connected to juvenile delinquency as well. Poor children are more likely to be exposed to environmental hazards, such as lead poisoning and dangerous heating systems. For example, children may suffer smoke inhalation or burns in homes heated with stoves or space heaters, and poor families are far less likely than others to have working smoke detectors.

Poverty for many kinds of children—not just those who experience downward mobility—brings quiet forms of shame. Kim Masters, a fourteen-year-old who grew up in Boston, arrives at school upset many days because he has no friends in his shelter and he is ashamed to live there—he does not want other kids to know. Louis, a homeless child from Boston, recently mustered up the courage to take on another twelve-year-old in his class who argued that the children of homeless people should be "put up for adoption and their mothers should be put in hospitals." Sometimes the daily indignities of poverty and health hazards are combined. In a housing project in Newark, New Jersey, some poor families, lacking refrigerators, keep their milk cold by storing it in toilets. Large numbers of poor children also suffer quietly from hopelessness

and fear—including fear of utter destitution and homelessness, the
worry that the wolf is at the door.

Many seemingly small, quiet problems can disrupt poor children's
learning, especially when combined. Overcrowding, utility shutoffs,
and inadequate heating can interfere with homework. Children
may be late for school because they don't have alarm clocks. As
Arloc Sherman of The Children's Defense Fund points out, many
poor families are unable to afford notebooks, textbooks or activities
that promote learning, such as family outings, hobbies, and camps.
Poor children have far less access than others to computers, and,
as Sherman notes, special fees for science labs, art supplies,
team sports, or field trips may be financially out of reach.

Mary Martinez is aware that many of her children are suffering
from one or another of these quiet hardships, yet putting out the
brushfires can take all her attention. Neglect does not get special
attention from her until it becomes severe. Whereas children like
Hector may secure attention because they are provocative or display
directly or symbolically how they have been hurt and abused
(children can be precise, even pedantic, symbolists), the counselor
at Martinez's school worries especially about neglected and abused
children who, instead of acting out, come to school dead to
the world, withdrawn. "Most of the kids I see here are very disturbed and act bizarrely. Some teachers don't notice kids who are
withdrawn, and some don't make anything of it. Withdrawn kids
get zero here. You have to be extraordinarily withdrawn to be
referred to me."

A counselor in an elementary school in the south side of Chicago
put it another way: "It's like an emergency room here. You have
to deal with the person with the heart attack even though someone
else has a broken arm. Kids who are neglected don't get the
attention they need." Whether or not a child's problem is uncovered
also depends on whether a parent has a visible trouble. A child is
likely to get attention if a parent always has alcohol on his or her
breath or comes to a parent-teacher conference on drugs.

When teachers find they cannot attend to or solve problems,
they may stop seeing them. Whole categories of children once
deemed worthy of special attention gradually slip off the screen.

Left unattended, these quiet problems can be devastating in
the long run, resulting in school failure and the problems that
spring from it—frustration, bitterness, alienation, and all too often,

bailing out of school, drug abuse, long-term welfare dependency. The tragedy is that many of these problems are entirely fixable— yet often no one takes responsibility for fixing them. It doesn't require a genius to ensure that children who have vision problems get eyeglasses or that children have clean clothes or adequate school supplies. Rather than focus solely on dramatic solutions to dramatic problems, we would do well to focus on accomplishing the small deeds and prosaic tasks that address these more pervasive threats to children's learning.

Broke but Not Broken: The Positive Fates of Poor Children

The underclass and similar concepts promote another dangerous myth about poor children—that they are doomed to lives of waste and failure, largely because poor parents are incapable of raising their children properly. Such images of poor families are not new. While there has also always been a tendency to romanticize poverty, to find in the poor grace and purity and innocence, these sentiments have long been buried in an avalanche of images of uncared for, benighted poor children. The inside jacket cover of a book by Robert Coles and Maria Piers, published in 1969, describes the poor this way (although the authors sounded the opposite theme): "The Children of the Poor: They endure emotional and physical neglect. Their learning power and will to survive are crippled. They do not know their parents in the same way that ordinary children do." Countless television documentaries evoking the plight of poor families and popular studies demonstrating that poor children are more likely to suffer problems in almost every area of childhood, important as they are, have only reinforced these images.

These stereotypes are so dangerous because they cause poor children to be stigmatized and shortchanged by professionals and other adults with great power over their fates. They lead many professionals to expect little of poor children—and to assume the worst about their parents. In one study, physicians provided with the same description of a child's injuries and the circumstances surrounding it were more likely to determine that the child was abused when told that the child came from a poor family as opposed to a middle-class home. In her book *Lives on the Edge*, Valerie

Polakow describes some teachers who presume that poor children, especially African-American poor children, mean "trouble" and lack creativity, intelligence, and rudimentary social skills. These teachers often blame these deficiencies on parents who lack the discipline to create safe and decent environments for their children. Both parents and children, moreover, are unable to wriggle free of these stereotypes; teachers brush aside information that collides with their presumptions.

Perhaps more often, negative assumptions about poor children take subtler forms. For example, teachers may start the year giving every child an equal opportunity to learn, but then make different attributions about poor children who are having difficulty learning than about middle-class children. A teacher may assume that a poor child has difficulty learning because he or she is poor, but assume that a middle-class child has trouble learning because of the nature of the material or the teaching method. A special education teacher in New York handicaps poor children in another sense: she believes that her poor children are bright, but that because of their poverty she has to baby-sit them and "provide a cocoon to keep them from failing" in order to boost their self-esteem, rather than giving them challenging academic tasks. These biases may undercut poor children in the long run, especially if they cause teachers to shunt the children into special education classes and remedial tracks, or to deny them access to challenging academic programs, based on scant evidence.

Although poor children are more likely to suffer an array of loud and quiet problems, the great majority of poor children are prepared to learn, at least when they begin school. Developmental delays and serious learning difficulties among children ages three to five are higher among poor than among middle- and upper-income children, but more than 90 percent of poor children in this age group are *not* reported by their parents to have serious developmental delays or learning disabilities, and the majority of children who are reported by parents as having such difficulties are not poor. Research suggests that over 75 percent of poor children ages 6–11 have never experienced significant developmental delays, or emotional troubles, or a learning disability in childhood.

Nor does poverty cause violence and crime. Most poor children do not engage in serious drug use—in 1993 about 14 percent of poor teen-agers reported using drugs in the previous year. Although children in ghettos are joining gangs and committing violent crimes in terrifying numbers, talking to professionals working with children in ghetto communities suggests that a substantial majority of ghetto children do nor commit serious violent crimes. Further, only a small fraction of poor children commit violent crimes. Poverty can create family and community stresses that, in combination with other circumstances, may lead to crime. Yet many such stresses are caused by factors other than poverty, and many children cope with family and community pressures without turning to crime.

Research also shows that most poor girls do not become pregnant in their teen years: 85 percent of girls who had been briefly poor did not become pregnant as teenagers, and about 67 percent of persistently poor girls did not have a child before age eighteen; whereas 30 percent of girls who did become pregnant as teens were *never* poor. There was a storm of concern about the spread of teenage pregnancy in the 1980s—and out-of-wedlock teen births have increased in the last few decades—but the reality is that both black and white teenage girls have been having *fewer* babies. Although the number of children born to teens has risen slightly in recent years, teenage girls bore fewer children in 1989 than at any time since 1940.

Whereas a disproportionate number of poor children are neglected and abused, the assumption that poor parents commonly neglect and abuse their children veers from reality. A recent study in Illinois showed that 6 percent of children born in 1988 to parents who were on welfare at some point in the first five years of their child's life were neglected or abused. Based on this sample, it is likely that 10 to 18 percent of poor children (in Illinois) are neglected or abused by their parents at some point in childhood. In addition, the incidence of at least one type of abuse—sexual abuse—appears to be only slightly lower in middle-class than in poor families.

Poor parents are not typically undisciplined or arbitrary, unable to provide structured, consistent, safe, and stimulating environments for their children. Poverty makes providing for the needs of children much harder, but at least one study suggests that most poor parents are able to scratch out adequate living conditions for their children. Many child development researchers assess the quality of the home environment using a checklist called the HOME Inventory, which measures such parameters as the responsiveness of the caregiving parent, the use of restriction and punishment, and the presence of appropriate toys and opportunities for stimulation.

These assessments are made by trained evaluators, who make observations in the home and interview parents. Although the test has methodological flaws and is crude in many respects, it does provide a rough sketch of the strengths and weaknesses of children's environments. The results of the test, administered in a nationally representative sample of homes, indicate that about 11 percent of American children grow up in deficient home environments. Of poor children, about 25 percent live in deficient environments, but 75 percent of poor families manage to maintain decent living conditions despite their poverty. According to these criteria, despite their poverty Cora has managed to maintain decent living conditions for Michael and Joe for most of their childhood. Studies also show that poor parents are responsible in another sense: they buy more nutritional foods than do other Americans. Ethnographic research suggests that even the majority of poor parents who live in ghettos manage to provide the basic ingredients of a healthy home environment.

Clearly, poverty can bedevil children, but most children overcome it, and the hardships they face and the paths they take are extremely diverse. The only thing that poor children have in common is poverty.

African-American Children

There is, of course, another assumption painted into the picture of poor children as ghetto or underclass children—the assumption that most children in the United States who are in trouble are African-American. Many people assume that most poor children are African-American and, conversely, that most African-American children are poor. They also commonly presume that poor African-American children are headed for disaster.

These assumptions are not manufactured out of thin air. African-American children are far more likely to suffer poverty and related problems. Black children are nearly three times as likely as white children to be poor, and they are likely to be poor for much longer. According to 1995 data, black children are nearly six times as likely as nonblack children to be poor for at least eleven years of their childhood. The chances are also astonishingly high that a black child born in the 1990s will spend part of his or her childhood in a single-parent family—nearly 70 percent of black children are now born to single mothers, and perhaps as many as 85 percent spend part of childhood in a single-parent home.

At the same time, poverty and growing up with a single parent are hardly black problems. As sociologist Andrew Hacker notes in his book *Two Nations*, Americans tend to think of white poverty as anomalous, as "atypical and accidental." Even those who concede that white poverty exists often imagine it as a kind of deformity: they conjure up images of imbeciles in bib overalls who live in the hills of Tennessee, or incest-ridden families in pockets of the Deep South, or other white trash stereotypes—overweight, unshaven, liquored-up, lazy, suspicious men and, as writer Randall Kenan puts it, "long-suffering, quickly aging, overly fertile, too-young-marrying, hard-headed women."

White poverty is far from anomalous. In 1993, about 40 percent of poor children were white, about 33 percent black, and about 25 percent Hispanic. The number of poor non-Latino white children (6.3 million) still markedly exceeds the number of poor black children (5.1 million) or poor Latino children (3.9 million). Even if there were no black children in this country, the child poverty rate in the United States would be 18 percent, higher than that of Canada (13.5 percent), France (6.5 percent), Germany (6.8 percent), Sweden (2.7 percent), Italy (9.6 percent), and the United Kingdom (9.9 percent). The number of Hispanic children in poverty is nearly equal to the number of black children in poverty, and Hispanics constitute the fastest growing poverty population. A white child's chances of spending part of childhood in a single-parent family are also high—about 50 percent. As conservative analyst Charles Murray recently observed, the number of white children now born to single mothers —22 percent—is approaching the number of black children born to single mothers in 1965, when Daniel Patrick Moynihan issued his famous report decrying the dissolution of black families. And the large, white, poor population—comprising mostly divorced mothers and their children and two-parent families with at least one wage earner—is, like every large population in this country, enormously varied in its moral and sexual behavior. What the white poor have in common is poverty, not depravity.

Nor are the great majority of African-American children headed for disaster. Many black children, including poor black children, have made significant gains in recent decades, and poor black children fare just as well as their poor white counterparts in important respects—a finding that should give pause to those who hold black culture responsible for failing to motivate or equip black

children. Poor African-American children are no more likely than
their poor white counterparts to drop out of high school. White
teens account for about 67 percent of today's teen dropouts; dropout rates for blacks *fell* from 28 percent in 1970 to 15 percent in
1988. Drops occurred even in ghetto areas. Moreover, dropout rates
for blacks have declined much faster than those for whites. As
sociologist Christopher Jencks puts it, "If not finishing high school
is a good measure of coming from an underclass family... the
underclass is not only getting smaller but getting whiter. Likewise,
if not finishing high school indicates that an individual will grow
up to be part of the underclass, the underclass will be smaller
and whiter tomorrow than it is today." If income is factored in,
African-Americans children are more likely to attend college
than are their white counterparts. Although basic reading levels
for blacks remain abysmally low, these levels have increased in the
last decade. And although black teenagers are more likely to bear
children than are white teenagers, the gap appears not to be
widening, as stereotypes suggest, but narrowing. According to
Jencks, in 1969 a representative sample of 100 black girls would
have had 80 babies by the time they reached the age of twenty. In
the mid-1980s, that number fell to 51. Among whites, the number
dropped from 40 to 21. Poor black children are faring just as well
or better than poor white children in other respects. David Hamburg
observes in his book, *Today's Children*, "when social class is
comparable, there are no differences between blacks and whites in
divorce rates, proportion of births to unmarried mothers, proportions
of children living in female headed families and proportions of
women working outside the home." There is controversy as to
whether, when economic class is taken into account, black
parents are more likely than white parents to physically abuse
their children, but there is strong evidence that black parents are
no more likely—and may be less likely—than white parents to
sexually abuse their children.

And black children certainly do not have a monopoly on
destructive behavior. All the forms of destruction found among poor
black children are found among poor white children who are encased
in extreme poverty—in South Boston, say, and in some all-white
small towns, such as Lewiston, Maine. Though these white communities do not suffer from gang violence on the same scale as
African-American ghetto communities, poor white children are
significantly more likely than nonpoor children to commit violent

crimes. One study in Atlanta indicated that blacks and whites who live in overcrowded homes have similar rates of domestic violence. Comparing this country with other countries further belies the notion that violence is a black problem. Young white males are at least twice as likely to die as a result of homocide in the United States than in other industrialized nations. Also, whites form violent gangs now and have in the past both in the United States and in other countries.

There are very strong reasons to be concerned about pervasive black poverty, but the notion that poverty is a black problem or that cultural deficiencies alone are undermining black children is not supported by the available facts.

Disadvantaged But Not Poor

Every day Sheila Woods, a short, stocky nine-year-old in a Houston school, brings the same meal for lunch: Coke and potato chips. When poor children are not eating well at Sheila's school they are usually detected quickly, their parents are contacted, and efforts are made to enroll them in a school lunch program. But school staff did not discover that Sheila was undernourished for several months because she is not poor. Her father is a lawyer and her mother is a doctor. (The discovery was made only when a staff member happened to see Sheila's lunch one day.)

Understanding the nature of childhood vulnerability in this country means understanding the plight of large numbers of children who are not poor. Even those Americans who do not strictly equate vulnerable children with ghetto or underclass children tend to equate vulnerable children with poor children. To be sure, most Americans at least have an inkling that the problems of American children are not solely the problems of poor children. Reports of affluent suburban children committing suicide, abusing drugs, or withering from neglect have pierced some layer of their consciousness. Many Americans know dimly, if not directly, about legions of latchkey children who come home daily to vacant homes. And many Americans puzzle about how children can suffer who are not poor or spurned or sick or oppressed, who do not lack choice or opportunity.

But circumstances conspire to create a distorted picture of the struggles of nonpoor children and to cause their numbers to be underestimated. Media attention focuses on extreme and flamboyant problems, such as teen suicide, and ignores the quieter learning disabilities and emotional problems that afflict large numbers of middle- and upper-class children. The enormous attention given to demonstrating the ill effects of poverty has also obscured the degree to which certain problems exist in the mainstream. Few Americans would guess that about 65 percent of the children who drop out of school are not poor at the time of dropping out and that the majority of children who drop out of school have *never* been poor. And most Americans simply do not associate certain kinds of problems with middle-class children. Americans seem to have an almost inexhaustible capacity to be shocked by the violence among middle-class children. This innocence was pricked by the 1991 Central Park wilding episode, when it became known that one of the assailants lived in an apartment with a doorman, and by the so-called preppie murder, when a Yale student brutally murdered his girlfriend. In fact, although violence rates are far higher in areas of concentrated poverty, it is hard to enter any high school in this country without coming across children who are violent.

There is, of course, something comforting in thinking of the problems of children as *their* children's problems, children who belong to other neighborhoods, to other cultures, to other economic classes. Robert F. Kennedy once called this conceit "the vanity of our false distinctions among men."

The blindness in this conceit is that millions of children, like Sheila Woods, are disadvantaged—they grow up in home environments that are deficient in one way or another—even though their families are never poor. If poverty were the only problem creating disadvantages for children, at least the goal of public policy would be clear: boost the income of poor families. But increased income will not ensure that parents do what it takes to raise their children properly.

To understand who these nonpoor vulnerable children are and what makes them vulnerable it is important to look closely at the basic home conditions that all children need in order to grow. While at bottom, every child needs a safe environment that meets their physical needs and an adult who is able to provide continuous, caring attention, psychologists can now spell out more exactly the critical qualities of this environment and this attention. Every child should have an adult who considers that child's existence at least as important as his or her own and who has at least a rudimentary understanding of the child's needs. Children need an adult whom they admire and who has some capacity to mirror them, to reflect who they are. Children of all ages should have a variety of opportunities for exploring their environment as well as language models and opportunities to talk with adults. In fact, research shows that when parents talk or sing or play with a young child they are doing something far more important than entertaining: they are providing stimulation that is critical to the development of the basic circuitry of a child's brain. Decent environments not only provide clear discipline and encourage children to absorb basic social expectations and norms; they also give children the kinds of knowledge and skills, the practical strokes—such as how to ask for directions or for change—that will enable them to swim in the mainstream. Parents do not have to be entirely consistent in these respects or perfectly in sync with their children—to develop effective coping strategies, children, in fact, need to learn to manage a certain amount of disappointment and conflict. Parents do have to be what psychoanalyst Donald Winnicott calls "good enough": capable of providing responsiveness at reasonable intervals, so that their children are not forced to endure extended disappointment and frustration.

All these ingredients do not have equal importance, and they interact in complex ways. Long ago Anna Freud observed that children who had sturdy, loving relationships with their parents, for example, could withstand terrible deprivations and traumas. An accurate scale of disadvantage would also be finely tuned according to children's different needs and capacities at different stages in development. Yet the absence of any one of these environmental conditions for a prolonged period at any age can hurt a child, and together these disadvantages can devastate a child.

Poor children are more likely to suffer these disadvantages for all sorts of reasons. It is simply harder for poor parents to provide for their children's material needs and to afford homes and neighborhoods that are safe, and the shame and stresses of poverty can grind away poor parents' responsiveness. Yet large numbers of children who do not receive these basic ingredients of sturdy growth are never poor. According to the HOME Inventory, more than half the children who grow up in a deficient home environment are not poor. According to a similar test, the chances of living in a home with unsafe play areas are far greater for a poor than for a nonpoor preschool child—1 in 6 versus 1 in 14. But a majority of children who live in such homes—60 percent—are not poor.

Further, other hardships may degrade children's environments more seriously than poverty, such as growing up with an uneducated parent. Many people assume that poor parents and uneducated parents are one and the same. Yet about 10 percent of American children live with a mother who is poor but educated, and about 10 percent of children—over 6 million children—live with a mother who has never obtained a high school degree but who is *not* poor. (Another 10 percent of children in the United States, like Michael and Joe, live with a mother who is *both* poor and without a high school degree.) According to the HOME Inventory test, children who grow up with uneducated parents who are not poor are more likely to live in damaging environments than are children who grow up with educated, poor parents. Children who grow up with an uneducated parent also have more school troubles than do children who grow up with poor parents. They are more likely to be in the bottom half of the class and to be retained a grade than are children who are poor only.

Many other sorts of parental troubles and deficits may undermine children more seriously than poverty. Growing up with a poor parent who is consistently loving and attentive might seem like a luxury, for example, to a child growing up with a middle-class single parent who is very depressed, or is constantly wracked by a serious illness, or is sunk in alcoholism, or who is narcissistic and cold.

Tewodros, an earnest, precocious twelve-year-old boy, is seriously disadvantaged in another sense. A new immigrant from Ethiopia, he does not speak English, and he knows little about American customs. His home environment is not preparing him for what is now his cultural and intellectual world, and his mother tends to isolate him from other children: she worries about his being exposed to lax American mores.

Three-year-old Melissa Carr has suffered yet another kind of serious disadvantage. Her language development is badly stunted because her mother has rarely spoken to her. Her mother simply did not know, until she was told explicitly by a social worker, that verbal interaction is important in the first years of life.

Several children in a small town in Arkansas are unkempt and starved for attention because they are deprived in still another sense: their parents, forced to work twelve to fifteen hours a day in poultry plants to make a decent wage, are rarely home.

Two-year-old Monica is endangered because her mother is immature: she leaves Monica in the car for hours while she shops in the mall. And children can be severely jeopardized by parents who are not only immature, but immoral, whether children are born to drug dealers or white-collar stock swindlers.

The Limits of Parental Responsibility

Keena Wells sits primly, her hair pulled back by a bright yellow ribbon, her long, thin arms dangling slightly over the edges of her desk. An African-American seventh grader in Little Rock who lives with both of her biological parents and comes from a middle-class home, Keena has the manner and the intelligence—the keenness and clarity of perception—of a much older child. Keena wants to be a child psychologist—she's interested in how a "six-year-old can think on a twenty-year-old level"—and her teachers do not doubt her potential. She's very bright, perhaps even gifted. Her parents have also, as she says, "thrown a lot of responsibility" on her to stay in school.

Yet when asked about school Keena's face betrays contempt; every day at school is for her unbroken misery. Keena says that she is "tired of teachers who just say write down this president, write down that president." One teacher says that when Keena is in school she is "in another world." Another confesses that he simply isn't trained to deal with bright students such as Keena who do not seem "to care about learning." Her grades are barely passing and her attendance is waning, and although Keena fancies herself as a kind of Houdini, escaping disaster at the last second—"I know how to get passing grades and I know when to pull together"— her teachers do not know how long she can keep pulling off these stunts.

In Tillie Olsen's short story "I Stand Here Ironing," a social worker expresses concern to a mother about her daughter's behavior in school and is reminded by this mother of the limits to the power that any one human being, even a mother, has over a child: "You think because I am her mother I have a key, or that in some way you could use me as a key? She has lived for nineteen years. There is all that life that has happened outside of me, beyond me." In a culture that often seems to trace every childhood failure back to some parental failure, this mother's rebuke underlines the simple fact that Keena and other children are not merely products of advantaged or disadvantaged home environments—they are not putty in their parents' hands—they are powerfully shaped by a vast array of circumstances in the larger world. Thinking of vulnerable children as poor or ghetto children not only ignores the many nonpoor children who suffer deprivations at home; it discounts these circumstances in the larger world that affect children of every race and class. Getting beyond divisive stereotypes and understanding the true nature of childhood vulnerability means looking closely at these circumstances.

It is, of course, impossible to catalogue all the circumstances in the outer world that shape children. Children are products of their moment in history, of prevailing conventions and wisdom, of social crusades. The civil rights movement changed the landscape of childhood for millions of children.

Yet it is possible to describe several basic conditions that should exist in every child's immediate neighborhood. Children should be physically safe in their communities, and they should have opportunities for accomplishment at close intervals in their communities and in their schools. Keena is denied these opportunities because her teachers do not know how to engage her. Such opportunities, including athletic and artistic activities, not only provide children with skills and confidence and self-respect—enhancing their capacity to withstand almost any kind of deprivation or difficulty—but also offer alternatives to smoking, drinking, and other destructive ways of allaying stress. A wide array of settings for accomplishment in schools and communities also puts children in contact with a rich variety of other children and adults and can be critical in providing children with successes to offset classroom failures.

Many children are imperiled not because of a lack of immediate opportunities, but because their future opportunities appear bleak. Some Little Rock high school students feel disillusioned and defrauded—their hopes watered by adults who preached to them that staying in school would land them good jobs, yet by tenth or eleventh grade they perceive that there simply are no good jobs in Arkansas, no matter what their qualifications. "Arkansas, the Land of Opportunity," jokes one tenth grader, mocking the state slogan. But the same sentiment could hold true in Long Beach, California, or Buffalo, New York.

Research on children who escape long-term poverty suggests at least one common denominator: these children typically have opportunities for work and other forms of accomplishment as teenagers, and these opportunities extend and improve throughout adulthood.

To function effectively in adulthood, all children also need to believe that there is at least some justice in the world, that there is a reasonable moral order maintained by trusted adults. I have spoken with many children who lose their way, who become dangerously passive or dangerously destructive, because they simply do not believe that their good intentions and hard work will be rewarded, or because they are convinced that they will never get a fair shot, that they are not playing on a level playing field because of their race, gender, ethnicity, or some other immutable characteristic.

With parents tied up by work and under stress, positive friendships have become even more important to children. Friends are not only a great joy of being human, but, research shows, they contribute to almost every important domain of children's development, including emotional, linguistic, moral, and cognitive development. Children also need adults in the community who can spot problems, point out routes to jobs, simply listen. Nearby adults can also be repositories of wisdom—"old wise-heads"—who confer to children a sense of solidity and continuity with the past. Sometimes a community mentor—a pastor, a recreation leader, an elderly neighbor—can be much more, providing the kind of steady encouragement and recognition that heals fractures in a child's basic confidence and trust. In adolescence especially, when children make sense of themselves in part by understanding how they are perceived by admired adults, developmental psychologists have long recognized that children are offered a kind of second chance, an opportunity to internalize the confident expectations of an adult other than a parent.

The tragedy is not just that large numbers of children are deprived of these basic needs, but that many of these deprivations are easy to remedy—if only someone would take responsibility for remedying them. Yet most city leaders do not think about how to create a rich variety of opportunities for children of all ages, or how to protect children from prejudice, or how to ensure that children have positive contact with community adults. Many school principals do not think about how to help children create positive friendships. Policy makers and the public are too caught up in debates about welfare and single parenthood and family values and the underclass. We need to inform the debate and look more deeply at these subtler deprivations that are every bit as much at the root cause of childrens' troubles.

The Real Roots
of Success and Failure

EVERY TIME WILMA MARTIN, A SINGLE MOTHER
who has lost the use of one leg, goes to the welfare
department, she is filled with trepidation. She is not
worried about losing her welfare benefits; she is worried about
losing her children. Even though she sees herself as a solid mother
and her children have never been reported for neglect or abuse,
her welfare worker has told her that she may have to report Wilma
to the state child welfare agency. Wilma believes that the welfare
worker has come to this point because she views Wilma as a
compendium of risk factors: "They never come in to see my kids,
to see how well they are doing. They deal with me as a category—
no money, handicapped, single mother. The handicap is a handful
right there. Oh my God, no money, handicapped and she's a single mother? Oh my God, those kids!"

About fifteen years ago a British psychologist named Michael
Rutter did some simple calculations that verified what many
researchers and practitioners had long intuited. Dissatisfied with
the limitations of any single explanation of children's problems,
recognizing that it is not simply bad home environments or poverty
that undermine children, Rutter sought to more accurately gauge
the likelihood of a child's failing by measuring the impact of multiple
risk factors, such as poverty, paternal criminality, and maternal
mental illness. Rutter discovered that as risk factors stack up,
the chances of failure multiply many times. One risk factor had
no connection to failure in adulthood; however, two risk factors

quadrupled the chances of serious failure, and four risk factors increased the chances tenfold.

The idea that multiple risk factors spell disaster for children has traveled fast and has deeply influenced a wide band of policy makers and professionals. Policy makers and administrators have been given a useful map for identifying populations of children, while they are still young, who are likely to struggle in school and in other areas of their lives. Rather than throwing money at problems based on race or class or simply hearsay, resources can now be more effectively targeted to those children most in need.

Yet the irony is that what has been useful to policy makers and administrators has in many ways impaired the work of teachers, police officers, and other professionals who are faced with individual children and all their particular complexities. Risk factors neither help these professionals understand what ails an individual child nor enable them to accurately predict an individual child's future. For two children with identical risk factors—two brothers in the same family, for example—can have radically different fates. And just as children and parents can be stigmatized because they are poor, parents such as Wilma Martin and children of such parents are often denied a clean slate by those who see them as bundles of risk factors.

Moreover, loose risk-factor thinking is being formalized in instruments used to assign children and families to programs and services. Just as health-care workers use risk factors to determine the probability of later disease, social workers and psychologists now use various risk-assessment instruments to determine the probability of numerous troubles in childhood, such as neglect and abuse, as well as failures in later life, such as dropping out of school. Although many of these instruments serve useful purposes, in many cases children and parents are stamped "at risk" based on factors that have no basis in research, but simply spring from presumptions that people carry in their heads. These assessment instruments do not typically assess strengths, either, and they are often not sophisticated enough to distinguish the fates of children who are alike in general respects but different in particular ways, such as two sisters living in the same family.

Those who run programs and work with children need a more complex model for thinking about why and how individual children are vulnerable. Such a model would not rely on general conditions, such as poverty, or on multiple, static risk factors. Instead, it would enable a professional to tell a story about a child that captures the interactions between the child and the environment and that is faithful to the dynamic qualities and complexities of the child's life. Such a model would also guide professionals in thinking of children not as blank slates, but as actively thinking, interpreting, meaning-making beings. Too often children are described as passive receptacles of their environments, as programmed by input from parents, schools, and communities, rather than as actively processing this input and shaping their own environment. Parental advice books especially, as child psychologist Jerome Kagan puts it, treat children as if they "have no mind."

Further, adults often predict children's fates based on their attributes and behavior in early childhood (in addition to risk factors). Yet large numbers of children fare well in certain stages of development and poorly in others. An interactive model helps illuminate the shifting nature of childhood vulnerability and resilience.

An Interactive Model

Michael Moran, described in the last chapter, seems to fall through a kind of hole in the world not because he is poor and has a learning disability and lives in a single-parent home. Nor is he simply having a peer problem. To understand Michael one must follow the interweaving of a dual narrative—one about Michael and another about the world he inhabits.

Michael's peer troubles, for example, destructively mix with his learning difficulties—children tend to make fun of him because he has these difficulties, which in turn heightens his self-consciousness and exacerbates the difficulties, causing him to further alienate his peers. Faced with this hostility, Michael has nowhere in his community to go. Unlike almost all the children in his neighborhood, he's interested in science, not sports, so it's harder for him to meet other kids and to develop friendships. At the same time, adults are not adequately supporting Michael or helping him manage these troubles. His teacher does not know that Michael has a learning disability and has no clue about how to defuse the hostility directed at Michael. New to this community, Michael also lacks a close tie to some other adult—a tie that could be especially crucial to him given the demands on his mother. At home he must share with his brother a mother who, despite her great strengths, is preoccupied with financial survival and who receives little support herself. Cora is often distracted, and when she does focus on Michael her tendency to hover around him may cause his self-doubts to balloon. Recall that Cora also at times responds to her own distress by hovering around her children.

All the neediness and self-doubt that Michael suffers is compounded by his particular stage in development. At nine years old, children are taking their first steps toward separating their views and values from those of their families and they are beginning to see themselves in the eyes of their peers. Children at this age, in fact, often have little capacity to clearly distinguish their own identities from other children's views of them. Like actors with stage fright, they anxiously register how their every gesture is being reviewed. The fact that Michael is trying to fit in in a new neighborhood in which children his age are extremely cliquish only makes things many times worse. Michael's poverty creates serious problems for him at this developmental stage as well. His clothes from Kmart, for example, make him an easy target for peers who have become keenly status and style consciousness. At nine years old, Michael does not have the capacity for self-observation and insight—or the capacity for self-empathy—that could help him manage this inner turmoil. Instead, he lacerates himself for his failures.

And Michael's problems did not suddenly appear. In countless ways, Michael's vulnerabilities echo the past and evolve from an interaction between the past and the present. Rejections bite so deeply in part because of the battle he is waging against his own tendency to distrust, born of a long history of disappointments, misfortunes, and losses. Every coping strategy also has its own complex history. Michael has learned through repeated trial and error that retreating from friends is his best mode of protecting himself, a strategy that has had, for him, complex costs and benefits.

These kinds of interactions damage many children's lives. Many children suffer because of an interplay between circumstances at home and at school. Research on children has tended to divide home variables and school variables, to explain children's troubles either in terms of school problems or in terms of family background. Yet these debates obscure the many ways in which circumstances at home and at school destructively mix. Becky, a Little Rock eighth grader, is not floundering in school simply because she is shy, but because she goes to a large school with crowded classrooms, where popular children tend to be assertive and where teachers are occupied with many other children with noisier difficulties. Many children have coping strategies and protective mechanisms that do not mesh well with their environment. Keena, for instance, is slipping in school not only because she is understimulated, but also because she reacts to boredom in a certain manner—instead of seeking more advanced work, she takes a detached, critical stance. Yet her teachers say they have little experience dealing with very bright students like her who seem to lose interest in learning, and meanwhile Keena continues to drift further.

Paradoxically, some children are in jeopardy in schools not because these schools aggravate their vulnerabilities, but because they destructively interact with their strengths. Research indicates that children who drop out of school, rather than being unintelligent, are often like Keena; they have sharp, critical minds and are thus more apt to bristle when school is mindlessly conforming.

Terrence Michaels, an African-American ninth grader in school outside of Boston is hurt by his strengths in school for another reason (as well as being hurt by a form of racism). Terrence, his parents say, is considered a "nice black boy," as opposed to other black children who "make trouble," so when his grades started to slip last year, his teacher, who looks to Terrence for hope and relief, brushed it aside. Research now shows that intellectually advanced black children tend to perform far below their capacity in school. When teachers feel besieged, many children with highly visible strengths fade into the woodwork.

Complex interactions between family dynamics and peer dynamics over time similarly direct a child's development, although these two worlds, too, are often treated separately. Research suggests that children who are difficult to comfort and whose parents respond to them negatively, for example, may become withdrawn and insecure very early in life. This behavior inhibits them in their contact with peers and deprives them at each stage of development of opportunities to gain the confidence and social skills that would launch them into more advanced stages of social interaction.

In some Asian communities today, many teenagers become estranged—and some seek to sever themselves from their parents entirely—because their parents' values, such as strict deference to adult authority, clash so severely with the values of their peers.

Often it is a chain of complex interactions among home, school, and peers that throws a child's life out of joint. Sally, a ten-year-old girl with Attention Deficit Disorder, has a highly anxious, fragile mother who can be irrationally critical, and a father prone to angry outbursts. Recently, career disappointments have escalated her father's anger, which increases her mother's anxiety and criticism. According to Sally's psychologist, Sally is furious at them and has withdrawn at home. At school, she has become increasingly disruptive and rude: She wrote on the chalkboard that her teacher is a bitch. Her teacher has little empathy for her, not only because of these attacks, but because she feels constantly harassed and criticized by Sally's mother. At war with both her parents and her teacher, Sally has increasingly looked to other children for support. Other children, however, find her needy and are put off by her rudeness. This appears to make Sally more provocative with her teacher, in a downward spiral.

When children develop destructive behaviors it is typically the result of interacting factors. Much research has hunted for a single cause of violence, has attempted to explain violence in terms of a single biological, cultural, or economic factor. However, Harvard researcher and psychiatrist Felton Earls, who is directing a major long-term study on the individual pathways to violence, is attempting to understand violence in adolescence and young adulthood by tracing many variables and their interactions over time. He suspects that certain disabilities and medical conditions, such as central nervous system disorders, as well as prenatal exposure to alcohol, drugs, and tobacco, are sometimes roots of violence, but that complex aspects of a child's character, gender, and temperament play a part. Most important, he notes that aggressive impulses can be channeled by friends, families, and communities in all sorts of positive and negative ways. Whether children have access to weapons, whether their older siblings are violent, and whether children learn from adults effective ways of resolving conflict may be especially important. As violence researcher Deborah Prothrow-Stith observes, some children "never know anyone who handles emotional crises and difficulties without violence." Alcohol or drugs may cause aggressive children to boil into violence, and Earls notes that certain children are more disposed to alcohol and drug abuse. Research suggests that early childhood experiences of shame and humiliation as well as poor communication skills, poor cognitive capacities, difficulties in school, and difficulty reading social cues are factors contributing to children crossing the border into violence. Psychiatrist Stanley Greenspan observes that children who cannot construct "internal dialogues"— children who can't reflect on or form a mental picture of their feelings—are often violence prone. The degree to which television contributes to violence among children is not clear, but research suggests that television is at least a thread in the story of how violence develops: in particular, television may validate violence as a means of resolving conflict, especially if adults are not actively invalidating violence.

And many children, like Michael and Sally, affect their environments in ways that boomerang. Among middle-class children especially, anxiety can result in overeating and hence obesity, which can cause a child to be ostracized, which can lead to more excessive eating, and on and on. Randall, an angry, provocative Little Rock seventh grader—the school principal calls him a "little asshole"—often finds himself in a very common type of escalating war with adults: he antagonizes adults, who respond by expecting the worst from him and threatening him with expulsion, which leads him to step up his provocations. Often these destructive cycles start at birth. A group of pediatricians at Boston City Hospital described a typical, destructive interaction that occurred between an isolated, depressed, poor single mother and her infant. The infant was born prematurely and following a three-week hospitalization tended to be unresponsive and passive. The unresponsiveness of the infant deepened the mother's sense of inadequacy and depression. The mother rarely interacted with the infant with enthusiasm, and in response the infant stopped looking to the environment for stimulation, only deepening the mother's depression and further hampering her ability to engage her child. By the age of two, the child had suffered clear language and cognitive delays.

Teachers, health-care providers, police officers, and other caregivers cannot be expected to fathom all the variables and interactions that imperil children. But they can be guided by an understanding of how certain basic characteristics of children— their temperaments, coping strategies, and primary vulnerabilities and strengths—interact with particular environments. This knowledge can assist adults in identifying destructive interactions and downward spirals and in finding points of intervention that may turn cycles of failure into cycles of success. This knowledge— combined with knowledge about risk factors—can bring both policy makers and professionals closer to understanding what is truly ailing so many children and can lead to policies and programs that stand a far greater chance of turning around children's lives.

Winner–Loser Myths

Melvin Butler's biggest problem in school is that, as he puts it, "too many girls are in love with me." An African-American classmate of Keena, Melvin is imaginative, nimble minded, and energetic—he seems to vibrate from head to toe. He also has an almost legendary tendency to exaggerate and self-dramatize—he calls himself "the equalizer," "the player," "the preacher," "the keeper of the peace," "the king of the seventh grade." Like some of his peers, Melvin carries on an almost constant patter. But while other children's patter is often just angry or empty, Melvin's patter is funny and infused with moral messages. "When kids get into a fight, I'm the one they come to," Melvin tells me, breaking into his friendly, pumpkinlike grin. "Color don't matter to me. It don't matter if they're Chinese or purple. I help old people. I help everybody."

Melvin suffers serious disadvantages. Melvin's father has been in jail for many years, and his mother has struggled to support Melvin and herself by doing clerical work on and off. Hampered by a learning disability, Melvin is frequently distracted in class, and his grades range from mediocre to poor. For many years school staff worried about Melvin's academic prospects. But they no longer describe him as "at risk." Melvin's spiritedness now endears him to adults: teachers seem willing to go an extra yard for him, and some adults recognize in Melvin's patter considerable verbal adroitness. Melvin's mother is closely involved with him as well, and she has worked with a social worker to keep Melvin interested in his classes. Melvin has no intention of dropping out—he recognizes his distraction as a problem, and he's intent on improving his grades. He has set his sights on finishing school and enrolling in a police academy, a goal that school staff now believe is within his reach.

Adults not only predict children's fates based on risk factors such as poverty and single parenthood, but they often assign children, even very young children, certain fates based on what they perceive as the children's fixed characteristics and abilities. Sometimes children who are combative and provocative, for example, are labeled hyperactive or simply as problem children, labels that are passed on year after year and that worm themselves into children's self-perceptions. Sometimes children are tagged as slow learners or as socially unskilled, tags that can have similarly large and lasting consequences. In these cases prophesies often become self-fulfilling. It is notoriously difficult, for example, for children placed in remedial tracks or special education classes to move upward or into the mainstream. Books such as Richard J. Herrnstein and Charles Murray's *The Bell Curve* suggest that we should limit the resources invested in the intellectual development of young children who appear, based on IQ scores, to have limited potential.

Conversely, it is often presumed that some children, such as Melvin, have certain strengths that will spare them serious suffering throughout childhood and adulthood. The now-popular notion of "resilient," or "invulnerable," or "super" children suggests that certain children have attributes that will enable them to weather almost any kind of stress and to bounce back from severe losses and blows. Books such as *The Stress-Proof Child* similarly sell the notion that children's vulnerabilities can be virtually eradicated (as well as the strange notion that life without vulnerability is somehow the ideal human condition). These prophesies, too, can be at least partially self-fulfilling. Adults are often more willing to invest in these children, which raises the children's confidence and motivation, which can in turn increase the adults' investment.

To understand the true nature of childhood vulnerability—and to avoid false, damaging predictions—it is critical to recognize that vulnerability and resilience are not static conditions. Because of complex interactions between children and their environments, children do not typically develop along some straight and narrow path. There are different pathways through every developmental stage, and children commonly zigzag, excelling in certain areas of development while lagging in others, struggling in certain segments of childhood while moving fairly easily through others.

This is not to say that children do not have some relatively fixed traits, nor is it meant to ignore children, such as Michael Moran, who develop problems early in life that plague them throughout childhood. Some children suffer serious organic impairments and deficits that cause them great pain and limit their potential throughout childhood and adulthood. And some children develop strengths and coping strategies that enable them to function effectively in a wide array of environments. These children appear to weather deprivations—for example, to tolerate serious poverty or unsafe and unpredictable environments—because, like Melvin, they have at least some of the ingredients for healthy growth. They have a stable and nurturing caregiver, they tend to engage both other children and adults, and they have certain innate traits that enable them to bounce back. Like Melvin, they tend to be intelligent and allergic to passivity. They commonly experience adversity as a challenge rather than as a threat and attribute failure to aspects of their worlds that they can change rather than to things about themselves that they cannot. These children typically have a variety of coping strategies that they use flexibly; many have strong religious convictions.

Yet the fact is that both of these groups combined—children with deficits that undermine their efforts throughout life and children with strengths that enable them to thrive throughout development—represent a small minority of children. The great majority of children are not doomed at an early age. Many children who scored low on IQ tests at early ages succeed in school and lead very productive lives, and sometimes the most unwanted, ugly ducklings do turn into swans.

Conversely, no child can be inoculated at an early age against any kind of hardship, and children rarely have strengths and coping strategies that will enable them to tolerate high levels of stress at every developmental stage in a wide variety of environments. Children are not resilient only because they have certain coping strategies and strengths. All children need ongoing nurturance from the outside world. Talk of "invulnerable," "stress-proof," or "super" children very wrongly suggests that children have walked through fire and turned into steel, becoming impervious to hardship. And many children, like Keena and Terrence, have strengths that negatively interact with their particular environments.

Looking at these types of interactions largely explains the shifting nature of childhood vulnerability and resilience. When a child is described as resilient, it is often because a slide, a snapshot of that child has been taken at a particular point in time. A snapshot taken five years later may reveal a child who is not weathering successfully the challenges and adversity presented by another developmental stage and another environment. Children described as resilient are often simply children who have not yet encountered an environment that triggers their vulnerabilities. A few years ago

Melvin's school prospects appeared very dim; now adults find strengths in Melvin that inspire hope. Yet strengths at Melvin's current stage of development may be of little use or may even create conflict for him at a later stage of development in another environment. That Melvin creates strong ties to teachers may put him in conflict with other children later in adolescence. His need to be a leader—the king, the preacher—may also create trouble for him in late adolescence, when he may be forced to choose between losing his popularity or joining a high-status gang.

New environments can also create new self-doubts and instabilities, in part because children's attributes have different meanings in different environments. Psychology researchers Lois Murphy and Alice Moriarty describe Susan, who was considered a hero in junior high because of her strength and courage in dealing with a crippling illness. When Susan entered a large high school, other children did not know how she had endured and prevailed. No longer held by others in the same high regard, Susan lost her social confidence and withdrew.

Sometimes children have strengths and coping strategies that serve them well in childhood but that work against them in adulthood. For example, coping strategies such as emotional withdrawal can help children survive chronic trauma in childhood, but can badly impair their capacity in later life to parent effectively, endangering the next generation. In one study, researchers attempted to predict which children in high school would thrive fifteen years later. They were well off the mark. Contrary to their expectations, a high proportion of high school students who were popular—primarily attractive girls and athletic boys—had serious difficulties in adult life, were "brittle, discontented and puzzled adults whose high potentialities [had] not been actualized." These researchers surmised that these children struggled in adulthood for several connected reasons, including suffering too little stress in high school to "temper strength" and becoming fixed on an image of themselves and on goals that did not fit with adult demands. Conversely, many of the children in this study who were functioning at high levels as adults had, as the authors put it, "severely troubled and confusing childhoods," which generated more evolved coping strategies in adulthood, including "sharpened awareness, more complex integrations, better skills in problem solving, clarified goals, and increasing stability." Parenthood especially offered the opportunity for many adults who had been hostile and rebellious as teenagers to take on responsibilities "that permitted dramatic modification of long established behavioral habits and induced new feelings of self-worth which liberated potentials for other adult tasks." Children's sources of self-esteem are also different from those of adults. For example, athletic ability is central to boys' self-esteem, but brings less recognition to adults in their forties.

Many types of destructive behavior, too, often appear and vanish throughout childhood and adulthood. Children who are violent at one developmental stage are often not violent at later stages, despite the fears of parents and professionals who witness violence in young boys and believe they see the handwriting on the wall. Violence researcher Felton Earls notes that boys in every culture become violent between the ages of three and seven—brandishing swords, for example, or turning sticks into swords when toy swords are not available—and the degree of young children's violent behavior is not highly correlated with violent behavior in adolescence or later life.

These discontinuities in development do not result only from interactions between children and their environments. They result from the capacity of human beings to learn from mistakes. They result, too, from accidents, and from good or bad fortune.

But they do seem to result primarily from these interactions and, more specifically, from the ways in which developmental stages and the attributes and structures of families and communities interact. For example, research on divorced families suggests that a strong identification with a custodial mother can safeguard preteen girls, but that such an identification can hurt a girl in late adolescence, when she is trying to piece together how to have her own relationships in light of her parents' failed one. Schools and communities, too, can support children at one developmental stage but leave them unprepared for later stages.

In *Friday Night Lights*, H. G. Bissinger describes a town in Texas that revolves around its high school football team: the community and the school worship young male athletes and pave the way for them to excel in sports. The well-being of the entire town seems to rest on the accomplishments of these athletes. Yet these children are given little help in making the transition from school to work; they are provided few tools for the more mundane task of holding down a job.

Keeping clearly in mind that children do not proceed along some straight and narrow path can lead to far more effective responses to a wide range of children. For example, fearing that displays of violence in young children are a portent, adults often respond to violence in ways that increase the odds of it reappearing in adolescence. Psychiatrist James Gilligan's work connecting shame to violence suggests that parents or professionals who are extremely punitive or recoil in shame when a young child is violent, for example, are far more likely to find their fears about this child realized than parents who, understanding that a child is passing through a stage, focus on teaching a child other ways of handling frustration and engage a child in a constructive activity.

Moreover, rather than having limited expectations of children who struggle at early ages, it is critical to seize the opportunities created by every developmental stage and to identify and pull on the strengths of every child—even, and perhaps especially, exasperating, embittering children such as Randall, described by his principal as "that little asshole," who elicit such hostility that their strengths become invisible to adults. And rather than presuming that some children are invulnerable, it is crucial not to miss the struggles of children at different developmental stages who have many visible strengths.

Irresistible as it may be to predict a child's fate, far too often these predictions are based more on adults' wishes and needs than on an understanding of children, and they don't stand up against life and time. Children can stay on track when they have effective coping and defensive strategies and when features of their environments continue to support their different developmental pathways. Public policies need to recognize these many pathways of healthy development. There are many roads to Rome. Staying focused on these different roads may not only help children overcome weaknesses and obstacles; it may help build in children some of the self-worth of which our current brand of deficit-focused paternalism deprives them.

The Mysteries of Childhood

At Randall's school, there is another child who is on the verge of being kicked out—Kevin Morgan. Kevin has recently brought a weapon to school and is suspected of belonging to a gang. He is flunking several courses and beats up other children for no apparent reason. Simply mentioning his name elicited gasps of fear from one group of students. Kevin is constantly under his teachers' skin;

he arrives late to class and takes some hopelessly convoluted and time-consuming path to his desk. On one occasion he found a teacher's paycheck and remarked that he made more money in a week dealing drugs than she made all year. Yet Kevin comes from a middle-class home—his father is a school administrator—and according to the social worker who works with his family, his parents are both loving and attentive. When asked why Kevin is self-destructing, his social worker simply throws up his hands.

All the knowledge that has accumulated about what makes children vulnerable and about what makes children resilient should not eclipse another truth: there remains a great deal that researchers and professionals who work with children do *not* know about what shapes their lives. There is no simple explanation for the troubles of a child such as Kevin, who has not suffered serious insults or deprivations, who appears to have strong ties to his parents, who has access to decent schools and to community adults. Journalist Brent Staples wrestles in his book *Parallel Time* with how he rose out of a ghetto while his brother, similar to him in so many respects, became a criminal: "Why was I successful, law-abiding and literate, when others of my kind filled the jails and the morgues and the homeless shelters? A question that asks a lifetime of questions."

It is true that sometimes the reasons that a child is in trouble can only be gleaned after many years of trying to understand and that sometimes it takes a highly trained clinician attuned to interactions between children and their environments to uncover these reasons. Yet the fact is that there are mysteries of development that have not been unlocked. Some children fare poorly in childhood and adulthood who seem to have all the makings of success. And some children succeed who would appear to be destined to failure—and who have few of the telltale signs of resiliency.

In many circumstances policy makers and caregivers simply need to move forward based on the best available knowledge. But these mysteries should also occasion great caution and care. At the very least, they suggest that there are ways to assess risk and ways not to—simply assessing the characteristics of Kevin Morgan's home will reveal little about his vulnerabilities. And they suggest that there is a sensibility that needs to guide both efforts to understand vulnerable children and attempts to help them. This sensibility should be abetted by knowledge and technical skill, but shaped by distrust of too-easy certainties, by constant curiosity and wonder, by a willingness to keep setting down alive the riddles and surprises in any child. "The only honest answer," Staples says, "is the life itself," and the lives of children contain mysteries that our formulations and statistical analyses have not touched. Ironically, public policies and professionals need to be guided not only by what is known, but by a deep and abiding respect for all that remains elusive about children and their development.

3

FAMILIES UNTIED?

A LTHOUGH FAMILIES ARE NOT THE SOLE influence on children's growth, any serious analysis of childhood vulnerability needs to look closely at families— and at how they are changing.

We have been told routinely for decades that American families are in crisis. Sunday talking heads, policy wonks, politicians in both parties blame family breakdown for almost every conceivable childhood trouble and modern ill: crime, school failure, urban decay, drug abuse, poverty, teen pregnancy, and a renewed cycle of family collapse. Popular images that evoke the damage done to children by divorce, unwed motherhood, and women in the workforce abound: working moms who park their young children in huge, sterile day-care centers and abandon their older children to malls; yuppies who parent on the margin, their nurturing roles assumed by au pairs; single parents who desert their children by throwing themselves into paid jobs or abandoning themselves to the welfare rolls. Many Americans, of course, fret that such families are failing to instill in children the right values. Compounding the troubles of these families, popular wisdom now has it, is the almost complete absence of extended family members who can pitch in, offer support, and provide a safety net in a time of crisis. A 1993 cover story in *Atlantic Monthly* announced that, according to the latest social science research, "Dan Quayle Was Right... the dissolution of intact two-parent families ... dramatically weakens and undermines society." The nuclear family in the next century, according to a 1992 article in *Time* magazine, is going to go "Boom." The result: "Think of Dickens' London," predicted Edward Cornish, president of the World Future Society. "Worse, think of Brazil, where there are armies of children with no place to go."

These images of families have roots in truth. Family decay is imperiling many children. For example, divorce plunged the Moran family into deep isolation, poverty, and uncertainty. It is estimated that 60 percent of children born in the early 1990s will spend part of their childhood, like Michael and Joe, in a single-parent home. Yet sounding alarms about family disintegration distorts important facts and drowns out others altogether. Arguments about the disintegration of families often take as their baseline images of a time that never existed. For much of our nation's history children have grown up in single-parent homes. Researchers Frank Furstenberg and Andrew Cherlin estimated that in 1900 about 1 in 3 children spent part of their childhood in a single-parent home, primarily because of the death of a parent. Images of roving armies of children untethered to an adult neglect the fact that considerably more children grow up with at least one parent today than did 50 years ago. In 1940, 1 in 10 American children did not live with either parent, compared with 1 in 25 children today. Similarly, changes in extended families have not been nearly as great as generally believed.

More important, apocalyptic images of the state of children vastly oversimplify the changes that children are now experiencing. Divorce, for example, is not a modern scourge; it affects children differently and typically has complex costs—and benefits—for children that depend on many family and community circumstances. Before blaming the troubles of a child like Michael on divorce, it is vital to consider how he would have fared had his parents' miserable marriage remained intact. Divorce and other modern trends need to be seen in terms of the kinds of interactions that imperil individual children and in light of the basic needs of every child. How do these trends affect whether children receive continuous, caring attention from a parent or guardian? How do these trends affect whether children are able to draw support from peers and community adults? How do they affect children's opportunities for accomplishment and recognition?

Good family policies cannot be forged when children are fictionalized, turned into characters in adult morality tales, and maneuvered in adult ideological wars. Viewing children in terms of these basic needs reveals that most children are not simply better or worse off because of these trends; they are likely to be vulnerable in different ways. Those who make policies and those who work for children need both to understand these differences and to identify the family, school, and community circumstances that will help children stay in one piece when both their parents are working or when their families are torn apart.

Divorce and Unwed Motherhood: The Distance between Rhetoric and Reality

When Fred Louis looks back at the suffocating misery of the previous year—the flight from school, the heavy drinking, the agonizing attempts to pass time—it seems that his parents' divorce a decade before was at the root. An earnest, barrel-chested seventeen-year-old with a broad smile, he didn't fathom the full extent of the damage at first. In fact, he thought he had come to a kind of truce with the divorce. The divorce sneaked up on him, uncoiled on him.

Sarah and Bill Louis divorced when Fred, their second of three children, was seven years old. All Fred recalls prior to the divorce is his parents fighting "about everything." Bill Louis had been attentive to Fred early in his childhood, but in the year before the divorce Bill was home only on weekends. Although he was pleasant with Fred, he seemed in another world, glued to the television or tinkering endlessly with his sports car.

Fred was aware of trouble in his parents' marriage, yet the divorce blindsided him. One day his parents were together, it seemed, and the next day they were divorced. His older sister told him that she had overheard a telephone conversation between their parents. Their father was not coming home again.

The marriage had begun to collapse about three years prior. Sarah worked as a secretary for Bill— he ran an insulation business out of their home—and she recalls his carping at her constantly: "I didn't talk right. I wore the wrong clothes." In the last year of the marriage, Bill developed a serious alcohol problem. When he was drunk, his anger spilled out viciously. When Sarah tried to cajole him to be nicer to her and more involved with the children, Bill responded with cold silence or tit for tat, pointing out some way in which she had failed as a mother.

Nearly every day of the last year of their marriage, Sarah weighed the pros and cons of splitting up. Her marriage was a constant, miserable battle, yet she hated the thought of her children growing up without a father in their home—she had grown up without a father, and she had made a covenant with herself that she would not allow her children to suffer this deprivation. She asked herself how she could raise three children alone. She had few friends; she had only moved to this neighborhood a year before. Because she worked for Bill, she knew that a divorce would wipe out her income. At the same time, this calibration of costs and benefits seemed abstract. When she was honest with herself, the thought of leaving Bill was simply too terrifying to consider seriously.

It rocked her to the core when Bill told her that he had been seeing another woman and was moving in with her. Bill also insisted that he needed the house to continue running the business, and that Sarah and the children would have to move out. He would help the family relocate.

Yet Bill never did help Sarah find an apartment, and he failed to pay child support. Sarah landed a part-time nursing job, but she was still unable to adequately clothe and feed the three children every day. Within a few months she found another job in the evening that kept the family out of poverty. She arranged to have a neighbor watch all three of the children.

Sarah thinks that Fred, of all her children, took the divorce the hardest, though at first the damage was not apparent to her, either. In fact, she leaned on Fred more than the other children after the divorce, expecting the most from him. By her lights, Fred had always had an inner sturdiness. He became a kind of partner to her, even though he was only seven years old. When she was upset, she depended on him to help with housework and to supervise his younger brother.

Fred, for his part, worried about his mother intensely. For hours, he recalls, she cried or stared blankly at the television. She looked like a zombie. Often he tried to buoy her, reassuring her that he and the other children were fine and that the pain would pass. And he hid from her how abandoned he felt by his father and his own fears. It seemed to him since his father had left that any number of things could go wrong, and he would have to protect the family.

His mother, Fred recalls, pulled out of her fog about two years later, and for a few years life at home seemed easier and more pleasant than Fred had ever remembered. Around the time that Fred turned eleven, however, his occasionally gusting anger at his father turned into a gale. He saw his father about once a month, but his father— wearing black leather jackets, driving a motorcycle, racing dragsters professionally—seemed pathetic, trying to deny his age. Bill Louis also married his much younger girlfriend, who Fred felt treated him like an interloper. Even more galling, Fred was told by his mother when he was twelve that his father was not paying child support.

Fred now believes that when he started to become cynical in the ninth grade, it was his disillusionment with his father that was the source. He became a leader of the druggie gang—though he was not a drug user himself—and fought frequently with rival gangs.

Although he managed to leave the gang, when he entered high school he lost contact with his father completely—"we just stopped calling each other," he recalls, and he found himself rudderless. The school seemed huge and impersonal. Not a single school administrator even knew his name. He had been a leader in middle school, but now he was "at the bottom of the totem pole." Nor could he turn to his mother for help. It seemed that Sarah was hardly ever home, and when she was she was distracted or critical of him. Sarah was frustrated in her own aspirations—she had always wanted to be a doctor, not a nurse—and Fred remembers her dismay that his grades were sinking. "You're the one with the good brain," he recalls her telling him over and over. "Why don't you use it?"

Every day it now seemed to him that he was "rotting," that "the sand was going in the hourglass." School seemed almost surreal: "I was there but I couldn't figure out what I was supposed to do." Sometimes passively, sometimes actively, he resisted his teachers, refusing to do work. In response, his teachers, it seemed, stamped him as a child with an attitude and became more demanding.

He began skipping school, sometimes persuading friends to skip with him. He stayed at his house drinking and listening to music, usually with friends and his girlfriend. Yet his girlfriend irritated him and he remained miserable. Again he felt that time was racing by.

Sarah was shocked when she received the call from the assistant principal at Fred's school. Fred had been absent for 30 days. Fred had had school troubles before; Sarah had tried many times to persuade teachers to look past the exterior, to understand that beneath Fred's fighting with other children and sullen defiance was a bright child who simply needed some adult attention. But Sarah had always assumed that Fred, the child she relied on so completely, was suffering the normal downturns of adolescence. When Fred recounted the day's events at school, she never dreamed he was creating pure fiction.

Even if there had been more obvious signs that Fred was drifting from school, Sarah may have failed to heed them. She was too consumed with Kim, Fred's younger brother. A few months before Sarah received the call from the school about Fred, she discovered that Kim was abusing drugs. After that, Sarah was on the phone constantly, talking to school personnel, to a lawyer, to a therapist, trying to get Bill more involved with his youngest son. If a school administrator was calling about one of her children, she didn't imagine it would be about Fred.

One night Fred came home drunk and blasted any remaining illusions she had about his taking the divorce in stride. All his troubles, he told her, stemmed from the divorce. Brimming with bitterness and disgust, he said that his father had betrayed him and the whole family. Not only had his father broken off contact with him; the man had ended up living quite comfortably, while the rest of the family had been dumped into poverty. The divorce, Fred said, had ruined it for all of them.

The number of American children whose parents divorce is staggering. Between 1960 and 1982 the divorce rate *tripled*. Perhaps as many as half of all children born in the early 1980s will be children of divorce.

The debate about how children are hurt by these changes is often perceived as a political debate, a debate between left and right over family values, but there are dilemmas at the heart of the divorce debate that blur standard political lines. Many people who assert that divorced families are not "atypical or pathogenic," as divorce researcher Mavis Hetherington puts it, are not simply mushy-headed liberals eager to relieve guilt-ridden parents; they are attempting to prevent the stigmatizing of children from broken homes. Those who emphasize the big troubles that divorce brings are not merely Bible-thumpers; Americans across the political spectrum are throwing their moral weight against parents who jeopardize their children by casually discarding their marriages. In the past decade, popular articles and books by liberal commentators, such as Sylvia Ann Hewlett's *When the Bough Breaks* and Judith Wallerstein and Sandra Blakeslee's *Second Chances*, have emphasized that divorce is emotionally disfiguring millions of children, while such conservative stalwarts as Ronald Reagan and his secretary of health and human services, as well as Newt Gingrich and Clarence Thomas, have defended their own divorces.

Nevertheless, those who comment on divorce almost invariably wind up polarized on the extremes, greatly exaggerating or greatly diminishing its destructive impact on children. No sound bite captures the impact of divorce on a child such as Fred Louis. Looking at children in terms of their basic needs and in terms of interacting factors reveals that both polarized views are myths and that the real story lies between them. It is a myth that divorce is a modern scourge, but it is also a myth that divorce is nonpathogenic or neutral. Reality is far more complicated.

Divorce does inflict certain kinds of highly predictable damage on children. Millions of children, like Fred Louis, will lose their fathers after a divorce. In some 90 percent of divorces, mothers are awarded custody of their children, who then tend to have sporadic or no contact with their fathers. Only one sixth of all children will see their fathers as often as once a week after a divorce, and close to one half will not see them at all. Ten years after a divorce, fathers will be entirely absent from the lives of almost two thirds of these children.

Vanishing fathers commonly mean vanishing income. About 41 percent of divorcing men, like Bill Louis, walk away without a child-support agreement; when child-support agreements are in place, nearly 50 percent of all fathers renege on the full amount. Even when child-support payments are delivered, they tend to be paltry—about $3,000 a year on average. Large numbers of custodial mothers are left to fend financially by themselves—no easy task for many wage earners who are trying to support families today, and an especially difficult battle for women, who tend to earn a good deal less than men. Children are almost twice as likely to be living in poverty after their parents divorce as before.

At the same time that children are losing their fathers, they are commonly enduring a mother, such as Sarah Louis, who feels some combination of defeat, fury, and deep anxiety about the future.

Custodial mothers are commonly moody and distracted, just when their children need stability and responsiveness. Over time, custodial mothers' sense of self and ways of relating to their children may change dramatically, as the old certainties of adulthood collapse and they are thrust, without coordinates or reference points, into an unfamiliar life—especially if they find themselves on welfare or entering school or the labor force for the first time.

Children do not absorb these changes easily. Like their parents, children often suffer many tangled feelings following divorce that evolve through multiple stages. Soon after a divorce, many children are flooded with anger, anxiety, and grief. Children at all ages commonly feel guilt—it is safer for children to blame themselves for divorce than to believe that their parents would knowingly send their children's lives crashing down around them. Divorce disrupts the consistency that is critical to young children. Confronted with the mysterious departure of one parent, very young children often fear that both their parents will desert them. Adolescents frequently suffer sharp disillusionment—a loss of idealized images of parents and of the ideals that these parents represent—and many children lose idealized images of themselves, images, especially, of their capacity to control events. Boundaries of parental authority are often broken or altered. Too many children, like Fred Louis, are saddled with inappropriate responsibilities, pressed prematurely into self-governing and caretaking roles, depriving them of necessary developmental opportunities to err, to test, to rebel. Conflicts with friends, delinquency, and school troubles often ensue.

Sometimes the worst effects of divorce are delayed. The impact of his parents' divorce hit Fred Louis hardest several years later, in early adolescence. In the teen years, boys tend to project themselves into the future by forming new, often intense identifications with male adults, especially fathers. At this critical point, Fred felt embarrassed by his father, who seemed ashamed of being an adult. For adolescents, loyalty, too, is paramount: Bill Louis's failure to pay child support thus burned Fred deeply. Moreover, after the divorce Fred became a caretaker and leader in the family, a role that made it easier for him to cope for a few years, but then contributed to trouble in early adolescence, when he slipped easily into a leadership role in a gang, and his need for independence and control embroiled him in escalating conflicts with teachers.

Sometimes the troubles created by divorce appear to drag children down in adulthood. Children of divorced families are more likely than children from intact families to be poor as adults, to earn less as adults, and to have marriages that end in divorce. Divorce—and especially the abandonment by fathers—may do particular violence to children's ability to trust others as adults. Children of divorced parents are significantly more likely to state that "other people will try to take advantage of" them and that other people are "just looking out for themselves." Wallerstein's work suggests that divorce may have a kind of sleeper effect for children as well: events later in life can suddenly open up a well of difficult, unresolved feelings related to their parents' divorce. Young adults entering love relationships suddenly find themselves, for reasons they do not understand, swamped with anger and anxiety.

But although those who warn of the destruction wrought by divorce are not crying wolf, they are dodging an obvious question: which is worse for children, divorce or perpetuating a destructive marriage? Sarah Louis and the children certainly suffered, as she predicted, because of the divorce. Yet in terms of their basic needs, it is hard to imagine that Fred and the other children, barring some major transformation in Bill, would have been better off had the marriage remained intact. Divorce brought many hardships to Sarah, but it also pulled her out of a dead-end marriage that was killing her spirit and badly compromising her ability to parent. And it was her parenting, not Bill's, that Fred relied on primarily. Studies suggest that over time, mothers tend to fare better after a divorce: they have more self-respect, and they are less likely to abuse alcohol.

Those who decry divorce do not, to be sure, argue that one must stay with an alcoholic and abusive spouse. They tell a different story about why couples are divorcing; they typically depict couples leaving each other casually and selfishly, because of boredom or a lack of fulfillment. They conjure up images of couples who are in the throes of midlife crises itching to fulfill vague, immature ambitions or flattering themselves with younger lovers. In this respect, Bill Louis is exactly the kind of parent that fuels the fire of divorce opponents.

Family therapists suggest, however, that although some people divorce casually, people divorce for diverse and usually serious reasons, especially when children are involved. Often spouses divorce because one partner or both lack the psychological maturity to communicate effectively and to work through the inevitable disappointments and compromises of marriage. Marriages end because one or both partners are unable to deal with a child who is seriously impaired or extremely demanding. Sometimes a marriage cannot withstand the long illness or depression of a partner. Alcoholism and other kinds of substance abuse are clearly not exceptional problems. Families can decay in many ways.

And children suffer from many kinds of family decay. Although statistics show that children from divorced families have more school and peer problems than do children from intact families, they do not indicate how children from divorced families would have fared had their parents *not* divorced, but stayed in rotting marriages. A study that tracked children in a Berkeley, California, nursery school beginning in 1968 shows that years before their parents' split, boys whose parents would eventually divorce were more likely to exhibit various behavior problems, such as impulsiveness and rudeness, than boys whose families stayed together (far smaller differences were found among girls). Other research shows that children in high-conflict homes are more likely to suffer depression than children in single-parent homes. Further, focusing on the damaging impact of divorce alone ignores the evidence that it is early childhood, and especially strengths and deficits in infants' attachment to parents, that is most central in shaping children's enduring traits and development, whether or not a divorce occurs.

Moreover, statistics show that even if every child in this country grew up in an intact family, we would still have high rates of many childhood problems. For example, the dropout rate for all children is 19 percent; the dropout rate for children from two-parent families is 13 percent. As divorce researcher Sara McLanahan points out, although single parenthood is one factor contributing to school, marriage, and work troubles, it is certainly not the root cause of these troubles.

Even though divorce often does contribute to problems in school and later life, it is essential to stress, given the tendency to stigmatize children from single-parent homes, that most children overcome these troubles. If 22 percent of white children who spend part of childhood in a single-parent family drop out of school, then 78 percent of these children do *not* drop out of school. Although children are twice as likely to live in poverty after a divorce, a large majority of families do not suffer long-term poverty after a divorce.

More important, the war over the precise damage done by divorce is in many ways beside the point. We need to get far beyond broad generalizations that describe divorce as good or bad for children. Divorce and decaying marriages tend to deprive children such as Fred Louis of basic needs—and especially of the ingredients of good parenting—in *different* ways. Fred felt ashamed and abandoned by his father after the divorce, but he may have felt ashamed and abandoned in different ways if his parents had stayed together, with his father remaining remote and continually berating his mother.

Consider Ann Waters, a ten-year-old child in Boston. Whereas many children assume caretaking roles after divorce; Ann spent a good deal of time taking care of her father *prior* to her parents' divorce. Jim Waters worked part-time and spent much of the day languishing around the house, often drunk and depressed. Ann's mother worked long hours, and every morning Ann awoke early to cook her father's breakfast. She also rushed home to run errands for him after school and to cook dinner. She enjoyed taking on these tasks, but her friendships suffered. Even when she had time to be with them, Ann often felt that she was too mature for her friends— an attitude that did not go unnoticed. Her friends called her bossy. In her free time she chose to read instead of spend time with friends.

After the divorce, Ann was referred to a therapist by her mother, who said she was having temper tantrums. Her therapist noted that Ann suffered a kind of "demotion in the family" post divorce. With her father out of the house, she was no longer a needed caretaker. Her mother was home more often, but did not allow Ann to play this caretaker role. "Instead of treating Ann like an adult," the therapist remarked, "Ann's mother treated her like she should treat her—as a ten-year-old—but Ann hated that. She became enraged about being treated like a child."

Although Ann was in turmoil after her parents' divorce, it is hard to argue whether she was better or worse off. She was simply vulnerable in different ways. Prior to the divorce, Ann was vulnerable because she shouldered responsibility for her father— a role that not only made it hard for her to make friends, but that made it hard for her to be a child. Had this marriage remained intact, these problems may have greatly intensified as Ann reached adolescence and sought some separation from her father. And although Ann struggled after the divorce because she felt infantilized by her mother, her frustration and anger may prove to be a necessary stage in her taking on a more healthy role in her family and with her friends. On the other hand, Ann's relationship with her father was not wholly negative. The divorce deprived her of the consistent warmth and love of a parent whom she loved and who provided her with the satisfaction of being needed.

The difference between growing up in intact and in divorced families is frequently greater still because for many children, divorce is only the beginning. Often children endure their parents' separation and divorce, life with a mother and her lover, and a remarriage: 75 percent of custodial mothers and 80 percent of fathers remarry. Remarriage may bring with it a new set of siblings and sometimes another divorce; the divorce rate is higher in second marriages than in first marriages. Thus divorce is typically not a single event for a child, but a series of events, and each new family arrangement protects children in certain ways and creates new vulnerabilities. According to David Kantor, a pioneering family therapist and the founder of the Kantor Family Institute, "We need to create entirely different models for understanding children in intact families and in divorced families."

Debating whether divorce is good or bad for kids is beside the point in another sense. It ignores the fundamental fact that whether children's basic needs are met after a divorce often has to do with many circumstances that have little to do with divorce per se.

Children are not only affected by how their parents handle divorce—by unexplained acrimony, for example, by being used as weapons or as messengers in divorce wars, by whether a custodial parent looks to them to emotionally replace a lost spouse—but by who actually lives in their house after a divorce. Sometimes families are split down the middle after a divorce—with siblings ending up in different households—and between 25 and 33 percent of custodial mothers elect to live with a relative after a divorce. In fact, despite increases in the number of single-parent families, children grow up with roughly the same number of adults in their homes as they did twenty-five years ago. The number of adults per family household has dropped only slightly, from 2.25 in 1970 to 2.20 in 1989, largely because of the presence of mothers' boyfriends and of relatives (and the number of adults present may be higher because some boyfriends and relatives are not counted by the census). Children thus often have opportunities to receive caring attention from adults other than their parents after a divorce, although there is, of course, a big difference between receiving the close, loving attention of two parents and growing up with one parent and an aunt, a mother's boyfriend or series of boyfriends, or a grandparent.

Children's experience of divorce is also shaped by whether they receive other key ingredients of growth and especially by their experiences with friends and adults in their schools and communities. Divorce and remarriage are commonly damaging to children because they force families to move. Studies that disentangle the effects of divorce and of moving to a new neighborhood after a divorce find that dislocation is more likely to hurt children's school prospects than divorce per se. Even when children do not actually move, divorce can untether them from supporters and loved ones, such as their father's family and friends.

Schools figure powerfully in this equation. Social worker and divorce researcher Dan Hertzel says that the damage done by divorce is often exacerbated because school staff don't know how to talk to children about it—many elect not to talk about it at all—deepening the shame that children often feel. Many children, Hertzel points out, provoke or test their teachers after a divorce. "They want to know if teachers, too, will abandon them, and sometimes they may secretly hope that causing trouble will get their parents to come to a meeting together." Yet teachers have little or no training in how to respond to this testing.

Hertzel adds that teachers are far more comfortable talking to children who have suffered the death of a family member than they are talking to children who have suffered their parents' divorce. "There are no rituals for school staff that can guide them in dealing with children after a divorce." Moreover, schools have few guidelines when faced with dauntingly complex decisions about, for example, whether to maintain the involvement of noncustodial parents, whether to encourage divorced parents to make educational decisions for their children jointly, and whether to include step-parents or cohabiting adults in school activities. When a child from a divorced family has a problem, sometimes school staff simply don't know which family member to call. High turnover among teachers and other personnel, especially day-care workers, often further compounds the damage done by divorce.

Most important for professionals, understanding the impact of divorce on individual children means looking at children in terms of an interactive model. This impact is usually the result of a chain of interactions, involving an individual child's attributes, parents' attributes, and the particular characteristics of schools and communities. Fred Louis is endangered not only because he was abandoned by his father at a critical developmental stage and copes with stress by taking control, but because he lost contact with his father just as he was entering a large, impersonal high school. He was facing another difficult transition that involved the loss of important sources of esteem and support: he left a small school, where he was a leader, and entered a large school, where he had little close contact with adults and where he felt lost and insignificant. His flight from school was made easier, too, by a pool of friends who were similarly disaffected. In adolescence, children also for the first time have the cognitive capacity to see their parents in a new and harsh way. According to psychologist David Elkind, adolescents "can conceptualize and attribute motives to their parents' behavior that they only intuited before. Many painful memories of childhood are resurrected and reinterpreted in adolescence. Hence young people begin, in adolescence, to pay their parents back for all the real and imagined slights parents committed during childhood that were suppressed or repressed— but not forgotten." At the same time, Fred's mother, strapped by two jobs and preoccupied with his younger brother, did not know about his drift and was not contacted by the school for a month. Fred is endangered by a chain of interactions, involving the loss of his father, his developmental stage, his specific coping strategies, his mother's coping strategies, his brother's troubles, a transition to high school, a sympathetic peer group, and an unresponsive school bureaucracy.

Children Born to Unmarried Mothers: Was Dan Quayle Right?

Children of divorce are not, of course, the only children in single-parent homes: more than 25 percent of children are now born to single mothers. And while divorce rates have leveled off, the number of children born to single mothers continues to grow. Despite the noisy backlash when Dan Quayle attacked television character Murphy Brown, it is these families that are commonly seen as a kind of separate, desperate species, as the rotten core of family decay. Americans have always viewed single parents across a wide spectrum. Widowed parents, especially widowers, have elicited generous public assistance and great sympathy. Two of the most popular television shows of the last three decades, *My Three Sons* and *Bonanza*, depicted widower-heroes and their thriving children. A spate of recent television shows and movies have portrayed—often sympathetically—children and widowed fathers, including *Lassie, Corrina, Corrina, Sleepless in Seattle, My Girl, Aladdin, Beauty and the Beast,* and *The Little Mermaid.* Parents who divorce fall somewhere in the middle of the spectrum. But very few Americans rise to defend children born to unwed mothers. In recent years the term illegitimacy has crept back into public discourse, including discourse among Democrats.

There's no question that children born to an unmarried mother are worse off in certain important respects than are children from two-parent families and children of divorce. They are more likely than children of divorce to be poor and to suffer other troubles, largely because their mothers are more likely to be young, uneducated, and on welfare.

Yet in terms of children's basic needs, much that is true of children of divorce is also true of children born to unwed mothers: these children are not some separate, desperate species. Children born to unwed mothers are likely to grow up in households that are quite similar to those of children of divorce. A large majority of these children spend part of their childhood living with two parents. About 25 percent of them are born to unmarried, biological parents who are cohabiting. Nearly 50 percent of unmarried mothers eventually marry—sometimes they marry their children's biological father (a smaller percentage of African-American single mothers marry). Children born out of wedlock are as likely to see their absent fathers on a weekly basis as are children of divorce. Moreover, like married mothers, most unmarried mothers, contrary to popular belief, are not teenagers. About one third of nonmarital births are teenage births. Children born to single mothers do tend to fare worse in school and in other respects than children of divorce, but not dramatically so. They are only slightly more likely to drop out of school and to become teen mothers, for example. The costs of raising children alone also need to be compared with the costs of exposing children to rotten marriages, since many parents choose to parent solo rather than enter shotgun marriages.

Yet the debate over which does more damage, unwed motherhood or divorce, in many ways ignores the real issue: the different ways in which children are vulnerable when born to unwed mothers. Most significantly, children born to unwed mothers are not likely ever to develop a strong, lasting attachment to a father, either a biological father or a stepfather. Children who suffer their parents' divorce, in contrast, are likely to grow up with their father in their early years and are likely to *lose* their fathers during childhood.

How children born to solo mothers fare also depends on many attributes of their families, schools, and communities. Unwed, middle-class, thirty-something mothers such as Murphy Brown are clearly better able, in general, than poor teenagers to provide their children with the security, responsiveness, and stimulation they need. Yet other attributes of children, parents, and communities may be just as important as poverty or a parent's age in determining the well-being of these children. A shy child born to a shy, suburban, middle-class single mother who is marooned in her community may struggle far more than an adaptable, gregarious child of a poor teenage mother who is adept at finding activities and resources for her child and who has many strong social ties.

Using Schools and Communities

Responding to the troubles of children in single-parent homes requires getting past the usual debates and taking up several compatible strategies. It is vital to educate young people in advance about the challenges of marriage and parenting, to emphasize the serious troubles that divorce and unwed motherhood can bring, to provide the support and counseling that parents need to stay together, and to remind parents, again and again, about their moral obligations to each other and to their children. It is crucial, too, to support and strengthen children in single-parent homes.

Research suggests that schools and communities can do a great deal to mitigate the specific vulnerabilities caused by divorce and unwed motherhood. Sociologist James Coleman's research suggests that children from single-parent homes are no more likely than children from two-parent families to drop out of school if their families are supported by community, educational, and religious networks. Yet the nation's major economic and social institutions are not designed to support single-parent families: they have not caught up with the realities of modern life.

Strengthening both custodial mothers and absent fathers and enhancing their parenting capacities has many dimensions, including improving the quantity and quality of child care, creating part-time work opportunities and flexible hours, and developing family-friendly management training. Just as important, children living in single-parent homes, and their parents, need a variety of ongoing forms of support. Given that children from single parent families are likely to tumble through various family arrangements, it is hard to exaggerate the importance of anchors in their lives— children and adults outside their families who are caring and attentive over time. Some communities and schools are now seeking to deepen and extend children's involvement with other children and adults. Many large high schools across the country are creating more personal environments—environments in which children spend the bulk of their day with the same group of teachers and students—by clustering teachers and students, for example, or by creating schools within schools or houses within schools. Multigrade classrooms, where children stay with the same teacher for two or even three years, enable teachers to deepen their involvement with children. Reducing teacher turnover and turnover among day-care providers—difficult as this task may be—can similarly give children greater ballast and a deeper faith in the solidity of adults.

Mentoring programs of various kinds have also sprouted up across the country in the last two decades. (See page 64.)

Supporting families also requires that schools and communities actively buoy single mothers and engage absent fathers. Minimally, schools need to work to eliminate tacit messages that single-parent families are deficient. Parent support programs and other kinds of help in reducing isolation are also vital to the growing ranks of single mothers.

Schools need to greatly expand their efforts to involve noncustodial parents in their children's education by, for example, inviting them to parent-teacher conferences and school assemblies, sending them report cards, extending the school day, and offering evening activities that expand opportunities for working parents to interact with their children. Researchers have identified certain reachable moments in fatherhood—moments in which fathers are engaged with their children, including the child's birth, entry to school, school graduations, and when a child is ill—and schools and communities might seize these moments to help children create more solid and lasting connections to their absent fathers. Because so many children live with a stepfather or their mother's partner, schools also need help in the complex task of determining how best to engage the various men who may be important to a child.

Because divorce is so deeply unfathomable to children, because

---

While mentoring programs are one way of deepening the investment of men and women, including senior citizens, in children's lives, mentoring programs are not the panacea they are sometimes touted to be. In an extensive review of mentoring programs, social policy researcher Marc Freedman found that ties between children and mentors are often tenuous and conditional—adults lose interest, for example, or are unable to overcome a teenager's initial resistance—widening the cracks in a child's basic trust that are supposed to be narrowed. Mentors can unwittingly create inflated expectations. In a program in Little Rock, many children seized on young-adult mentors, who quickly became important—sometimes larger than life—and were tacitly expected in some cases to perform miracles of compensation for the deficiencies of other adults. Some mentors signified every good thing that a child's parent or stepparent was not. One seventh grader, reveling in the attention of her mentor, lashed out at her father for "acting so silly" as he, anxious to please her mentor, fumbled for words and for social grace and apologized repeatedly for his failures. In these circumstances, a mentor can undermine a parent or parent figure whose tie to a child is fundamental. Moreover, children need contacts with different adults at different stages in their development. An adult who is helpful to an isolated and lonely ten-year-old girl may not be helpful to that same child when she is sixteen and in anguish over a new romance.

At the very least, mentors need to think of their roles not only in terms of strengthening children, but also in terms of strengthening their families, which can and should safeguard children throughout childhood. Ideally, children should grow up in what Freedman calls "mentor rich" environments, environments in which children have access to an array of community adults.

it renders them so helpless, because they are so likely to feel rejected and disillusioned, it is critical that children have opportunities to talk to adults who are able to help make this experience comprehensible. As Hertzel points out, school staff need to develop rituals and nonintrusive ways of letting children know that the staff are aware that a divorce has occurred and are available to talk about it. Sometimes even a small amount of empathy and responsiveness can make a critical difference. Fred Louis skipped school in part because he had no connection whatsoever to any adult there.

School staff must also be able to recognize when a child should talk to a counselor or social worker. Health-care providers and others who work with children need to be similarly sensitized to the problems of divorce and given rudimentary training in how to talk to children about it. Groups for children in the midst of divorce and groups for children who are having difficulties with stepparents are cropping up in some schools and offer other useful opportunities for children to come to terms with foreign family arrangements. Because for many children, like Fred, the worst consequences of divorce are delayed, it is vital to create ongoing opportunities for them to make sense of the experience rather than reaching out only when they are in the immediate wake of a divorce.

The happy irony is that many of the strategies for helping children in single-parent homes—such as supporting parents and involving fathers in the children's education—will not encourage people to divorce or to bear children out of wedlock, but will help families stay together. These various community supports thus serve two key aims of any sound family policy—keeping families together and keeping children in one piece when they are born to single mothers or when their families come apart.

Butted Children and Other Myths about Maternal Employment

In 1972, two pediatricians published an article entitled "Maternal Attachment: Importance of the First Postpartum Days" in the *New England Journal of Medicine*. The article described the behavior of certain animals, particularly goats, when mother and baby were separated after birth. What the researchers discovered was striking. Mothers and babies never reunited: in fact, the mother goats butted away their young. Emboldened by their findings, these researchers proceeded to study humans and claimed to find evidence of diminished attachment in infants deprived of contact with their mothers.

The notion of bonding was popularized—infants deprived of extensive maternal contact might not actually be butted by their mothers, but their chances of normal development could be squashed—and was quickly embraced by those critical of mothers who chose to work outside the home. Here, finally, was hard and fast proof that however uplifting entering the labor force might be to mothers, it spelled trouble for their butted children.

Large increases in maternal employment in the last few decades have changed the landscape of childhood in this country. Recent data indicate that 67 percent of mothers work at least part-time outside the home, as do 50 percent of mothers with children under age five. Among children living with single parents, about 70 percent live with a parent who is in the workforce.

Yet as with the other villains in the alleged family debacle— divorce and unwed motherhood—there is little solid evidence that maternal employment is the root cause of the problems of today's children. Even though research has powerfully influenced social attitudes and social policy, it has distorted far more than it has clarified. It is now widely recognized that many of the most often cited studies of the effects on children of maternal employment have suffered from major methodological flaws. Wide holes have been blown in the methodology of the goat study in particular. More recently, methodologically careful research has shown that no single sound bite can capture the effect on children of maternal employment. Children with mothers in the workforce are likely to be vulnerable in different ways from children whose mothers stay home, and, in terms of basic needs, maternal employment has many costs and benefits for an individual child that change over time. Moreover, as with single parenthood, whether parents are able to meet their children's basic needs has less to do with maternal employment per se than with how maternal employment interacts with the attributes of children, families, and communities.

For many years Cora Moran has worked on and off and weighed the costs and benefits for her and her children. Many circumstances drew her to work. She is able to earn more money working and avoid the humiliation of welfare dependency. By and large, she finds working energizing and gratifying, in part because it creates a community for her. Most of her close friends she met while working as a secretary for an electronics company. Because of these gratifications, she describes herself while working as a more energetic parent. Yet concerns about Michael and Joe have often outweighed these benefits. In Michael's and Joe's early years, Cora felt that she could not afford adequate child care for them. When Michael entered school and developed learning and social difficulties, she needed to be his advocate at school and she wanted to be home for him after school because he was friendless and because she could not afford an after-school program. Given that every day at school was a trial for Michael, she also knew that by the end of the school day he was at the end of his rope and needed focused attention. She has worried far less about Joe, who had always made friends easily. Michael himself said that for many years he bitterly resented his mother's working after school, but that in recent years he has resented her being home all the time: he feels suffocated.

Many of the variables that Cora has been juggling are typical and powerfully shape the effect of maternal employment on children. Whether children continue to receive responsive parenting when their mothers are employed depends on whether work reduces isolation and stress for mothers and is gratifying and challenging. High-quality child care is not only important for children, but it reduces stress for working mothers. The needs, strengths, and coping strategies of children such as Michael and Joe, and the qualities of their ties with other children, are equally important.

Fathers are not innocent bystanders. Research suggests that when mothers are employed, children fare better academically when their fathers contribute significantly to child rearing. Extended family and community adults, too, can be critical in picking up the slack. For Meissa, a bright, energetic, eleven-year-old Mexican-American child, coming home from school every day to two grandparents whom he adores and regularly spending time with adults in his neighborhood have made a world of difference.

Perhaps most often, a particular interaction of circumstances determines how a child fares when a mother works outside the home. Six-year-old Betsy had temper tantrums and told her mother that she hated her not only because her mother started working long hours: Betsy had entered a new school, her two siblings were demanding much of her mother's attention, her father suffered from depression, and she was unable to entertain herself easily.

More commonly, interacting factors result in children's developing not only new vulnerabilities, but new strengths as well when their mothers are employed. For example, some children become more mature and capable of taking on greater responsibility. This constellation of costs and benefits changes at different developmental stages. A child like Michael who needs his mother's focused attention at age ten, increasingly recoils from it as he moves deeper into adolescence. A child who is excited about taking on greater responsibility at home at age twelve may similarly find responsibility more and more oppressive as he or she moves further into adolescence.

The greatest concern about maternal employment is that it cuts so deeply into the amount of time that mothers spend with their children. It is now widely claimed that children spend far too little time with their parents—not just because of maternal employment, but also because of lengthening workweeks, the decline of leisure time, and the absence of fathers—and soothing clichés such as "quality time" have been ripped apart. This time squeeze is not new, however. It is hard to imagine that parents who worked family farms fifty years ago, for example, had much leisure time with their children (*The Wizard of Oz* opens with Aunty Em, pressed for time, shooing Dorothy away). Moreover, there is little hard proof that this time deprivation is damaging to children. Those who decry the damage often hang their claim on a thin reed—a single study conducted in southern California on latchkey children that shows that these children are more likely than others to abuse alcohol and drugs; other studies have shown no effects of the time deprivation.

Nevertheless, it is certainly preferable, in general, for children to spend a significant and consistent amount of time with a parent, and a good deal of clinical and anecdotal evidence suggests that some children, like Michael in his early teens, can be harmed if they spend less than a few hours a day with a parent or some other stable caregiver. Children themselves feel this vacancy: the results of one large survey indicate that a high proportion of teens want their parents more involved in their lives. Child psychologists also report that it is especially harmful to children when parents are locked into rigid work hours and cannot be available at times of crisis or for important events, such as school plays. How parents explain their absences, too, is critical. Meissa's mother communicated to him that she must work, and she obviously enjoys the time she spends with him. Journalist Richard Louv interviewed children whose mothers work, and found that some children receive muddled messages or see their parents' working as flat-out avoiding them.

If there is a bottom line about maternal employment, many social policy analysts conclude, it is that it is generally best for children when mothers work part-time. (The benefits of fathers' working part-time are unclear; this alternative has been given little attention by analysts.) The problem is that many mothers are not supported in working full-, or part-time. Even though the typical American family now has two wage earners, both social policy and social attitudes lag behind this reality, as they lag behind the reality of single-parent families. As family historian Stephanie Coontz observes, "Work, school and medical care in America are still organized around the 1950s myth that every household has a full time mother at home, available to chauffeur children to doctor and dentist appointments in the middle of the day, pick up elementary school children on early dismissal days, and stay home when a child has the flu."

But perhaps the bottom line about maternal employment is that there is no bottom line—because there is no typical employed mother. Much of the war about maternal employment stems from the fact that, as with divorce, Americans hold quite different beliefs about why mothers work. Some people imagine narcissistic women who take parenting responsibilities lightly and crush their children under the weight of their careers. Others imagine women who seek desperately to balance legitimate self-interests with their children's needs. Still others think of parents such as Sarah Louis, who need to work desperately long hours simply to feed and clothe their children.

The reality is that each of these stories describes some women. Rather than warring over the precise impact of maternal employment on children, it is far more important to develop compatible strategies for improving the lot of children in these very different families and for supporting these children along their different developmental pathways. At the very least, parents, employers, and the government need to be reminded of the importance of parents' spending "quantity time" with their children and of discouraging parents from finding easy substitutes for their steady, enthusiastic love. In addition, opportunities for employed parents to spend time with their children should be expanded through flexible hours, job sharing, and part-time work options. To increase the amount of focused attention children receive from adults other than parents, the quantity and quality of child care and after-school programs need to be improved. Finally, professionals need a map of the various child, family, and community attributes that influence how a child weathers parental absences, a map that will enable them to fashion their work with children based on a child and family's particular capacities and needs. These strategies, together, can greatly expand the number of children who receive the responsiveness from parents and other adults that so many children are now so clearly denied.

4

LOOKING
INSIDE FAMILIES

T HAT SINGLE PARENTHOOD AND MATERNAL
employment are not the scourge they are made out to be
raises an obvious question: why do so many children
experience problems that are clearly rooted in their families? The
answer to this question lies beyond the structure of families and
the employment patterns of parents. It lies in the qualities of
parenting and in sibling relationships and family patterns. In addition
to the issues of single parenthood and maternal employment, an
understanding of these aspects of families needs to guide the efforts
of policy makers and professionals to strengthen children.

Many Americans, of course, blame the plight of children today
on parents who lack values, who have abdicated some fundamental
sense of responsibility for their children—or who have entirely lost
their moral bearings. These images have been fed almost daily
through the 1980s and 1990s by newspapers and talk shows that
grimly parade stories of children brutalized by their parents;
children chained to bannisters, stuffed into garbage cans, even
immolated by their parents. In 1994, Speaker of the House Newt
Gingrich, prompted by the story of Susan Smith—the mother
who drowned her two sons and then pleaded publicly for help in
finding them—promised to attack the "sickness" in American
families. Some of these stories describe middle- and upper-class
parents, including suburban parents who leave their children home
alone and all-American families in which sexual abuse is rampant

("Unspoken Traditional Family Values: Abuse, Alcoholism, Incest," reads a Vermont bumper sticker). A proliferating self-help literature and at-risk family industry also trumpets the notion that self-indulgent middle-class parents have blighted their children's development, leaving children as adults, as best-selling author John Bradshaw puts it, with a "wounded, neglected child within." (Without a hint of irony or self-consciousness, two specialists in the at-risk family industry declared that 96 percent of American families are dysfunctional.) Yet the bulk of these stories describe poor parents, especially poor, crack-addicted mothers who visit horrors on their children. A small but growing number of Americans now clamor to solve this problem of depravity by removing children from their homes, by yanking them out of these moral swamps.

These images depict some families. Some parents appear to have lost some basic moral sense. Parents who sexually abuse their children have surely lost their moral compass. Workers who investigate neglect and abuse cases can reel off chilling accounts of very immature, narcissistic parents whose gross self-indulgence jeopardizes their children, such as parents who, wanting to party downstairs, lock their toddlers in an upstairs room. Teaching parents about their moral responsibilities and helping parents learn how to transmit important values to their children surely has to be part of our nation's efforts to strengthen children.

But these images distort and misguide on several counts. Most forms of neglect and abuse do not appear to be more prevalent today than they were in previous eras; some forms of neglect and abuse were far more widespread in other times. Child labor laws passed in the 1920s, for example, redressed a pervasive form of child maltreatment.

Most important, these images obscure a wide range of problems undermining parents that have little to do with defects or morality. If we are concerned about creating healthy conditions in which all children can grow, we need to find ways to help parents who suffer chronic stress and depression. Children are far more likely to be deprived of their basic needs by parents who are depressed, who feel helpless and hopeless, than by parents who are depraved. Similarly, although media attention has focused on the destruction caused by single parenthood, whether a primary caretaker is seriously depressed is more important to children than whether two parents live in a home. Behind every case of neglect and physical abuse there is a complex story, but it is stress and depression, not depravity or single parenthood per se, that typically play prominent roles. Moreover, when parents are depressed, children can be deprived of basic needs in subtle ways that do not constitute serious neglect or abuse. Poor parents in particular are more likely to experience not only hopelessness and the humiliation of unemployment and welfare dependency, but also health problems, mental illness, accidents, the death of family members or friends, hunger, eviction, among other difficulties, that create grinding anxieties and miseries that undercut their ability to meet their children's basic needs—and that sometimes lead to serious neglect and abuse.

Depression affects a staggering number of parents in the United States. Young children depend heavily on their mothers, and 12 percent of mothers of young children are depressed according to strict diagnostic criteria, and 52 percent report depressive symptoms. These parents are far less able than others to provide their children with almost all the ingredients of growth. Research shows that depressed mothers are less able to enter into the world of their infants and to be the physical, warm, encouraging, "I'm behind you, I'm with you, I'm here for you" presences that infants need. They have more difficulty mirroring their infants' facial gestures, and they tend to be less vocal and proximal (they play at a distance).

In addition to suffering from their parents' unresponsiveness, children of all ages sometimes play destructive roles in relieving their parents' misery. Sheila, a Boston parent, admits that before entering a family support program, when she started to feel helpless and overwhelmed she would hit and scream at her children because "they were the only things in my life I could control." A 16-year-old in Little Rock says that when her mother is depressed "she tries to drag me down with her." Bill, a parent in Baltimore, concedes that he looks to his eight-year-old daughter to buoy him, saddling her with what he knows is far too heavy a burden. Children faced with the mystery of a parent's depression may come to feel defeated and deficient. Diana, an eleven-year-old in Chicago, tells her therapist that she is worried that something is wrong with her because she can't cheer up her mother. Research shows that depressed parents also often resolve conflict with their children in ways that require little effort, either dropping initial demands at the first hint of resistance or issuing unilateral commands, and that measured, consistent forms of discipline tend to fly out the window. As child-development researcher Vonnie McCloyd writes: "Rewarding, explaining, consulting, and negotiating with the child require patience and concentration—qualities typically in short supply when parents feel harassed and overburdened."

Many areas of children's lives are affected by parents' depression. Because they are more likely to smoke, drink, and abuse drugs, including during pregnancy, depressed parents can be hazardous to their children's physical health. Maternal depression during pregnancy has been linked with low birth weight and with inconsolability in infancy. Behavior problems, somatic difficulties, learning problems, slow growth, emotional illness, even accidents are more likely to befall young children with depressed mothers. Failure to learn from parents effective strategies for dealing with stress and depression may also undermine children's friendships and romantic ties throughout childhood and adulthood and impair their own capacity to parent.

What makes this situation even more tragic is that depressed parents are likely to be keenly aware that their depression is sabotaging their parenting, understanding all too well that they are unreasonably impatient, for example. Yet given how dragged down and embattled they feel, they cannot do any better or stop their detrimental behavior.

Of course, parents do not need to lead consistently cheerful and frictionless lives to parent effectively. Children typically have little trouble rebounding when a parent suffers a temporary problem, such as an acute illness or an accident. Chronic, unrelenting stress or depression is another story, however. One study of unemployed fathers found that the likelihood of a father's describing his child negatively increased with the length of time he was unemployed. Children may be especially endangered when a parent who is frayed by long-standing problems must suddenly confront a crisis, such as the death of a family member or an unexpected financial burden. Abuse often occurs because an already depleted parent is pushed over the edge by yet another battle to be fought, another loss to be absorbed, another disappointment to be endured.

How badly children are hurt when a parent is depressed is, again, connected to many other, interacting circumstances. The child's temperament and coping abilities, the parent's coping strategies, whether the child is heavily dependent on the parent, how depression is explained to the child, whether the child is able to draw on the support of siblings, friends, or community adults, and whether families have resources to deal with crises all determine the extent and nature of the damage. Children in poor families often fare the worst not simply because poor parents suffer more crises, but because they have fewer means of coping with crises and releasing stress and typically have little time to recuperate. Research shows that crises in poor families' lives often come in rapid succession.

Parents cannot be protected from depression and other forms of mental illness that have a strong biological basis. Some parents also will suffer unrelenting stresses and hardships that plunge them into a depression that lasts many years. Yet the good news is that even when depression cannot be prevented or cured, parents can meet their children's basic needs. Research shows that knowledge should not be underestimated, that even when parents remain depressed they can learn parenting skills, such as effective disciplining methods, strategies for constructively expressing anger, and strategies for getting children to comply with requests, that keep their children on healthy developmental paths.

Basic knowledge about children and their development appears to be key in keeping depressed parents from becoming verbally or physically abusive. Research shows that abusing parents often greatly overestimate what children can do and attribute to babies hostile intent. For example, an abusing parent is more likely to think that a baby is crying because he or she is annoyed with the parent rather than because the baby is simply irritable. In one study, parents who received simply a newsletter instructing them about the developmental needs and tasks of infants and suggesting coping strategies were significantly less likely to hit their children than were parents who did not receive this newsletter. High-risk parents, including socially isolated parents and poor parents, were most likely to benefit.

Many sectors of our society need to be engaged in relieving stress on parents and in helping parents deal with depression. Employers who seek to reduce stress for parents, city governments that respond to parents' needs, parent and family support programs that help people support one another and that deal directly with stresses in parents' lives can all make a difference. Greater knowledge about which families are likely to suffer stress and depression, about the many ways in which children can be undercut by the troubles and limitations of their parents, about ways of preventing depression, and about parenting techniques that can allay the damage caused to children by parents' depression needs to be built into every layer of public policy—from how teachers and health-care workers tend to children and parents to how politicians think about large-scale public programs.

Siblings and the Architecture of Family Life

Glenda Michaels is a lovely, lanky twelve-year-old girl living in New York City. She has a smile that slips on softly and easily—there is nothing to suggest its newness. For most of her childhood she has tried simply to survive. Glenda has never known her father, and her mother, Frances, was lost in cocaine for the first six years of Glenda's life. At nine years old, Glenda was sexually abused by her uncle. As recently as a year ago, Glenda was a different child—tense, agitated, unwilling to respond to simple requests, a cyclone of disruptive activity in school.

Glenda began to feel steadier when her mother stopped using cocaine, but it was not until a year ago, when her older brother, Ronnie, received a scholarship to attend a private boarding school in upstate New York, that her life changed dramatically. With Ronnie home, Glenda always felt pushed out. Ronnie and Frances have an intense bond. Frances hated Ronnie, her first child, when he was little—"I couldn't stand him," Frances says. "I didn't hug him until he was nine years old"—and beat him frequently, nearly strangling him once. When Frances talks about Ronnie now, though, she becomes swollen with feeling. Frances is grateful to him, both because he shows few signs of residual bitterness toward her, and because he became a kind of partner for her, helping her with the younger children. "Ronnie and I are survivors of the house," she says. Ronnie's departure left Frances feeling not quite whole, not quite herself.

With Ronnie out of the house, Glenda blossomed. She was glad to be free of Ronnie, who had found great sport in humiliating her. More important, her mother began to lean on her more, and she liked the special status and authority of being the oldest in the house. Her school performance improved.

When Ronnie comes home, however, even for a few weeks, Glenda often cannot maintain her newfound equilibrium, and problems with school and friends erupt. Glenda feels that her mother turns against her. "It seems like I can't do anything right," she complains, "when Ronnie's home." Ronnie has also begun to protect Glenda from boys who he thinks are just interested in sex. This paternalism enrages Glenda, who believes it is not motivated by concern about her but by concern about his status— it embarrasses him if boys talk about his sister.

Ronnie's leaving has been a mixed blessing for the youngest child in the family, seven-year-old Larry. Sweet and impish, Larry is a deft manipulator—a quality, he plainly asserts, that he acquired from his mother. When Larry wants something or when he feels aggrieved, he pouts and often employs an extensive arsenal of threats. On several occasions he has threatened to run away; a few times he has threatened to jump out of the car while it was moving at a high speed. These manipulations often work on Frances, but they also infuriate her, causing her to enter into escalating conflicts not only with Larry but also with Glenda. Glenda often takes care of Larry, and their relationship is close and relatively friction free, yet Glenda stays clear of the fighting between Larry and Frances. Ronnie, however, serves as a buffer between Frances and Larry. These manipulations are transparent to Ronnie, and he doesn't brook them. When Ronnie leaves, it is both good and bad for Larry. Larry doesn't like Ronnie's heavy-handed discipline, but he admires Ronnie, and he knows that Ronnie's leaving seems to create trouble for him and his mother.

Blaming children's troubles solely on single-parent families or on parents' deficits or depravities—or focusing exclusively on parental stress and depression—distorts children's worlds in another profound sense. Siblings and intricate webs of family relationships as well as parents determine whether children's basic needs are met. The interlocking needs and limitations of different family members affect whether children receive continuous support and whether they are given appropriate roles and responsibilities in their families. The consuming demands on parents of a severely retarded or disabled child, for example, can leave other children in a family stranded or thrust them prematurely into caregiving roles. Sometimes two children in a family are deprived because they have to share or compete for basic material necessities. In a Boston suburb last year, two brothers came to school on alternate days because they had only one pair of shoes between them. The number of children in a family also clearly affects parents' capacity to support and nurture. Research shows that the greater the number of young children in a family, the more likely a mother is to be depressed. Siblings influence one another's development in many powerful ways. For a significant number of children, including siblings who are buffeted among foster homes throughout childhood, siblings are the only family they have.

Moreover, complex psychological patterns or structures powerfully influence whether children receive the basic support and guidance they need. For example, Ronnie's leaving for school enables Glenda to become far closer to her mother, and his return home triggers predictable tensions not only between him and Glenda, but between Frances and Glenda, and between Frances and Larry. In Eugene O'Neill's great tragedy *Long Day's Journey into Night*, Edmund, the second child, is a replacement—the first child born after an infant in the family dies. Terrified of losing another child, his mother clings to him with all her might. Yet her clinging dislodges the oldest son in the family, James, who has nowhere in the family to go: his father, on the rare occasions when he is home, drinks himself into oblivion.

Because of these patterns and structures, solving one child's problems may ignite troubles in siblings. Family therapists note that children sometimes create trouble and draw attention to themselves when they are afraid their parents will divorce—children learn that by creating trouble they can unite their parents in responding to them rather than tearing each other apart. Yet solving the problems of one child can lead siblings to create trouble to attract attention—they take on the role of salvaging the marriage. The family therapy movement was born in the 1950s largely out of the puzzling observation that improvements in one family member often brought not relief but anxiety—and sometimes disturbing symptoms—in other family members.

According to Anne Peretz, the founder of a family center near Boston that serves hard-pressed families, the slew of problems that Americans are most concerned about are often "symptoms of problem[s] that are deeply rooted in a complex family system." Peretz describes a teenage girl who became pregnant because she fantasized that a child would win from her mother needed attention, dislodging an older sister as her mother's favorite. Similarly, juvenile crime, dropping out of school, teenage substance abuse, and suicide are often symptoms of problems whose roots lie in family patterns. Peretz points out that, although all families suffer from some destructive patterns, these destructive patterns are likely to be more severe in poor families because of the stresses created by poverty.

Teachers, police officers, health-care providers, and other professionals cannot be expected to be well-versed in family patterns and dynamics—or to become family therapists—but the reality is that the problems of many children will *not* dissipate if they are not seen in the context of their families. Understanding these family patterns can have a crucial bearing on whether a professional responds successfully to a child's problem. Without grasping how Glenda's performance in school is pegged to her difficulties with Ronnie's being home, a school psychologist simply has no way of understanding why her performance in school suddenly plummets and might attribute the change to irrelevant or erroneous factors. Other professionals, too, can benefit from at least some understanding of certain basic family patterns that undermine children. Family therapist Lyn Styczynski trains pediatricians about the common ways in which the birth of a sibling or a parent's remarriage can influence family patterns and a child's well-being.

And the fact is that schools, health-care agencies, and other caregiving institutions are constantly influencing family patterns, wittingly and unwittingly, and these influences, if better understood, can be positively directed. How a school chooses to deal with parents after a divorce, whether it works actively to engage both noncustodial and custodial fathers, whether it encourages children to enlist parents and siblings in homework, and how it deals with potential sibling problems—whether it places twins in the same class, for example—can have a significant bearing on how a family relates and on who in a family is vulnerable. Schools routinely influence children in ways that reverberate widely through their families, both negatively and positively. When children learn literacy or computer skills, for example, it often sparks parents' and siblings' interest in developing or improving these skills. Schools and other institutions, by paying attention to how their activities reverberate through families, stand a better chance of strengthening whole families and of generating far more enduring cycles of success.

5

THE ROOTS OF
GANGS AND CLIQUES

ALMOST EVERY YEAR A TELEVISION STATION IN Boston airs a story about the stretch of old U.S. Highway 1 that passes through Saugus, a town of 25,000 about ten miles north of Boston. Perhaps the gaudiest display of outdoor advertising east of Las Vegas, this strip boasts a giant neon cactus, an oversized replica of a Spanish galleon, a "Leaning Tower of Pizza," an orange dinosaur, and other extravaganzas promoting the restaurants and malls that now occupy about a third of this town's land mass. The Hilltop Steakhouse—a massive restaurant with metal cows grazing on its front lawn—is the town's single largest employer, and increasingly the economy of this old Yankee town, once powered by a large iron mill, revolves around the highway restaurants and stores.

A motorist on Route 1 would never know about Saugus's several lakes or that over a third of Saugus is an astonishingly pretty wooded area. Rocks that jut out of one lake, clearing the water by several feet, are used by children as diving boards in the summer. Well-heeled professionals, some of whom commute to Boston, live in large houses that speckle and skirt the woods. Much of Saugus consists of working-class Italian neighborhoods, block after block of midsize houses with large picture windows, bright aluminum siding, and unfenced, square front lawns. Saugus also contains fairly large islands of poverty.

Sunvalley Estates is one of these islands. Its waiting list is long because the housing units are in decent shape, the grounds are clean and uncrowded, and eligibility is based on a single criterion—an adult or a family has to demonstrate that its income is below the poverty line. Oak and fir trees are scattered around the buildings, spaced well apart. A circular road travels through the estates with starchy white, colonial-style buildings on either side. Many families as well as a large number of elderly residents and disabled adults have been drawn here.

Around the estates boys and girls, from about eight years old on, walk in packs of three and four, gossiping, teasing, poking one another. Last year, a group of about eight children, all around 15 years old, decided to form a gang. They called themselves the S.E.B.B.— the Sunvalley Estates Bad Boys. Early on members of the S.E.B.B. occupied themselves in ways that were merely annoying—one common prank was to hide with a remote-control channel selector under the window of elderly people who were watching cable television and randomly change channels for them. Recently, though, the pranks have become far less innocent. The S.E.B.B. is no longer a "baby" gang, a group of boys playing at being a gang. Several members have been involved in vandalism, fighting, and intimidating younger children. Some have become seriously involved in drugs.

Fourteen-year-old Stephen Bremer, one of the founders and leaders of the Bad Boys, is handsome and lumbering, with bright blue eyes. Brown curly hair sprouts, like an unmowed patch of grass, from an ellipse about four inches long and three inches wide on the crown of his otherwise shaved head. Unlike many children his age, Stephen listens carefully—he is right there when you talk to him—and he is deft at reading social cues. He prides himself, in fact, on his ability to play possum: "When kids first meet me, they think I'm just some stupid grub. But I'm seeing a lot of things other kids don't see." He is also an articulate observer of popular culture and a connoisseur of horror films, with an uncanny ability to summon up the tiniest details of Jason's terror tactics in the *Friday the 13th* series.

In the last several months, Stephen has spent nearly all his time outside school with the Bad Boys. Much of the problem, Stephen says, is that there is nothing else to do. Despite the various job opportunities and activities in Saugus, children at the estates are marooned. Occasionally they go to the mall or to the lakes for a swim, but aside from buses that come infrequently and cover only a small part of the city, there is no public transportation in

Saugus. Some older children work along the highway, in fast-food restaurants, as clerks or waiting on and busing tables, but many teens cannot get to these jobs because they do not have access to a car. According to a social worker, the only activity that occupies large numbers of children in Saugus is team sports. Yet Stephen is ineligible for school sports teams because, although he is bright, his grades are poor.

What makes being trapped at the estates far harder for Stephen is that he hates being home. His parents divorced several years ago, and he lives with his mother, Anne, and his older brother, Kevin. As recently as a year ago, Stephen felt very close to Anne and was protective of her—he took it upon himself to screen her suitors. Now he says that she spends little time with him and that she is almost always consumed by the demands of his older brother. Kevin has a learning disability and has had various emotional troubles, and Anne spends a good deal of time advocating for him at school or transporting him to one kind of counselor or another. Stephen also thinks that his brother manipulates his mother into paying attention to him.

At home Stephen plays Nintendo, watches television, or takes refuge in his room, where he pumps iron, surrounded by posters of sports heroes and bodybuilders. He becomes bored easily and is often drawn into fights with Kevin. Sometimes Stephen lashes out at his mother, simply refusing to do anything she requests of him. He has threatened to run away from home.

For Stephen, hanging with the Bad Boys not only gets him out of the house, but gives him status at school, and he has a prestigious role within the gang—bodyguard. Stephen says that other kids depend on him for protection and that, because he's funny, he's extremely popular. Unlike when he is with his family, with his gang he's "secure" and gets "respect."

Yet as the activities of the S.E.B.B. have become more destructive, Stephen has been getting deeper and deeper in trouble. Stephen and a gang friend set out one day to harass another boy who was a kind of pariah in the estates, a "weird" kid. They threw rocks at his house. When this boy's mother appeared and threatened to "whip their ass," Stephen pulled down his pants, mooned her, and retorted, "Whip this." About an hour later Stephen was arrested for disorderly conduct. Stephen has been reprimanded or suspended for fighting in school so many times that he is in danger of being retained a year. His bodyguard role has brought on numerous consequences that Stephen did not bargain for. Parents have begun to see him as the evil force driving the whole gang. He has contemplated easing up but is worried that if he steps out of the bodyguard role, other boys, with whom he feels competitive, will step in and claim his status within the gang.

Anne is also distressed about how Stephen talks to girls. Stephen's clique is the most popular at school, and several girls call him almost constantly. When Anne overhears Stephen on the phone she is appalled by how abusive he is. It is especially frightening to her because it reminds her of too many men she has known, including her ex-husband. Stephen claims that telling girls to "shut up" or "piss off" is just the way kids talk to each other and that the girls, unlike his mother, know he's kidding.

———————◻———————

While researchers have been amassing literature on the impact of parents on children, it has been chiefly novelists and filmmakers, not social scientists, who have sought to capture the intimacies, vagaries, and anguish of children's friendships. These artists, far more than social scientists, appear to be in sync with the concerns of parents. Americans have become increasingly troubled by the influences of children on other children. Teenage peer groups, as peer group researcher Bradford Brown notes, are typically viewed as inherently "irresponsible, hedonistic and recalcitrant." Fears have been primed in the last decade by the sheer amount of time that children spend with other children, receiving from them— rather than from parents or other adults—their social and moral education.

These fears are not manufactured from thin air. Any serious effort to understand childhood vulnerability today needs to look closely not only at families but at friendships, in part because many children rely on other children to fulfill basic needs once met by the family. Escalating numbers of children with single parents, such as Stephen Bremer, or with both parents in the workforce have resulted in some children being left alone at home and in some children's increased involvement with other children. Smaller families may also lead children to lean less on siblings and more on friends. While at other times in our history children have relied heavily on peers, children's dependency on other children today is great: high school students now spend twice as much time with peers as with parents or other adults. In this country, teenagers average twenty hours per week of nonclassroom time with peers, compared with two to three hours reported in Japan and the former Soviet Union.

Yet to cast peer groups as a kind of monolithic, destructive force recalcitrant to adults distorts on several counts. Spending a large amount of time with friends is not necessarily—or even typically—negative. Studies show that peer groups often counteract children's destructive tendencies, encouraging children, for example, to *stay* in school and to *avoid* smoking. Being a member of a clique in adolescence is a significant predictor of adolescent emotional well-being and ability to handle stress. Debating whether peer groups are good or bad for children is itself largely beside the point. Most children who spend more time with peers are probably not more or less vulnerable, better or worse off, than other children; they have different types of relationships, different modes of understanding moral problems, and different strengths, limitations, and vulnerabilities.

What is important is understanding why some peer groups become destructive. Stephen's peer group is not a mysterious force that drags him into destruction. Children's peer groups tend to become destructive when children lack a basic ingredient of healthy growth: positive sources of recognition, especially meaningful opportunities that extend into adulthood. Stephen has few day-to-day opportunities for achievement: he is failing in school, he is excluded from team sports, and, despite living in a town that is prospering, he is cut off from after-school activities and jobs. Stephen feels that he receives little recognition from his mother, who is distracted by the demands of his older brother. That Stephen comes to feel powerful by tormenting other children and that he stakes so much of himself on the approval of this group of friends—that he is even willing to take a role in this group that compels him to fight constantly—is his way of adapting given his inability to find more positive sources of affirmation.

Every destructive peer group also has its own particular story— a story in which, among many factors, messages from the larger culture, children's specific attributes and coping strategies, parents' wishes and needs, family dynamics, and many attributes of schools and communities form the plot. Understanding these factors is critical as well in fashioning interventions to prevent peer groups from taking a destructive form. Stephen cannot entertain himself easily by reading, playing music, or watching television: he is intensely social. As bodyguard, Stephen recapitulates in his gang the familiar and comfortable role of mother's protector that he once played in his family. It is also perhaps not accidental that Stephen singles out a "weird" child in his neighborhood to abuse, given his embarrassment about having a "weird" older brother and his anger at this brother for consuming his mother's attention. And Stephen's gang bravado and abusiveness stir up his mother's old angers toward men, which may drive him further into the gang, in an escalating cycle.

Added to this mix is the peer group's idiosyncratic attributes. Like families, peer groups develop their own particular coping strategies, communication styles, and dynamics, both constructive and destructive. In his peer group, Stephen must compete with other boys who want his position in the gang—a competition that plunges him deeper and deeper in trouble.

Children will not be spared the destruction of peer groups if teenagers are seen simply as victims of bad crowds. Nor will children be spared this harm if adolescence is seen simply as a time when moral development is thrown into reverse and when children become impervious to the influences of adults. To spare children this destruction, those who make policies and who work with children need to understand how children are hurt when they lose basic opportunities for recognition, and they need to understand the various family and community circumstances that pull children into cliques and gangs and that cause these groups to become destructive.

Gangs

To understand how children's friendships are affected by the absence of sources of recognition, it is important to look at the nature of adolescence. For while adolescence is not inherently immoral, the destructiveness of teenage gangs and cliques is deeply rooted in the nature of this developmental stage.

Adolescents typically vacillate between feeling powerful and feeling powerless—for example, powerful in relation to younger children, and then inadequate in the face of perceived adult tasks; powerful because of new physical capacities, but deficient in their ability to manage these new urges and capacities. Adolescents are also highly prone to shame, in part because their bodies have been thrown out of control—they are being visited by unfamiliar sexual longings and physical changes—at the same time at which they are intensely preoccupied with how they are viewed by others. For many adolescents this shame is deepened because they recognize the defects of their parents and other adults for the first time, adults with whom they have identified and often whom they have idealized.

A good deal of psychological and sociological literature suggests that teenagers are disposed to violence when they suffer shame and helplessness in relation to basic life tasks. Sociologist Elijah Anderson suggests that it is the fear of overwhelming shame that propels teenage violence in inner-city neighborhoods—hence teenagers' extreme sensitivity to being disrepected or "dissed." So threatening is this shame, Anderson argues, that teenagers strike preemptively to remove the prospect of losing respect and feverishly obliterate disrespect. The risk of shame can be worse than the risk of death (to be shamed publicly—exposed as weak— may also increase one's chances of being killed). Psychiatrist James Gilligan interviewed dozens of prison inmates who had committed serious violent crimes and found that these criminals had been chronically humiliated—they were commonly the whipping boys in their families—and were similarly obsessed with maintaining respect. According to Gilligan, violent criminals manage to briefly inflate themselves by rendering others helpless; they eradicate their shame by destroying other people's capacity to induce shame, by destroying others' "eyes." (It is thus perhaps not accidental that maintaining eye contact for too long, as Anderson observes, is a classic form of "dissing.")

Both researchers suggest that poor and minority children are more likely to become violent because they are more likely to feel the shame of social and economic inferiority and less likely to have alternative means of gaining recognition and prestige in school and in their communities. Lacking such means of recognition, they, like Stephen Bremer, are more likely to cling to the status of gangs. One Boston gang member described to violence researcher Deborah Prothrow-Stith why teens find gangs appealing: "They just want people to know their name."

The great majority of children in adolescence do not, of course, suffer the kind of shame and helplessness that catapults them into violence, and many teenagers adapt to feelings of shame and helplessness in ways that do not involve hurting others. Michael Moran responded to shame by withdrawing and berating himself mercilessly. Yet when shame and helplessness become intense, when violence is seen as a legitimate means of resolving conflict, and when children have few day-to-day opportunities to gain respect and prestige, the chances of their crossing the border into violence or degrading other children are multiplied many times. Moreover, when children such as Stephen Bremer lack other opportunities for recognition, they are far more likely to give other children significant power in defining what is valuable and virtuous about them, and they are far more likely to look to peer groups for some sense of belonging. They are thus more easily drawn into forms of destruction that run against their natural inclinations.

This lack of opportunity goes a long way toward explaining the prevalence of violent gangs in ghetto communities. Poet June Jordan wrote: "This is the meaning of poverty: when you have nothing better to do than to hate somebody who, just exactly like yourself, has nothing better to do than to pick on you instead of trying to figure out how come there's nothing better to do. How come there's no gym/no swimming pool/no dirt track/no soccer field/no ice skating rink/no bike/no bike path/no tennis courts/no language arts workshop/ no computer science center/no band practice/no choir rehearsal/ no music lessons/no basketball or baseball team?"

In many affluent communities, children are also denied meaningful achievements. Many cities and schools fail to run quality after-school programs even though large numbers of children come home to vacant houses. Many parents and professionals simply fail to recognize the importance of engaging children in meaningful activities. Logistical and practical problems, such as the lack of good transportation in Saugus, are also common.

Moreover, children are not simply creatures of the present: they are heavily influenced, especially when they become teenagers, by their perceptions of the future. Stephen Bremer lacks immediate opportunities, but adolescents feel similar feelings of helplessness and shame and similarly cling to other children when they are unable to see themselves prospering as adults. Without meaningful future opportunities, children also have less reason to be afraid of the repercussions of their destruction because they have fewer deterrents; it doesn't matter if they are expelled from school or in some other way jeopardize their future because they have no valuable future at stake—this is the greatly destructive freedom of not having anything to lose.

When, in Lakewood, California, in 1993, a group of about thirty middle-class boys known as the Spur Posse vandalized homes and tyrannized younger children in their neighborhood—as well as embarked on a highly publicized sex spree, a contest to see who could sleep with the most girls—it was this loss of future opportunities that appeared to be at work. The Posse has been variously cast as a classic example of a bad crowd and as a symbol, as Jane Whitney described on her talk show, of the "souring of American values." In fact, what appears to have provoked these boys to destruction was a sharp downturn, brought on by the recession, in the aerospace industry. By 1992, the major aerospace industries in southern California, the industries that employed the breadwinners of Lakewood, were laying off thousands of workers. For these boys, many of whom had been star athletes and town heroes, the imagined road ahead suddenly vanished. "When towns like these came on hard times," Joan Didion described in the *New Yorker*, "it was their adolescent males, only recently their community's most valued asset, who were most visibly left with nowhere to go." Didion also noted that for most Lakewood residents obtaining jobs in the aerospace industry and joining this community had been a step up and a source of pride, a signal to them and to others that they had joined the upward stream of prosperity of the American middle class. For many residents, according to Didion, the sense of presumptuousness and shame connected to losing jobs, to losing hold of middle-class status, was acute: "At the center of every moment in Lakewood [are these questions]: What had it cost to create and maintain an artificial ownership class?... What happens when that class stops being useful? What does it mean to drop back below the line?" (At one point these class sensitivities boiled quite publicly to the surface. One Spur Posse member, Chris Albert, bitterly retaliated on a talk show when a young black woman suggested that the Spurs were unintelligent: "Where do you work at? McDonald's? Burger King? $5.25? $5.50? I go to college.")*

---

*A wife of an aerospace engineer in Orange County told Robert Scheer of the *Los Angeles Times* of an especially painful moment in the history of the class sensitivities of this town. "One of our sons was on the football team in the high school in Costa Mesa about 12 years ago. They had a great team and they were beating the pants off one of the schools in Newport Beach and the Newport stands started to cheer, "Hey, hey, that's okay, you're going to work for us one day."

In many kinds of communities, when children feel this despair about the future, their peer groups become destructive. Studies of ghetto gangs have described how shame and despair drive destruction, how children deprived of future opportunities learn to look to each other to define their worth at the same time that they are learning to inflate themselves by degrading others. Elijah Anderson describes how the desire of many African-American ghetto males to do right by girls is corrupted by gangs and poor economic prospects. The fear that they will be unable to materially provide for a future spouse in a traditional way makes these boys, according to Anderson, much more likely to succumb to peer pressure to exploit girls. In some ghetto communities, children at young ages may begin to perceive large impediments to obtaining mainstream jobs.* According to James Comer, a black Yale psychiatrist, children begin to understand in about the third grade whether they are part of the American mainstream or some tributary, and sometimes the distinction dawns earlier. Moreover, perception can be as potent as reality. Journalist Nathan McCall, who, as a teen, along with a group of friends raped, robbed, assaulted, and terrorized widely in his working-class black community, explains that he and his friends perceived their choices as "somewhat limited," even though "the reality may well have been that possibilities for us were abundant."

Yet some children with ample opportunities join gangs, and some children without opportunities do not join gangs, and it critical for those who work with children to understand the many deciding factors. Some children have virtually no choice: to avoid gang membership is to suffer brutal abuse or even death. Some children are compelled to join gangs because gangs fulfill basic needs,

---

*Some ghetto children in the seventh grade in Little Rock talk vigorously and insistently about wanting to be sports heroes or high-powered lawyers (here television shows such as *L.A. Law* played a part), but lacking adults who can bridge the two worlds—and the seemingly low ceiling created by most of the community adults surrounding them—eventually presses down their ambitions. The gulfs that often separate ghetto children from the mainstream economy also create practical problems that are now familiar and that flatten ambition. Even when ghetto children stay in school, they often do not know about available jobs, lack access to adults who themselves have good job connections, do not have the knowledge or the skills necessary to engage in a successful job hunt, lack transportation, and have a sense of how to conduct themselves in the mainstream that has often been distorted by television images.

including providing food, clothing, shelter, safety, and emotional support. Terry, a Boston teenager, initially rebuffed an African-American gang, yet because he attends a largely white school where he is regularly physically threatened and called "nigger," the shield offered by this gang became a necessity.

Often when children join gangs, as in Stephen Bremer's case, a complex interplay between the child's attributes, the gang's attributes, and the attributes of the school and community are at work. To avoid gang membership in some communities means enduring unpopularity or friendlessness. In his book about children in a Chicago housing project, *There Are No Children Here*, Alex Kotlowitz describes a twelve-year-old boy, James, who says that the only way to resist gang membership is to isolate oneself, "to try to make as little friends as possible." Children vary widely in their capacity to endure unpopularity and isolation. Gangs also provide rigid hierarchies, structure, and activities that are well suited to some children. Randall, the Little Rock seventh grader described by the school principal as "that little asshole," has attributes that constantly drive other children away from him at school—he has little capacity to negotiate, to engage in friendships that are mutual, or to delay gratification—but these attributes may be supported or at least tolerated by his gang. Children may be more likely to join gangs when they lack some positive tie to an older child or adult. Some Asian refugee children appear to join gangs and rely inordinately on other children in part because they lack adults who can help them navigate the transition to mainstream society: they do not perceive their parents as powerful or competent in the new world, and they do not have long-standing or trusting connections to American adults.

Cliques and Other Problems in Friendship

The amount of attention male gangs receive often obscures the other serious peer problems in adolescence. Many children are unable to form friendships, and many children form cliques that are destructive both to their members and to other children who are fenced out or scapegoated. Studies now suggest that prolonged isolation and rejection by peers—the kind of rejection that Michael Moran suffered—is not only an immediate agony, but a source of long-term damage, implicated in juvenile delinquency and in dropping out of school. African-American children may be especially vulnerable to scapegoating and rejection by other children because they often feel spurned by mainstream culture from early ages. Children from other marginalized ethnic and religious groups may similarly suffer double rejection.

To a certain degree, forming cliques, conforming, and scapegoating are, of course, a natural part of development. In her book *You Can't Say You Can't Play*, teacher Vivian Paley describes children who engage in the complex process of sorting some children in and others out—an activity that is extremely difficult for teachers to alter—as early as kindergarten. Faced with Paley's insistence that they stop excluding, one girl wails, "But then what's the whole point of playing?" In adolescence, sorting and scapegoating become even more pervasive and intense, in part because children respond to the complex demands of identity formation by becoming brutally clannish, defining themselves in terms of who they are not.

Yet in some communities, the problems of cliques become severe, and, as with gangs, the severity of these problems appears to be rooted in part in a lack of meaningful opportunities. Anderson points out that inner-city girls, as well as boys, are extremely sensitive to being "dissed" because they, too, lack sources of esteem. These girls' cliques are often characterized by intense, corrosive competition and conflict over status, beauty, and boyfriends.

The problems of cliques may be exacerbated in many communities because girls tend to have even fewer opportunities for meaningful achievement than do boys. Psychologist Lyn Mikel Brown notes that although sports provide "one of the few legitimate avenues where girls can enact and experience a sense of power and efficacy," many girls are still tacitly discouraged, if not openly ridiculed, for participating in sports. For girls to be interested in sports may also seem to involve devaluing their feminine identity. To be interested in sports is still to be a tomboy, which means, as Brown points out, "not a girl at all, but an honorary boy." Although the number of girls participating in sports has increased greatly, it remains only half that of boys.

Recent studies also reveal the intense pressure that many girls in the United States feel to diminish their intellectual accomplishments, to dumb down, and to defer to boys in class. Often girls are not provided with images of adulthood that can help them find meaning in their day-to-day activities as preparation for later roles.

In different ways, parents, teachers, and cultural values can directly aggravate these destructive tendencies of cliques. In their book *Meeting at the Crossroads*, Brown and psychologist Carol Gilligan describe parents and teachers at the Laurel School, a private school in Cleveland, Ohio, who fail to provide girls with effective strategies for dealing with conflict among friends. Many parents and teachers inundate girls with the message that keeping friends means never venting feelings that might be abrasive to others. One mother instructed her daughter not to have a best friend, because it would create jealousies and conflicts. Some teachers arrange girls in ways that break up cliques—they instruct girls to walk in straight lines to prevent gossiping, for example—rather than talking to girls directly about teasing or spreading rumors.

Often teachers simply see working with peer problems as outside their job descriptions. Valerie Polakow, in her book *Lives on the Edge*, describes some teachers who are all too ready to accept, rather than to challenge, children's cliquishness, no matter how exclusionary. Michael Moran was furious at a teacher who failed to keep his tormentors at bay. As Vivian Paley puts it, "Just when the old fashioned city bosses have all but disappeared and the once-exclusive dining clubs are opening their doors to strangers, we still allow children to build domains of exclusivity in classrooms and on playgrounds."

Helping children deal with the conflicts and costs of gangs and cliques means recognizing the influences that teachers and parents have, both wittingly and unwittingly, on children's peer groups influences that, if understood, could be positively directed. Although parents often believe that they have little influence over their teenagers, that teenagers have spun out of their parents' orbit, studies show that teenagers trust the counsel of their parents more than that of their peers in making key decisions about the future and that teenagers are powerfully affected by their parents' values. Parents' choices, including choices of schools, churches, and neighborhoods, also strongly influence children's friendships.

Teachers, parents, and community adults can give children sound ways of coping with peer troubles and pressures. Many schools and communities now teach children conflict-resolution strategies, including ways of saving face when insulted. The Harvard School of Public Health's "squash" program, modeled after successful public health efforts to stop smoking and the designated driver campaign to stop drunk driving, is designed to help children con-structively respond to aggression by making it cool to walk away from a fight.

Guided by the conviction that violence is a preventable and controllable public health problem, the Violence Prevention Project, established in 1986 as a community-based program of the Boston Department of Health and Hospitals, mobilizes communities and schools around the idea that nothing is gained by fighting. Included in the project are a ten-session school-based violence-prevention curriculum, a series of public service announcements, a peer leadership program, and a clinic program that assists in caring for children victimized by violence. Staff members of youth agencies are also trained in violence-prevention approaches.

The Resolving Conflict Creatively Program, now in over 150 New York City public schools, trains teachers to deal with conflict by providing students with nonviolent alternatives and negotiation skills. Students are trained as mediators, and parents attend workshops to learn strategies for handling conflict at home.

Schools can adopt many other strategies to reduce peer troubles. The core curriculum of schools should include readings and discussions to help children understand peer difficulties and how to resolve them. Schools and classrooms can be organized in ways that discourage cliques; certain teaching practices such as co-operative learning, group projects, and peer learning can help break down destructive cliques. One study shows that teaching children social interaction skills can lead to marked and lasting increases in peer acceptance. School policies and practices as well as teachers also need to constantly affirm the importance of inclusion. Emphasizing inclusion means, minimally, actively insisting that exclusion is unacceptable, openly discussing stereotypes and prejudice, and constantly surfacing commonalities among students. For example, one teacher drew a grid on the wall with her students' names listed on both axes; she then asked students to find something they had in common with every other student in the class. Many aspects of school climate—such as ensuring that schools are safe and that school staff consistently express positive moral messages—can reduce peer troubles. It is also critical for schools to obtain effective counseling for children who have little capacity to form friendships or who consistently play destructive roles in peer groups. Interventions may be most effective when focused on certain critical junctures in the school experience, such as the transition from middle school to high school, when dividing and excluding are very common and cliques and gangs commonly emerge.

Research shows that parents, too, can do a great deal to help with peer troubles by teaching social skills, listening, and advising children on ways out of stubborn difficulties. Children who play positive roles in their families also often slip into these roles with their friends.

Key to any good intervention or program that seeks to mitigate the destruction of peer groups are several principles and practices. Stephen Brion-Meisels, who has worked extensively with teachers and children in urban schools, notes that it is critical for adults to listen to children and to start with the child's point of view in dealing with peer troubles—too often adults are too quick to judge children and impose premature solutions. It is critical, too, for adults to model in their relationships the values and problem-solving skills that they hope to generate in children.

Effective interventions also need to tap the many strengths in children's friendships, the great capacity children have to console one another, sacrifice for one another, constructively challenge one another, support one another. I recall watching a seventeen-year-old Little Rock boy listen intently and empathically to a sixteen-year-old girl, a friend, who had been raped the day before. Another Little Rock seventeen-year-old told a friend, whose mother had told her that she would never make anything of her life, "You show her, don't let her take you down with her." The film *Stand by Me* depicts the great empathy and healing capacity that even eleven-year-old children bring to their friendships: these boys help each other understand their parents' neglect and destructiveness and consistently find ways to affirm one another's worth in the face of their parents' harsh assessments.

Most important, responding to the problems of gangs and cliques means providing children with opportunities connected to meaningful adult roles. Harvard psychologist Jerome Kagan observes that programs and parents often attempt to prevent violence by telling children about the harmful consequences of violence. Yet children, Kagan has observed, understand these consequences quite fully—what they cannot control is the shame and helplessness that fuel their destructive impulses. Conscious efforts to provide children with a range of exciting opportunities and to connect children to adults who affirm the importance of those opportunities are essential. Some schools now provide apprenticeship experiences in local businesses and community agencies. Individual citizens, too, can make a difference. A couple in New York started a Cub Scout pack, a Girl Scout troop, and the local Little League, which, combined, have provided activities and recreation supervised by adults for 600 children.

The rungs on the ladder of opportunity also must be clearly and regularly defined for children. Childrėn need to see how their day-to-day activities are connected to the next stage in their development as workers and responsible family members, and how each stage is connected to their ultimate goals. In a shifting and complex economy, adults in some communities will have to take on the enormously difficult task of creating new ladders of opportunity, of charting out clear paths for children to decent jobs, even if it means encouraging children to leave their own familiar neighborhoods.

One thing is clear: adults cannot simply wring their hands about the vagaries of adolescents or intervene punitively after gangs and cliques become destructive. Children's well-being depends on adults playing many positive and proactive roles in children's friendships on many different fronts. Both private citizens and public agencies—not only schools but, as I discuss in later chapters, the police, health-care agencies, human-service departments, youth employment divisions—can guide children toward meaningful opportunities and help them develop the skills needed to build and sustain good friendships.

6

COMMUNITIES:
MORE THAN KIND
AND LESS THAN KIN

IMPORTANT AS FAMILY AND FRIENDSHIP ARE TO children, across the political spectrum there is growing consensus that both children and parents depend on wider nets of social ties, on communities—"It takes a village to raise a child" according to the popular African proverb—and that the disintegration of communities has placed children in serious jeopardy. We are routinely told that unraveling communities as well as unraveling families are at the root of rotting schools, elevating crime, widespread greed, and anomie. As early as 1960, sociologist Kenneth Keniston blamed the "shattering of community" for Americans' pervasive sense of "uprootedness" and "homelessness." Teenagers now lack mentors and role models in their communities. Because of increasing geographic mobility and growing anonymity among neighbors, children no longer grow up laced together with other children and caring, watchful adults who are themselves warmly and confidently tied. Moreover, this sort of informal caring network, popular wisdom has it, is no longer undergirded by the formal affiliations that families once maintained through religious, political, and social institutions. Children have lost a kind of paradise—sometimes the whole country seems to be mourning this drowned innocence—with large costs to them and to our culture.

There is a great deal of truth to these laments. Ties with other families can be a vital safety net when one's own family is pained or struck by calamity; families can greatly benefit from watchful neighbors; and children surely suffer if they are cut off from the caring and wisdom of community adults. But some of this nostalgia for communities is based on half-truths—and some is pure confection. Americans have pined for communities for decades, yet they have pined for an era that never existed. For various reasons large numbers of American children have never planted deep roots in communities. Historical studies suggest, for example, that nineteenth-century Americans were just as mobile as are twentieth-century Americans. One study has shown that geographic mobility was higher in Boston in the mid-1800s than in the mid-1900s. Nor is alienation from communities a modern theme—uprootedness and wandering have occupied American novelists since Melville. The exodus from small towns in the early decades of this century was in part a flight from precisely those communities that Americans are supposed to cherish.

More important, communities in the past have hardly been frictionless nor unconstrained for many families. In every era and in every part of the country, communities have not only included and supported, but they have scapegoated and exiled. Salem, Massachusetts, was a community, but it was a community that condemned people for witchcraft. Those who wax nostalgic about communities cannot be thinking about how communities have commonly treated homosexual children or members of religious and ethnic minorities. Michael, Joe, and Cora Moran, the family described in Chapter 1, were scapegoated because they were poor and not natives of their town. They moved into a tight-knit community, but it was not *their* community.

Communities have also always taken very different forms and have supplied very different things to their members. Some people experience their community as an extended family and submerge a large part of their identity in their community— sociologist Kai Erikson, in *Everything in Its Path*, describes members of a rural community as part of the same "tissue." Other people deposit little of themselves in their broader community, drawing the boundaries of their world to encompass only their families and/or a few friends. Different members of a family may have different experiences of a community. Although Michael Moran was largely isolated in his immediate neighborhood, Joe tended to have close contact with a wide range of adults and children.

Further, these one-dimensional images of community ignore the fact that many families are involved in multiple communities or social networks that are not defined neatly by geographic boundaries and tend to presume that membership in a single community is preferable for families. The workplace is perhaps the most common community today, not only for American men, but increasingly for American women as well, and membership in both an immediate neighborhood and a work community can create opportunities—can even be a key to emotional survival—as well as problems for families.

The desire to recreate happy, seamless communities also forgets that today and in the past community adults have not uniformly or wholeheartedly embraced children. In the 1950s, much-publicized juvenile delinquency, made famous by such movies as *Rebel without a Cause* and *West Side Story*, exposed wide gulfs between adults and children. The 1960s proved a great watershed in terms of generational conflict in some U.S. communities. Today, inundated with media reports about dangerous and depraved children, many adults fear children and avoid them. As Lisa Sullivan, a black Yale graduate student and community activist, told *New Yorker* reporter William Finnegan, "It's much worse than it was to be a teenager in the forties, when people were afraid of the Klan, of being called 'nigger,' of having somebody spit on them. These kids know that the whole society hates who they are. And they can't help who they are. Why do you think their favorite band calls itself Public Enemy Number One?" One Little Rock seventh grader reported being the victim of a mass judgment orchestrated by her minister, who pulled her to the front of church and read aloud her grades—a common Sunday ritual—and then asked the congregation to pray.

Nostalgia for traditional communities is misguided in another sense as well. Although geographic mobility is not a new feature of American life, millions of children's basic needs are threatened today because they move repeatedly during childhood. Seeking to re-create traditional communities will do little for these children. We need new community structures and strategies to reduce mobility and to deal with the toll taken by constant uprooting.

Traditional communities, too, often deprive children of the ingredients of sturdy growth. Even if we could wave a wand and create communities across the country based on some exact model of a traditional neighborhood, it would be unwise to try. Public policies should embrace certain characteristics of traditional communities while recognizing the flaws of nostalgia. The bottom line is that we need a new model of community that enables us to strengthen neighborhood ties while creating opportunities for children and families to participate in multiple communities.

Stressful Social Networks and the Importance of Multiple Communities for Parents

Sharon Rogers is a self-assured African-American woman with a quiet, husky voice. She has lived in a homeless shelter for almost a year with her two children, Matthew and Gloria. The shelter is clean and pleasant, and each family has its own room, but residents pitch in to help one another with baby-sitting, grocery shopping, and other errands.

Yet when Sharon Rogers talks about her neighbors in the shelter she complains. Other women rely on her, and she is tired of dealing with so many parents who have troubles and of "petty things blowing out of proportion." She feels forced to socialize with many people for whom she feels little kinship. She is worried about her children being exposed to other children who are sick and to a seven-year-old boy who frequently pulls down his pants in front of other children. Organized weekly meetings attempt to foster cooperation among residents, but Sharon resents these meetings: she does not want to be pushed deeper into these other lives. She cannot wait to leave the shelter—not because she dislikes the people—but because she wants some freedom from them.

When parents are marooned, their children are endangered. Parental isolation has been linked with everything from decreased cognitive abilities in children at eight months, to behavior problems among five- to-eight-year-olds, to lower IQ scores at four years, to a higher incidence of child abuse. Yet social ties can create burdens of their own. In a study of forty-three low-income parents living in varying housing circumstances in the Boston area, psychologist Deborah Belle found that low-income women such as Sharon often come to depend on other parents and adults when available because these women have a need for both emotional support and concrete assistance. Poor women who have close neighborhood ties to other parents also glean some psychological advantages. Belle found that such women feel "more secure" and have a greater sense of "mastery"—they feel more in control of their lives.

Yet these webs often simultaneously drag down and entangle, stirring up hostility and anxiety. Belle discovered that many low-income women feel constantly burdened by friends or relatives with illnesses or problems—a relative who drinks or a friend who is in constant financial crisis. For these women, generosity may have a zero-sum quality: to give something is to suffer an acute loss to one's self and to one's children. Belle observes, "the woman who lends her neighbor a pint of milk also needs that pint of milk, and the woman who tends her neighbor's children for an afternoon expends energy and attention on these children that she may well need for her own young ones." Like Sharon Rogers, many parents resent their lack of privacy and deeply resent forming friendships out of necessity rather than affection. Not surprisingly, anthropologist Carol Stack, a leading scholar of families' social networks, found that low-income women, given an opening, tend to opt out of these mutually dependent relationships. Belle also found that women who were not greatly stressed by the immediate demands of their lives would often opt out of these networks.

Many women revitalize themselves and temper their dependence by belonging to multiple communities. Other women in Sharon Rogers's shelter felt they were able to bear the burdens of neighbors more easily because they belonged to social groups outside the project, which provided affirmation and support. Toby Herr, the director of Project Match, a program for welfare recipients in Chicago, notes, "Many low-income mothers do not want more involvement with their neighbors. They want to meet other women and get involved with activities outside the projects. They might want to send their kid to a class downtown. They want the kinds of opportunities and communities that middle-class people have."

Single, isolated communities create another kind of serious burden for low-income parents. Sociologist Mark Granovetter argues that people who are embedded in single, close communities can be seriously disadvantaged because their access to economic resources tends to be defined and bounded by the resources of this group. While Granovetter does not describe poor communities specifically, this problem is surely greater in low-income communities where resources are scarce. Granovetter makes a case for the "strength of weak ties"—ties to many different communities that generate economic opportunities.

Not all low-income families live in sealed worlds, and many friendships among low-income parents are *not* overwhelmed by these burdens. Cultural differences in the purposes and patterns of social interaction also clearly shape the degree to which low-income communities create friction for families. Nevertheless, large numbers of poor parents are entangled in social ties that hamper their ability to parent.

Nor do low-income communities have a monopoly on these problems, although middle-class parents, to be sure, have fewer troubles and tend to have more choices about whom they associate with and how and when they associate. Well-heeled urbanites and suburbanites may lament the fragmented nature of their lives because their choices lead them to belong to many different communities—a work community, a social club, a political organization—rather than to one seamless community, but it is precisely these choices that low-income Americans lack. Middle-class Americans are far more likely to have access to technology that gives them access to many communities. The diverse virtual communities created by computer technology are largely inaccessible to poor families; many poor citizens lack basic telephone service or cannot afford long-distance calls.

Generosity in middle-class communities also tends not to have a zero-sum quality; there are more resources to spread around. Research indicates that parents in middle-class neighborhoods are more likely to consider their ties to neighbors unstressful and helpful. These harmonious ties to neighbors are so taken for granted in fact, that they tend to be in the background, whereas in poor communities the problems of privacy and burdens created by others are constant and nagging concerns.

Nonetheless, the problems of ties among neighbors are clearly not limited to impoverished communities. Many social problems found in low-income communities are also found in all sorts of communities where significant numbers of people are under stress—for example, in neighborhoods comprising large numbers of new immigrants, or on military bases where numerous families are missing a parent and suffer the additional stress of moving repeatedly from base to base, or in towns whose economies depend on a single industry that is failing or threatened with closure. Psychologist Dan Frank's study of a steel-mill community fallen on hard times shows that in these situations many people suffer stresses and a loss of control that causes relationships to fray. Many kinds of families are forced into affiliations with those with whom they feel little kinship or who violate their privacy. For countless parents, small towns can be airless and intolerant. Families can be bound to a neighborhood for racial, ethnic, or religious reasons or because of work, yet feel little else in common with their neighbors.

Some new immigrants from Liberia are repeatedly directed to a Boston community where they are welcome but feel ill at ease. This community revolves around a church where Liberians congregate, but there is a civil war in Liberia, and there is tension in this community because members come from opposite factions in the conflict. Some of these new immigrants also want to develop ties to non-Liberians and feel confined by this community.

Susan Grace is a young mother whose family moved to Utah when her husband was transferred by his company. Their new neighborhood is predominantly Mormon. Most neighborhood children are heavily involved in church-sponsored activities, ranging from Bible study to craft classes. Susan has never been involved in organized religion, and although her family is welcome, she finds it awkward and stressful when her family participates in these activities.

The reality is that Americans deeply value both their community and their independence—according to a recent survey, 58 percent of Americans describe themselves as "very private"—yet many kinds of living circumstances can make it difficult to realize both these values. Every parent also needs a balance between closeness and distance, and striking this psychological balance can require delicate choreography. In a sense, poverty can impair parents' capacity to strike this balance, as can various other social and economic circumstances. A parent's particular emotional needs and limitations can also make the necessary choreography complex. Sociologist Robert Wuthnow describes forty-two-year-old Don, who has grown distant from his church community because he feels that "some people ask for help too much" while others are "too private" and don't ask for help when they need it. Some parents can only stave off debilitating anxiety and loneliness by sustaining involvement with a wide range of other nearby adults; whereas other parents want freedom from all the social contacts of a tight-knit neighborhood—all they need is the responsiveness and encouragement of a spouse or a few friends. Research indicates that the presence of *one* significant source of social support can make a huge difference to some families.

Unable to match their needs with the shape of their communities, many Americans are isolated, and many feel trapped in communities that create stress. Many others seek alternatives. Research shows that 40 percent of Americans now opt for support groups—from Bible study to Alcoholics Anonymous. As sociologist Robert Wuthnow explains, these groups serve individual goals and affirm the self yet, unlike tight-knit neighborhoods, make no onerous, lasting demands.

All these factors make the task of giving parents the support they need, while no less worthwhile, far more complex. Ideally, parents should be given resources and assistance so that they can function effectively in the parent communities in which they are embedded, opportunities to belong to multiple parent communities, and the freedom to avoid membership in a parent community altogether if that is right for them.

Multiple Communities for Children

Children are also far more vulnerable when they are dependent on a single group of children for friendship. They are more likely to be dragged into destruction by a clique or gang when the alternative is social isolation. Children who depend on one social group are more vulnerable to its brutal qualities—to the competitiveness, scapegoating, narrow typecasting, constant sorting in and out—and they are far more exposed to the various problems of other children, from aggression to contagious illnesses. The worlds of poor children especially are more likely to be defined in ways that limit their ability to escape the problems of other children. A prime example is Sharon Rogers's complaint—a complaint echoed by other low-income mothers who do not live in the confines of a shelter—that her children are constantly sick because she cannot shield them from other children who have viruses and her despair about her daughter being exposed to a boy's inappropriate sexual behavior. Many poor parents fear that their degree of entanglement with other families increases their children's exposure to the anger and violence of other children and adults. Another mother in Sharon Rogers's shelter wondered whether her children were also becoming frustrated and violent—fighting with each other and with other children—because they were forced into relationships with children whom they would otherwise avoid.

Children reap many benefits from access to different social groups and to diverse friendships. Psychoanalyst Erik Erikson underlined the importance of adolescents' exploring various social roles and affiliations—"trying on" various identities. Research has underscored that such exploration is critical to identity development. Children often report a greater sense of self-worth in high school than in middle school because they are able to find a niche amid a diverse array of peer groups. In one especially intensive study, David Kinney, a University of Chicago psychologist, chronicled the transition from middle school to high school of a group of nerds—a tag often applied to Michael Moran. Kinney found that in middle school children often felt that there was only one popular crowd and that they were either in or out. Thus the nerds typically felt like pariahs in middle school. In high school, however, with a large array of social groups, they typically found a sufficient group of kindred spirits to ameliorate their perception of themselves as rejects. "We got nuked in middle school," one of these nerds said. "Now we're normal." Children who find their neighborhood or school peer group oppressive and bridle about their lack of privacy—everyone "knows your business" says twelve-year-old Stephanie—may successfully regulate their involvement with their immediate peer group by finding additional communities. Such communities may lead to academic success. Research shows that children who are unpopular in school do better academically if they have friends outside the classroom.

Such research has significant implications for social policy. Many parents and community leaders, for example, oppose busing and school-choice plans in part because they believe that children should attend a school in their neighborhood. Neighborhood schools are a venerated American tradition. Yet there are advantages to belonging to a neighborhood community and a different school community. In a separate school community a child can explore different roles or even gain some freedom from a neighborhood in which he or she has been narrowly typecast or scapegoated. Cities and towns make hundreds of other decisions about what kinds of activities to provide for children and where and how to provide them—whether to make a teen center available to those only in a particular neighborhood or to teens across a city, whether to require children to play on the Little League team that represents their geographic area. These decisions of private citizens and government leaders would often take a different shape if they were informed by the value not only of strengthening children's neighborhood ties but of giving children access to multiple communities.

Geographic Mobility

> My mother was married to my father. After that my mother went away to New Jursey. There she found my new father. He took me to age of 3. And then we came to New York. We lived in manhatin. And there they robed us. And then we moved to Stagg. There we had trouble with the landlord. we moved to Nicker Bocker. There we had to move because we had trouble with the water and the service. And from there we move to Major. There we are having trouble with service and my father got in jail for a day. And there I stayed and went to school and hope that I'll never move.
>
> (Lorenzo, eight years old, diary excerpt)

Seeking to re-create traditional communities will do little for the millions of children like Lorenzo, who are constantly in motion, who never live in the same area for very long. Although in the past many children migrated one or more times during childhood, family migration in the United States today is high: nearly 20 percent of families change residence every year. Children from poor and single-parent families in particular are driven from place to place by troubles similar to those that uprooted Lorenzo: a mother's remarriage, neighborhood crime, trouble with a landlord, a plumbing problem, a father's incarceration. I have spoken with single mothers in homeless shelters who have moved up to ten times in their child's first five years of life. Children in poor families move about twice as often as children in other families, although large numbers of families who move repeatedly are not poor. Poor children are also more likely to cycle in and out of schools as well as child-care situations as their mothers cycle on and off welfare and as their eligibility for child-care programs changes.

Compared with other problems of childhood, such as violence and single parenthood, repeated moving has received little attention—it is often not considered a problem at all. Yet repeated moving may be just as damaging as the more often acknowledged problems. Constant mobility can deprive children of nearly all the ingredients of sturdy growth, creating stresses on parents that impair parenting, robbing children of opportunities for lasting achievement, and hindering children's ability to draw on friends and community adults.

Beth, a Little Rock eighth grader, hangs on the rim of her school's playground, watching other children play. She has moved from school to school so many times, she says, that she no longer expects to have school friends.

Peter, a migrant child described by psychiatrist Robert Coles, longs for lasting friendships. Because their relationships are fleeting, children who frequently migrate do not have the opportunity to work through conflicts or disappointment with other children and adults. Some children who do not plant deep roots may have difficulties engaging in school and staying with tasks or may never develop the basic sense of security that continuity brings: "I had a fourth grader who moved to this school midyear and spent the first three weeks with a coat over his head," a school principal reports. "I found out this was the fifteenth school he'd been to in four years. His teacher is working hard to engage him, but he's sullen and seems apathetic. He probably knows he may leave again at any moment. You can't expect a child to feel secure or to get into the rhythm of a class who is always on the road."

Instead of a growing sense of mastery, some children feel that much that is important to them is out of their hands. Moving also forces children to rely far more on their parents and siblings— sometimes it throws children back on their parents precisely when independence is important for development—and can thus exacerbate almost any kind of family problem.

When children move constantly, it is extremely difficult to help them overcome the wide range of troubles that require sustained attention from professionals, and the gains that children make in dealing with problems are often swiftly undone. In Little Rock, I followed twelve children for three years who were identified as at-risk and who were receiving school-based services. By the third year, seven of these children had either changed schools or moved away from Little Rock.

According to recent research, repeated moving can seriously unbalance all types of children in the long run. The more children move, the more likely they are to drop out of school, even when poverty, ethnicity, marital status, and a mother's education are taken into account. Each move diminishes a child's chances of finishing school, on average, by 2.6 percent.

At the same time, many children clearly survive repeated moving unscathed, and the damage caused by moving depends on the attributes of families, schools, and communities. In the early 1900s, families moved at high rates, but they tended to move to join other family members or relatives, and how these relatives integrated them into a neighborhood was crucial. Today, it appears that families move to find jobs, and they depend more on work communities to absorb them. Whether children and parents stay attached to a school community matters as well. Changing schools repeatedly is harmful to children such as Beth even when a family's residence does not change. Conversely, moving repeatedly may be far more endurable if families stay attached to the same school community. How children fare also depends on the degree to which adults are moving around them. For some children, adults cycle in and out, appear and vanish, a part of the rhythm of everyday life. "Kids in the hallway stop me and ask, 'Where are you going next?' a school principal laments. Turnover among day-care providers and teachers in many neighborhoods is especially high. The average center-based early education and care program suffers the loss of approximately 25 percent of its teachers every year.

Many child and family attributes matter as well—attributes that are important for those working with children to understand. It is one thing for a socially adroit, adaptable child from a well-heeled, gregarious family to move; it is quite another for a child such as Michael, who lacks social confidence and skills, whose family doesn't have the financial means to utilize a wide range of activities and resources in the new community, and whose mother is isolated and overwhelmed.

Parental stress may be the single most important factor in determining how children adapt to constant motion. Psychologist Tim Daley, who works with children on army bases, notes that mobility for children in the military is often destructive because low pay and unpredictable changes in work shifts create great stress for parents: "parents often feel they have no control over their lives."

When children have suffered major family disruptions and dislocations, such as divorce or the sudden illness of a parent, moving may cause deeper damage. One of Daley's patients, Eric, a ten-year-old who suffers severe depression, has moved five times and experienced several losses and traumas—he has lived with an abusive father and stepfather, his mother has been divorced twice, and his current stepfather is never home. Daley believes that Eric has had great difficulty coping with these hardships in part because constant moving has been unsettling to him and depleting and distracting to his mother—she has been unable to give him focused attention.

Moving has a different impact on children at different developmental stages—young children especially rely on consistency and reliability—and the effect of moving repeatedly may change over time. A child who adapts to moving by becoming skilled at forming casual friendships may fare quite well in middle childhood, for example, but may have trouble in adolescence, when greater intimacy is commonly expected in friendship.

When other children move constantly, there may also be serious harm to children who remain stationary. Ellen O'Brien, the principal of the Healey School in Somerville, Massachusetts, observes, "When half the children in a class disappear in the course of a year and a dozen new kids arrive, it's not only terribly stressful for the kids who move, it's stressful for everyone else. It's stressful for all the children. It's stressful for teachers and administrators to bring in all these new kids. The paperwork itself consumes enormous amounts of our time."

Sparing children the difficulties of repeated moving means dealing with the conditions that force families to continually pull up stakes. Dealing effectively with these conditions means taking on huge and complex problems, including providing better income support and job programs, strengthening efforts to keep families intact, and improving schools. Many parents try to avoid moving if they believe a move will jeopardize their children's education.

Cities and schools can adopt more direct strategies to significantly reduce mobility. For example, cities can help tenants and landlords resolve disputes. Isabel Mendez, a Boston school principal, notes that some children change schools repeatedly because their parents distrust schools, based on their own experience and the experience of their children. These parents are skittish: they push on to a new school the first time a problem crops up. Mendez and teachers at her school go out of their way to tell both children and their parents that they are wanted, and they insist that parents work problems out. "We won't let kids feel that they have failed at another school," Mendez says. "We tell them and their parents, we're going to make it work here." When children must move, it is important to create other oases of stability whenever possible by enabling them to stay in the same school, club, or activity.

Meanwhile, schools and other community institutions need to help ease transitions for children and parents who are bouncing from place to place. This work will not be simple. Schools and communities must have a culture that embraces new children. Creating such a culture often requires not only working against children's natural clannishness, but rooting out the many tacit, unseen ways in which schools and communities deny entry to outsiders or relegate outsiders to lower, marginal statuses.

The good news is that at least some schools are now taking on this responsibility. Some schools pair new children with a classmate and create rituals for teachers that guide them in both welcoming and parting with children, such as asking every child in the class to share a positive memory of a child who is leaving. Schools need similar rituals for welcoming and parting with parents. Health-care providers, police officers, and other professionals, as well as other community adults who interact with children, also need to create and participate in these rituals. Daley suggests that parents and professionals can help children by supplying elements of predictability—by letting children know well in advance when a move is going to occur and by describing what the new place will be like. Professionals must also be attuned to other factors in a family's life that might make moving especially hard to bear, such as the occurrence of a divorce. When the number of dislocations a child suffers cannot be reduced, such measures can give children a stretch of greater security and calm—and perhaps enough faith in the solidity of others on which to build a sturdy sense of self.

THE TROUBLES OF GHETTO CHILDREN

FAMILIES NEED OPPORTUNITIES TO PARTICIPATE in multiple communities and help in staying in one place, but they also need to live in neighborhoods that are safe and predictable and at least minimally responsive to their needs. American neighborhoods are often assumed to be built to meet the needs of children and to simplify the complex task of parenting. Families, in fact, are considered the soul of the community, the foundation for a neighborhood's existence.

Many American neighborhoods, however, do not accommodate parents and children, especially young children. Adequate child-care facilities do not exist in the typical U.S. neighborhood. Many neighborhoods are unresponsive to parents of young children in hundreds of small ways—there are not adequate playgrounds or sidewalks, pharmacies and stores do not have hours that make sense for working parents, and restaurants are not welcoming to infants and toddlers. These failings can create particular strain for single-parent families, and demographic research indicates that a high percentage of U.S. neighborhoods comprise large numbers of single-parent families.

Some U.S. neighborhoods are far worse than simply unaccommodating. To understand the range and severity of children's vulnerabilities today, it is crucial to understand the particular plight of children in ghettos. In terms of meeting children's basic needs, ghetto neighborhoods differ from other neighborhoods in crucial respects. Children in ghetto neighborhoods are not only far more likely than other children to be exposed to violence, but they are also far more likely to suffer deprivations and abrasions that generate quiet troubles—from learning difficulties to medical problems to serious anxiety. Moreover, once a problem erupts, it is likely to take a longer and more harmful path in a ghetto. Individuals and institutions in ghettos possess many and great strengths—the church is one obvious example—yet because of the absence of basic resources, and hope, problems that may be relatively easy to contain in more affluent communities can easily spiral out of control in ghettos. Often children are not affected by a particular problem at one point in time only, but are undermined as they move through every developmental stage.

Neighborhoods everywhere can do better by children. Yet the particular—and the especially serious—troubles of children in ghettos call for more concerted efforts and for special strategies. These strategies at the very least should be aimed at mitigating the destructive effects of violence on children, preventing a wide range of quieter troubles, and containing troubles at early stages.

Violence

Every decade, Americans appear to seize on a single explanation for the plight of children. In the 1970s, poverty and hunger were in the news nearly every day, and researchers and policy makers focused their attention on eradicating poverty. Single parenthood came into vogue in the early 1980s and brought a new generation of reports, findings, and legislative proposals. More recently, single parenthood appears to have been edged out by violence as the number one problem afflicting American children. Cover stories in both *Time* and *Newsweek* in 1993 suggested that violence everywhere is on the rise and is changing the fabric of childhood.

Parents share this concern. According to a survey conducted by the National Commission on Children, parents believe that they can control their children, but they do not believe that they can control their neighborhoods. Nearly half of all parents report that there was "no safe place in their neighborhood for children and teenagers to gather, other than their own homes."

Significant as these fears are, it appears that violence has not risen markedly in the great majority of U.S. neighborhoods. What newspapers are accurately depicting is the sharp increase of at least one type of violence, children killing other children, in ghetto neighborhoods. This trend may continue: more and more children may be involved in violence because it appears that increasing numbers of children will reside in ghettos. It is critical for policy makers and professionals to understand how violence affects children and to identify the many family and community factors that can mitigate the damage done by violence.

Beyond the danger to life and limb, chronic exposure to violence can erode the soil that children need to grow, and threaten every aspect of their development. Many children, sometimes for the entire course of their childhood, are robbed of the most elemental sense of safety and security. Research shows that children exposed to violence often suffer post-traumatic stress disorder, the disorder, formerly called shell shock, that incapacitates combat veterans. These children experience nightmares and flashbacks and are hyper-vigilant, always braced for the next attack. Just as serious, violence often severs children from friends and community adults and deprives them of normal developmental opportunities for achievement and mastery. In a violence-riven area of Boston, small children, rather than roaming in playgrounds, are placed in a wooden corral during the day to protect them from gunfire. Willie Whitaker, described in the *New York Times*, likes to play at a local McDonald's because there he can climb into a giant steel hamburger and "bullets can't get through." Maria, a nine-year-old in an elementary school in southwest Los Angeles, explains that she sleeps in class because at night she must sleep on the hard bathroom floor to avoid stray bullets: the bathroom is the only room in the house that has no windows. Sometimes children cannot concentrate in school because violence is an immediate prospect. At one Chicago high school, file cabinets are pressed against windows to protect children from stray bullets. At another Chicago school, children talk of warring gang members who have on different occasions thrown each other down stairwells.

Instead of feeling a growing sense of mastery, some children feel increasingly helpless and small. Sometimes children cling to parents at precisely those developmental moments when it is normal and healthy to seek greater separation; sometimes the dangers of inner-city life demand that parents rigidly control their children's actions and require unquestioning obedience; and many children develop coping strategies that are destructive to themselves and others. Like combat veterans, in vain attempts to manage their vulnerability, some children become addicted to danger, thrusting themselves into treacherous situations, or they seek to obliterate their helplessness and rage through primitive forms of vengeance. In *There Are No Children Here*, journalist Alex Kotlowitz describes Ricky, a child in the Henry Horner Homes in Chicago, who responded to the murder of a cousin by waging war: "Now it seems like when I get into a fight, I don't care if I kill or something. It be like, we be fighting, we be fighting other people. Someone be telling me in my mind, 'Hurt him, just don't worry about it.'" Other children, such as nine-year-old Diante, another child living in the Henry Horner Homes described by Kotlowitz, become numb, helpless, bitterly fatalistic. Diante's older brother was fatally shot in an argument with a friend, and two weeks later, gunfire nearby, "Diante remained glued to a playground swing," repeating over and over while his friend begged him to take cover, "'I want to die.'"

Sometimes children develop coping strategies in the face of violence at one stage of development that increase their vulnerabilities and level of exposure to violence at a later stage. Tim, a six-year-old boy who lives with his mother and four younger siblings, has responded to violence with swaggering bravado; he thinks of himself as the "man" in his family. Whereas bravado might be adaptive to Tim at six, at twelve years old the odds of his becoming a casualty will rise dramatically because of his refusal to back down in the face of a threat. Tim's swaggering could also set in motion destructive family dynamics that may impair him in the long run. Remember that the swaggering of Stephen Bremer, the fourteen-year-old from Saugus, reminded his mother of her former husband, an arrogant, abusive man, and escalated her fights with her son.

In ghetto neighborhoods, where parents or community adults are apt to feel harassed and are sometimes victims of violence themselves, children are more likely to adapt to violence in ways that are primitive and self-destructive. Studies of children growing up in war zones reveal that the level of distress suffered by parents—not a child's direct exposure to the brutalities of war—is the most important factor in a child's ability to cope. A study in Israel of children on kibbitzum that had been shelled found no correlation between the level of shelling and a child's anxiety; parents' level of anxiety and children's level of anxiety, however, were linked.

How children cope with violence is directly connected to their parents' coping strategies. Tim, the six-year-old, has had great difficulty coping with exposure to violence, according to his therapist, in part because his mother was exposed to violence when she was twelve years old—she witnessed her mother's murder and her uncle's suicide—and remains badly damaged by this trauma. She adapted in ways that make her unresponsive to Tim and hamper his ability to manage his fears. She drinks heavily, is depressed and withdrawn, and frequently watches *Friday the 13th* films with her children. These films have directly fed Tim's fears.

The damage caused by violence is likely to be deeper when a child's tie to a primary caretaker is ruptured, when children are bounced among caregivers, when children suffer serious neglect or abuse, or when children witness frequent domestic violence. When children are repeatedly exposed to violence in their homes, they often feel that there is no sanctuary in their lives, and they are far more likely to see violence not as something aberrant in human nature, but as a norm. For these children, neighborhood violence, as violence researcher James Garbarino and his colleagues point out, can be a kind of "last straw," utterly shattering their trust in others.

Yet devastating as violence can be, many children who grow up in the thick of it are not broken or disfigured. Whether violence does lasting damage depends largely on whether parents and communities continue to provide children with at least some of the conditions of healthy growth. Children especially need meaningful opportunities, some sense of predictability and control in their immediate environments, and stable, supportive connections to adults who exert even greater control over the spaces that children occupy. In contrast to Tim's mother, Marsha Allen has been steadily affectionate, calm, and sensitive to the needs of her daughter, Avery, after Avery witnessed a brutal murder. Marsha managed, even in the chaos of a shelter, to create a miniature, stable environment. Avery, according to the family therapist, has emerged from the storm of this trauma entirely intact.

Children are less likely to be scarred by violence when they are able to talk to an adult soon after their exposure to it, when they have ongoing opportunities to discuss their fears, and when adults are able to give violence some meaning that is logical. Some children may develop more complex understandings of human nature and morality if adults can engage them in understanding violence. Parents and community adults may also impart religious beliefs that give violence a meaning and sustain hope. One significant difference between affluent and ghetto neighborhoods is that typically when violence occurs in affluent neighborhoods, exposed children receive immediate professional help and have other opportunities to talk to adults. When a group of youths savagely attacked another teenager in a serene suburb of Philadelphia, high school students were encouraged to go to a drop-in counseling office and a coalition of youth organizations, parents' groups, and religious institutions organized to counsel children and their parents. Immediately after an emotionally disturbed woman shot several children in a school in Winnetka, a tony Chicago suburb, teachers received instruction on how to talk to the children, and a crisis team of psychologists and social workers was assembled. In contrast, when a nine-year-old survived being shot in the back of the head in the Henry Horner Homes two days later, no one counseled either him or his friends. His friends simply prayed for him.

The age at which exposure first occurs is critical. Sometimes the neurological development of infants and toddlers who witness violence is impaired. Children under twelve years of age who are exposed to violence are three times more likely than children exposed later in life to suffer post-traumatic stress disorder. For young children, the horrors of community violence can merge with the frightening figures of the fantasy world, a situation described by Garbarino and his colleagues as "Godzilla joins the gangbangers." Younger children also often have difficulty talking about how violence affects them—there's no place for it in their cognitive or moral framework—making efforts to help them more difficult.

Along with parents, teachers, health-care professionals, police officers, recreation leaders, and other adults who work with children need some rudimentary knowledge of the factors that determine how children react to violence as well as training in how to talk to children about violence. Professionals also need to provide children exposed to violence with daily opportunities for accomplishment and mastery—especially opportunities that enable children to feel that they can affect their environment—to counteract the helplessness that witnessing violence brings. Teenagers should be encouraged to be activists, working with schools and the police to reduce violence and to educate other children about how to identify and avoid dangerous situations.

Parents can help children by taking active steps to combat neighborhood violence and by supporting their children's activism. Moreover, community institutions need to enable parents to talk about their responses to violence. Some parent support programs now emerging in ghetto neighborhoods are designed to help parents cope with violence and to give them practical advice about increasing their safety and the safety of their children. Until violence is reduced, the damage it causes can be greatly allayed by building on children's and parents' strengths and adaptive capacities.

The Quiet Troubles of Ghetto Children

The two central children profiled in Alex Kotlowitz's *There Are No Children Here* are Lafeyette and Pharoah, brothers, eleven and nine years old, who are trapped in the Henry Horner Homes in Chicago. Violence is rampant in this housing project. These boys regularly witness gunfire; they have heard about a brutal quadruple murder across the street; Lafeyette has witnessed a firebombing of a nearby home; they have lost friends to violence. But violence is not the only hazard these boys face. Nearly every day seems to bring unwanted intrusions that could fire the most colorless imaginations, let alone the active minds of these children. Darkness engulfs the hallways of their building—even in the daytime residents must carry a flashlight—and strangers pass freely through these tunnel-like corridors. Robbers have broken into their home. Some older children from a nearby gang intimidate them. In part because of these pressures, Pharoah has developed a serious stutter, which causes him to be ridiculed by other children at school and to keep to himself.

Other physical hazards—especially the risks of disease—abound as well: the basement of one of the buildings is littered with animal carcasses; parking lots are covered in waste; because of difficulties regulating the heat in their apartment, Pharoah develops bad cough.

Faced with these hazards, the boys have few sanctuaries. Pharoah's only places of refuge are a small plot of land abutting a railroad track and a small lawn in a nearby, somewhat more pleasant, project. As in other ghetto neighborhoods, productive activities and diversions are scarce: church activities, Scouts, and boys' and girls' clubs have dwindled or vanished; there are no public libraries, movie theaters, skating rinks, or bowling alleys; and parks and playgrounds, rather than providing stimulation and relief, can be menacing and reminiscent of harrowing scenes of shoot-outs and killings.

This neighborhood also saps their mother. She worries about her children constantly. In addition to caring for five children by herself, she tends to the needs of many neighbors. Many young people call her Mom. She is extremely generous with help, but, like other mothers in communities where stress is high, her generosity is sometimes abused. (She hides the toilet paper in the kitchen because it has been stolen several times.) She, too, lives with fear of violence and intruders. The nerves were severed in two fingers while she was fending off the attack of a robber in her home, and a drug-addicted man harasses her on the street. Her children worry that she might be killed. The infrastructure of the Henry Horner Homes has so deteriorated that nearly all the basic activities of daily life have become trials for her. There is no nearby bank or check casher, and prices at nearby grocery stores are exorbitant. Public-aid checks are sent to the local currency exchange, because the mailboxes have all been vandalized. Taxis will not enter the area, and stores will not deliver; even furniture must be carted home. The two neighborhood health clinics are on the edge of bankruptcy. Once there were thirteen social-services agencies; now there are only three. These tasks of daily life are even more difficult because she has no telephone. The neighborhood has become for her, in Kotlowitz's words, "a black hole." In part because of these stresses, the boys' mother battles sleeplessness and persistent colds and headaches for prolonged periods. She feels that her insides are "nothing but threads."

Nor can these boys turn readily to older siblings or friends or to community adults for support. One older brother, who cares deeply for these boys and wants to be good role model, is incarcerated. Women in the neighborhood tend to have their hands full meeting their own children's needs—and often the needs of their grandchildren and great grandchildren. "Many of the adults had aged with the neighborhood," Kotlowitz writes, "looking as worn and empty as the abandoned stores that lined the once-thriving Madison Street." Men are scarce; Pharoah's school is focused on recruiting male teachers. Elderly residents do not appear to figure at all in these boys' lives. A few incidents of being falsely accused by police officers—including being roughed up by a racist cop—have not only broken Lafeyette's faith in the police but aggravated his growing distrust of authority. Community institutions that reach out to children have also broken down— churches for Horner residents have "lost their authority." Because of the loss of these institutions and because of widespread fear and distrust, it seems to residents that the community has no collective conscience, no moral center. Over time, living in a world with few children or adults whom he trusts—a world of terrible, random events, in which people he cares about are killed for no reason, a world that no longer seems to recoil from and mobilize in the face of injustice—Lafeyette sinks into a deep fatalism and cynicism.

Despite the media attention that ghetto violence receives, children in ghettos are more likely to be undermined by quiet, insidious difficulties. The perils and abrasions of life in the Henry Horner Homes are typical of ghetto neighborhoods. In part because of menacing intrusions and exploitation of different kinds, children in ghettos are more vulnerable not only to various anxieties that can produce physical symptoms, such as Pharoah's stutter, but also to many other emotional and learning difficulties. In addition to diseases, accidents—especially head injuries—are more likely to befall ghetto children than others. Dangerous intersections are less apt to have crossing guards, information on childrens' safety is less available, and safety accessories, such as bicycle helmets and car seats, are scarce or unaffordable. Ghetto children are more frequently exposed to toxic chemicals and pollutants that have been linked to behavior difficulties, brain damage, and damaged immune systems, among other problems.

Unlike other communities, ghettos have been stripped of the resources and supports that children need to cope with problems. Thus almost any problem, however minor at first, can fester. Ghetto children are less likely than other children to have productive activities and ties to stable, unstressed adults, in part because there are simply fewer adults per child in ghettos.

Schools and services in ghettos do not typically help children weather these abrasions and deprivations. Health and social services are not only scarce, but are often of miserable quality. Even when good health services exist, ghetto families often lack adequate health-care coverage. With the exception of the Headstart program, formal child care tends to be unavailable or unaffordable in ghettos, and child-care providers in ghettos tend to be less well-educated than those in other neighborhoods. Among schools, those in ghettos commonly have the fewest resources and the most difficulty attracting high-quality teachers. Although some ghetto children have ties to police officers, others are loathe to seek help from the police—"We are our own police," a ghetto teenager in Chicago told reporter Michael Marmot. "I'm not calling 911."

At the same time, ghetto communities constantly assault children's own inner resources and coping capacities. Children, such as Lafeyette, often are subjected to senseless, incomprehensible suffering, are unable to exert control over their environment, and lack faith in the trustworthiness and fairness of authority. Many children feel an acute sense of injustice and lack faith in the future. They come to believe that hard work, intelligence, and admirable intentions will not be rewarded—in particular, that there are no routes to meaningful jobs—and that a meritocracy does not exist for children such as them. These conditions breed resignation— or rage, not resilience. Psychologists have also long recognized that the self is a kind of mirror of the outside world and that constant images of stagnation, decay, and disease can over time insinuate themselves into a child's self-image.

In these environments bereft of the basic nutrients of the self, environments that do so little to buttress children's and adults' coping capabilities, small problems constantly erupt and are not adequately resolved. Everything that "goes wrong keeps going on and everything that's right doesn't stay right," Lafeyette says. Pharoah's stutter is continually exacerbated not only because he is repeatedly subjected to violence and intimidation, but also because he is greatly distressed by his brother's incarceration and because his mother is pulled in a thousand directions and cannot focus attention on him.

Small problems quickly trigger other problems, undermining children in many areas of development. As social policy researcher Lisbeth Schorr observes, ghetto children, because they are more likely to be malnourished and to live in unheated apartments, are also more susceptible to ear infections. An ear infection may not be detected at an early stage, because caretakers are often overwhelmed with other problems. Even after an infection is detected, health care may be inaccessible or of poor quality. An untreated ear infection can lead to a hearing loss, which can set off a whole slew of other difficulties for a child in a ghetto neighborhood. A hearing loss makes schoolwork far more difficult, and an overwhelmed teacher in a ghetto neighborhood may not be able to attend to these difficulties. Worse, a teacher or community adult under stress may mistake a child's difficulty hearing for a serious learning disability, stubbornness, or defiance and meet it with punishment. Further, frightening and isolating as a hearing loss can be for any child, the difficulties and dangers of navigating in a ghetto are compounded many times for children who have lost some capacity to sense their surroundings. And difficult as it is for children from ghettos to make the transition to mainstream employment, the task can be utterly overwhelming for children who have never developed an adequate sense of competence in their own surroundings. Physical and learning disabilities and vision impairments—almost any kind of problem— similarly feed off the aggravations of ghetto life and persist in ways that can impair children at every stage of development.

Creating environments within ghettos that meet children's basic needs—preventing these quiet troubles— and intercepting troubles early is clearly not a simple matter. Although good social services, sound health care, and strong schools are surely part of preventing and responding to these troubles, they will not by themselves spare many children persistent difficulties where poverty is rampant and many adults are overwhelmed or despondent. Nor can the various economic development strategies now being implemented themselves turn ghettos around. New job opportunities are meaningless to children who cannot seize them because they are debilitated by physical or psychological problems or lack basic skills.

Further, positive reforms are not likely to take root in communities such as the Henry Horner Homes, where social institutions responsible for children have evaporated and where there is little civic involvement or civic pride. In an extensive, landmark study of the properties of strong communities in Italy, Harvard political scientist Robert Putnam found that civic engagement—a commitment to and involvement with neighborhood life—is the single characteristic that most clearly separates prosperous and failing communities. Communities in which civic engagement is high protect children and generate crucial resources and support— job ideas, religious groups, informal networks. Putnam points out that in this country, too, inner-city youths, regardless of race, who live in neighborhoods in which there are collaborative ties among neighborhood adults are more likely than those from other inner-city communities to finish school, hold jobs, and avoid drugs and crime and appear to be less likely to become pregnant as teens.

What is most promising are current efforts that seek simultaneously to provide parents and children with necessary services and supports, to strengthen civic involvement, and to create economic opportunities. In Sandtown-Winchester, an extremely poor area of Baltimore, community residents, city government, and the Enterprise Foundation embarked in 1990 on an especially exciting partnership utilizing many strategies, including housing development, community building, education, health and human services reform, expansion of job-training opportunities, commercial development, and community policing. Significant gains have been made in all these areas. Several hundred housing units have been renovated or rehabilitated. The community building project has led to nearly 90 projects and services, including the upgrading of more than a thousand housing units, a new community center, a health outreach program to provide mothers with prenatal and infant care, and the establishment of a residents' food and clothing cooperative. Specific education goals have been created, such as improving children's readiness for kindergarten and increasing attendance, and progress has been made toward achieving them; parent academy and parent training programs have been established in elementary schools, all school staff have been trained in the Efficacy Institute philosophy that all children can learn, and a full-day kindergarten has been instituted. Many pieces of what will be a comprehensive health-care system available to all Sandtown residents have been implemented. A newly formed Sandtown Employment and Training Center provides skills testing, training, job placement, and follow-up assistance to residents. This center focuses both on entry-level jobs and on creating long-term career paths. An extensive community policing effort has been launched, and more than 120 block captains have been recruited for Block Watch and Neighborhood Watch programs. A variety of recreational and artistic opportunities have been created for both children and adults. Residents themselves have taken leadership roles in these transformations. Key to this success has been the ability of the Enterprise Foundation's community organizers to work with residents to fashion together a long-term vision according to Sandtown's particular strengths and needs.

Other promising multidimensional strategies have appeared in the realm of community economic development. Shorebank, based in Chicago, is collaborating with leaders in the Austin neighborhood to create jobs and to train residents for these new jobs. This collaboration is also developing family service and grassroots "affinity" organizations of peer groups and other vehicles to reconnect people and support their work toward self-sufficiency.

These many interventions involve significant expenditures and extensive planning. But ghetto communities are not going to be transformed inexpensively. If we are to stop violence and its many destructive repercussions, if we are to prevent and stem early the quiet troubles of ghetto children, we have to stop thinking about single solutions or quick fixes. We need to think instead about using many different tools simultaneously to undertake the painstaking work of re-creating in ghetto neighborhoods the soil that all children need to grow.

8

WHY OUR EFFORTS TO
HELP CHILDREN FAIL

I N OCTOBER 1987, TWO MONTHS AFTER HIS ELEVENTH
birthday, Michael Moran was admitted to a psychiatric hospital
for children. What triggered the hospitalization was not
Michael's taking refuge under his desk and screaming, "Go away."
After that episode he regained his bearings fairly quickly, largely
because he was returned for part of the day to a special education
classroom, in which his learning difficulties were addressed.

But, eighteen months later, when Michael entered junior high
school, a group of children ganged up on him, just as another group
had when Michael first moved to Ferguson. His concentration in
class began to crack. This time, under the constant pressure of
the teasing and the anxiety of not being able to focus on his
schoolwork, Michael found himself barraged with strange,
frightening thoughts. Sometimes it seemed to him that everyone,
including his mother, Cora, hated him and was out to hurt him. If
Cora suggested that he take a walk, he thought she wanted him
to get hit by a car. He developed compulsive behaviors. He rubbed
his wrists almost constantly. He chewed his nails down to his fingers.
He thought about suicide and went so far as to make a noose one
day. It seemed to him that everything was "caving in."

Cora did not know how to break his fall. She had lost her ability
to communicate with him. When she asked him to tell her about
his day, he would start one story—usually about a vicious attack
he had suffered—and jump to another midstream. She worried
that he was becoming, like her uncle, schizophrenic.

A psychiatrist whom Michael had been seeing for several months reassured Cora that Michael was not schizophrenic, but expressed concern that stress was badly distorting Michael's thinking and that Michael was losing the ability to handle almost any type of day-to-day pressure. The psychiatrist was leaning toward temporarily hospitalizing him. Cora dreaded the thought, but she had lost faith in her ability to help.

Initially, Michael was terrified of the hospital, and his experience during the first week of his stay only confirmed his fears. His roommate woke up howling and thrashing and had to be strapped to a bed. One of the first nurses he met was "creepy": "nice to parents, but the terminator with us." Within two weeks, however, he had become attached to two other nurses and had made two friends. In many ways, he began to feel more at home than he had ever felt anywhere. Never had he been around so many people who were nice to him. His progress seemed so solid that after two months his mother and the hospital staff felt that he was ready to return home, although with certain conditions.

His hospital records described Michael as prone to "major depression," a child who "desperately needs safety and structure." The staff recommended—and Cora agreed—that Michael be placed in a special school where his learning problems would be directly addressed and where he would be less likely to become prey to his peers. While Michael awaited placement, his old school agreed to provide him with support. For a month a tutor came to the house. Then a temporary support system was established for Michael at school. He had access at any time to a guidance counselor and to the assistant principal—a man named Fred Barton—whom he knew and trusted.

The support team proved indispensable. Michael continued to be hounded, and several times a week he retreated from the battleground of the classroom or the hallways to the assistant principal's office.

But after several months there was still no movement toward placing Michael in a special school. Part of the problem was that the hospital had no capacity to press the school system for such a placement. The hospital did not even have a staff member who could attend a meeting at Michael's school, and the school, Cora was told, did not have a representative who could attend a meeting at the hospital. The assistant superintendent, Tim Downey, told Cora that even if a representative were available, Michael did not need special placement. "Taking some heat from other children should toughen Michael up a bit," Downey said, and he asked rhetorically, "If Michael's not hurting other kids, why put him in one of those places?" He also suggested that the teasing might be defused if Cora could find Michael some "nicer, more stylish clothes."

Cora thought Downey was working another agenda, that he was simply trying to avoid a costly special placement. Yet even Fred Barton, the assistant principal and Michael's confidant, expressed concern that Michael might be worse off in a special school, surrounded by many other children who had been out of control in regular classrooms and who might be more abusive than Michael's current classmates.

Meanwhile, Michael's designated support team was evaporating. Fred Barton became the principal and had little time for Michael. Because of budget cuts, the counselor's hours were cut back, too.

Michael plummeted again. For the first time, he developed severe headaches. His doctor ordered a battery of tests, but found no organic cause. "School is making him sick," the school nurse told Cora. At home his temper flew.

Cora was enraged. It seemed to her that the school was subjecting Michael to another form of abuse. And this was not the first time that she had felt that Michael was being mistreated by one of the long line of professionals who were supposedly charged with helping him. She was losing faith in the whole lot. Although many of these professionals, such as Fred Barton, had been both able and kind, far too many had been indifferent, insensitive, even cruel. One teacher, in a moment of exasperation, had called Michael "a retard" within his earshot. One psychologist had told Cora that Michael "would be fine, he's just a nerd...he'll go to MIT and be a big success." Questions had been raised about Cora's mothering that burned deeply: one psychologist had suggested that she was suffocating her children because she was deprived as a child; a teacher had told her that she was "overnurturing" and "feminizing" her children because she wouldn't let the boys fight; a social worker had thought she had put her finger on the real source of Michael's distress—"Do you think Michael has seen you engaged in sexual intercourse?" With her son in agony, here was the assistant superintendent suggesting that the problem was wearing the wrong clothes! Why did Tim Downey obsess about Michael's sweatpants, Cora thought, rather than credit her with getting him to school in the first place? There was also the mass of labels that followed Michael—Michael had always especially hated "emotionally disabled"—and the jargon, the psychobabble.

Cora had heard one of Michael's diagnoses—"secondary emotional problems due to hyperactivity and attention deficit"—so many times she could recite it in her sleep. Adding insult to injury, it seemed to Cora that all the various professionals working with Michael—teachers, psychologists, and nurses—had different understandings of Michael's problem and different methods for solving it. It was like the blind men feeling the elephant.

Cora had had enough. She declared war. She pulled Michael out of school altogether. The school urged her to return him, but that was out of the question, in part because Michael made it so: "You send me back to school," Michael told her, "and I'll throw myself out of the car."

Downey met with her twice about Michael's absences, but she felt that every time she insisted that a special placement be made, he found some way to stall or dodge her. Finally, he agreed to call a meeting of Michael's teacher, an advocate from the State Office for Children, a school psychiatric consultant, and Cora's lawyer to decide Michael's fate. At various points during the meeting threats were exchanged. Downey threatened to file a Child in Need of Services (CHINS) petition with the state. Downey claimed that Cora was neglecting Michael by keeping him out of school, and the petition, he said, would enable the state to force Michael to attend. But Cora wouldn't be bullied. Political activity over the past few years had given her a few media contacts, and she threatened to let a reporter know her version of events: Michael had been denied a desperately needed and promised special placement so that the school system could save money. Whether or not he took the threat seriously, Downey agreed to a special placement in a school for emotionally disturbed teenagers.

None of this filled Michael with hope, however. What would be better about this special school? Would he be spending all day with "a bunch of retards"?

Cora worried, too. It seemed to her that she had been a victim of dirty play and that it might not be over. And Fred Barton's concern echoed in her head: how would Michael do in a special school for emotionally disturbed children? Would he feel more alone? Would he be less—or more—abused?

When children's basic needs are not met, when children do not receive the kind of nurturing they need from families and communities, many come to depend on the web of care provided by schools, health-care agencies, and other caregiving institutions. Many children also need special health, social, and educational services to deal with inherited deficits, ailments, and disabilities or with problems such as Michael's that develop as a result of complex interactions between inborn traits and environmental conditions.

Yet these caregiving institutions are now widely seen as failing to meet the needs of children, and such criticism has generated no shortage of reforms. Every institution has its own reform industry. Every year education advocacy and research groups recommend new teaching methods, for example, that are more responsive to vulnerable students. Health-care advocates regularly seek to sharpen responses to specific diseases. Individual programs and professional disciplines have evolved in response to problems that have attracted widespread public concern. In the 1980s, for example, a high rate of teenage pregnancy was "discovered" by the media. Legislators scurried to create programs to drive these rates down. Private funding also tends to chase media attention, reinforcing the patterns set by the public system. As a result, schools, health care, and social service agencies—bolstered by academic specialists—have developed better ways of curbing many specific problems.

Yet this collection of institutions and programs, this system of care, disarmingly simple in conception, is too splintered and complex to administer effectively, and it does little to prevent problems, to ensure that children such as Michael receive the basic ingredients of sturdy growth. Not a single institution, for example, takes responsibility for supporting and strengthening parents such as Cora.

Moreover, the system fails to stem problems at early stages, and it deals inadequately with many children and families once their problems become serious. Children like Michael who have multiple problems are often buffeted among institutions that, because of their different funding and bureaucratic and professional requirements, have different ways of defining the issue, different modes of providing help, indeed, different ways of defining whether a child has a problem at all. In the musical *West Side Story*, Riff and his gang, the Jets, mock exactly this aspect of the system. In the song "Officer Krupke," Riff describes his tortuous path through various institutions that are supposed to help him. He is first labeled as a delinquent and sent to a judge, who declares that his real problem is that he is emotionally troubled; the judge refers Riff to a psychologist, who defines the problem as a social ill and fobs him off onto a social worker; and so on. Teachers, health-care providers, and other professionals also often lack the resources, training, and support they need to move outside rigid bureaucratic and professional boundaries to respond to children who do not have tidy problems but who have multiple and messy difficulties.

And although many good programs and services around the country deal with discrete problems, the reality remains that vital services simply don't exist in certain communities, and far too many services are of miserable quality. Once problems develop, many children and families, like the Morans, feel not only frustrated, but degraded when they seek assistance from professionals— whether teachers, health-care providers, welfare workers, or social workers.

Focusing on improving individual institutions' responses to certain high-profile, discrete problems—important as that is—will do little to improve the prospects of large numbers of vulnerable children. Improving these children's prospects requires simultaneous changes across many institutions, and it requires reversing the basic motion of our efforts to care for vulnerable children. We need a system of care that is not driven by concerns whipped up by the media and molded by legislative, bureaucratic, and funding requirements. We need a system that enables professionals to work respectfully, collaboratively, and proactively with families and that takes its shape from children's and families' needs.

Why the System Fails

Psychology researchers and practitioners have learned a great deal in the past several decades about the nature and course of children's and families' problems, but this knowledge has had little influence on the basic structure of child and family services, driven as they are by funding and bureaucratic mandates. The web of care for children is not governed by any coherent philosophy about the nature of child and family troubles, about the basic needs of all children, or about how to promote healthy child and family development. As a result, the system fails many different kinds of children and often fails one child and family in many different ways.

Consider the many ways in which the system failed to prevent or to deal with the troubles of the Moran family. Like most children's problems, Michael's problems did not suddenly explode—they escalated in stages. Michael moved to a new neighborhood where he was teased. The teasing upset his concentration in class. Michael was frustrated by the teasing and his inability to do his schoolwork, and his behavior became increasingly strange, which elicited more teasing, which further undermined his school performance. Yet the system did not respond to his problems until they were full-blown. Michael only received concerted attention from school staff when he wound up under his desk screaming or his mother pulled him out of school altogether. Similarly, Mathew, a sixteen-year-old from Boston, had a learning disability that went undiagnosed, making schoolwork extremely difficult. He eventually dropped out of school and joined a gang. His learning disability was not addressed until he was arrested for assault and a concerned family friend, a psychologist, sought tutoring for him. Occasionally a social worker who becomes involved in a juvenile delinquency case is the first to detect such long-standing difficulties.

Health-care providers also miss early signs of distress. Neglect and abuse are often not discovered by pediatricians until they are contacted by a child protective services worker who is conducting an investigation. Only then, in response to such a report, do pediatricians ask parents whether they are having difficulties with their children. Too often problems are only uncovered when a child is unusually frank and brave. "Mommy drinks too much liquor," a nine-year-old told Lisa Forest, a Boston pediatrician. This statement prompted Forest to ask several questions that revealed this mother's serious alcohol problem. Because basic mechanisms for identifying and intercepting problems early are not in place, many children receive preventive care at the wrong time for the wrong reason. Sometimes teenage boys, for example, do not receive their first physical exam until they are incarcerated.

Family problems also escalate in stages, yet are rarely intercepted early. In the Moran family, a divorce threw Cora onto welfare, and the stresses of poverty and single parenthood made it far more difficult for her to cope with Michael's problems as they developed over time. Fred Louis, the Little Rock high school student, struggled after his parents' divorce. His mother had taken two jobs to make ends meet, and because she was working and then became preoccupied with the drug problem of Fred's younger brother, she failed to notice that for months Fred had been drifting out of school. Families such as the Morans or the Louises typically do not receive help until a child is in crisis. Sometimes the problems of several family members have to veer out of control before anyone intervenes.

Once problems escalate, the system often fails in equally serious ways. Because each profession views children through its own particular professional and institutional lens, care providers may fail to discern that a problem has a symptom in one domain and a cause in another. Michael's pediatrician ordered a battery of tests to identify the source of Michael's migraines; he never asked Michael how he was faring in school, so he never discovered that Michael was under terrific stress. Diane, a ten-year-old in Seattle, was distracted and restless in class, yet no one learned that she was being sexually abused until she was referred by a school outreach worker to a medical clinic for a possible urinary tract infection. An exam revealed that the infection was caused by a sexually transmitted disease, which was eventually traced to her uncle.

Teachers often have a hard time discerning whether a concentration problem in class is due to an emotional difficulty, a learning disability, or a physical problem such as hunger or illness. And problems such as violence that have many different roots in children's families and communities are often not effectively addressed by the system.

Once problems have become serious, the system fails doubly: not only does it view each problem in isolation, but it views children and their troubles in isolation from their families. In addition to ignoring family patterns and dynamics, programs often ignore the most elementary ways in which family members influence one another. Individual systems tend to treat every family member as an isolated unit. The many professionals working with Michael failed to help Cora deal with her debilitating anxieties. Ryan, a Little Rock high school student, had to stay home to take care of his depressed mother after his brother was shot and killed because no one at the school could help her find a counselor. Often children who stay home from school to baby-sit for a younger sibling could attend school if schools could help parents obtain child care. Yet schools are not structured to solve this kind of problem.

Conversely, services designed to help parents often ignore their children. Cora's doctor discovered that she was depressed during the period prior to Michael's hospitalization—she had lost sixty-five pounds in three months—but never asked her about Michael and Joe. No one in Michael's life sought to understand how his peer problems, his migraines, his learning difficulties, and his mother's depression might be intertwined and reinforce one another and how this downward cycle might be broken.

Hard as it is to coordinate treatment for families at one point in time, the system often makes it even more difficult to provide and coordinate care for children such as Michael *over* time. The problems of a child such as Michael won't go away unless they're given sustained, continuous attention, yet Michael's support team vanished when a key member took a new job. Often services for children are covered by public or private insurance only for short periods of time. Individual counseling and psychiatric hospitalizations, for example, are commonly covered for a few months or weeks. When children turn eighteen, they may be terminated from desperately needed programs. Child protective service agencies generally terminate cases of neglected and abused children when they turn eighteen. These children often lose Medicaid benefits as well, even though they are at high risk for pregnancy, sexually transmitted diseases, and substance abuse. Transitions, even positive ones, sever parents and children from vital programs. A new job can place parents in an income bracket that disqualifies their children from a needed child-care or after-school program. Care may be disrupted not only when families move, but even when they remain in one neighborhood. Children are often handed off clumsily from one program to another—there's no underlying framework, no scaffolding that connects programs for children over time—or simply leave programs with little or no follow-up. In Little Rock, many junior high school children became attached to young men and women through a mentoring program, yet when these children went to high school, the mentors picked up a new group of junior high school children.

Some institutions and programs do stitch together their understandings of children and families and develop coherent, coordinated, long-term plans for responding to the various problems a family presents. But many obstacles stand in the way of this kind of collaboration. Often institutions are not structured for collaboration—in Michael's case, neither the hospital nor his school could afford to devote a staff member's time to easing his transition back to school. Turf problems torpedo collaborations: Institutions see a child with multifaceted problems as primarily their responsibility or, conversely, institutions are eager to pass the buck when children have problems that cannot be easily solved or that do not fit cleanly into their guidelines. Sometimes teen mothers are denied access to drug treatment programs, for example, if they are on welfare.

Another problem is that professionals have different data about children. Teachers make judgments about children's difficulties based primarily on direct observations, grades, and attendance. Although contact with parents is regular, it is typically scant, so that teachers typically understand little about children's family situations and often have little knowledge of their neighborhoods. Health-care providers usually see parents and children irregularly; contact is extremely brief, and they have no opportunity to observe children and parents in any natural setting. Police officers and social workers see families in their homes and sometimes in their neighborhoods, but they generally see families only when they are in crisis. Because these different caregivers have limited information, they often have limited comprehension of how a family functions as a whole. Because they draw on different sources of information—a teacher sees Michael in class but does not know his mother or see him outside of class; Michael's counselor sees him in counseling but nowhere else—and use different methods of analysis, caregivers often come to different understandings of children's and families' problems and develop strategies for solving those problems that often bear little relation to one another.

Faced with a system that is fragmented in these ways, many parents, like Cora Moran, manage to coordinate their own care. Much can be said for a system that enables families to piece together services for themselves rather than relying on professionals. Yet surveys suggest that the system is a bewildering, dizzying maze to many parents, that many parents simply don't know that services exist or where to obtain them, and that cities' information and referral systems are inadequate and confusing. Parents are sometimes daunted by the huge effort of tracking down even a simple service, such as a lead-poisoning test for a child. Once located, a service may be difficult to access because of a long waiting period or because it is far away. Transportation problems are significant for many parents. And, whereas Cora was able to use a media contact to force the school principal to find Michael a special placement, most parents have neither the contacts nor the skills to advocate effectively within the system.

A system that is fragmented fails children such as Michael who have many persistent problems, and many other children as well. Because there is no framework for checking in with children at regular intervals, children who suffer problems that have delayed effects often never receive decent care. Although schools sometimes reach out to a child in the immediate wake of a divorce, the full impact of a divorce often does not hit children until years later, as with Fred Louis. Schools and other programs sometimes try to reach children immediately after exposure to violence, yet the disturbing reality of post-traumatic stress disorder is that the most distressing symptoms caused by witnessing violence often do not boil to the surface until months or even years later. Because the system does not have routine check-in points when children and parents are able to talk about their concerns and fears, it also responds sluggishly to children who do not have highly visible symptoms and to those whose families present no easy markers of distress. Recall Sheila Woods, whose poor eating habits went undetected by school staff because her parents were both successful professionals.

The Shackles on Caregiving Professionals

Twenty-four-year-old Bill Davis is now in his second year as a teacher at a public elementary school in South Central Los Angeles. Usually clearheaded, direct, unequivocating, lately, confronted with the many troubles of his students, Bill feels at sea. He is especially concerned about two children: Lakeisha, who comes to school listless and sleeps in class, and Carlos, who has recently witnessed the shooting of his father. Bill can't figure out how to help. The school counselor is not an option; her position was recently eliminated because of budget cuts. He has consulted with other teachers, but they have given up. One teacher remarked that Bill should be grateful that one of his students was sleeping—"a sleeping student is one less student to have to teach." Talking to the principal is out of the question. He is bogged down, he tells Bill, in an "ungodly amount of paperwork" and has stated clearly that he cannot be consulted about individual students. Bill has called Carlos's mother, but she does not speak English. He is also worried about spending too much time with any one child—he has thirty-two children in class—and he fears that he is not equipped to deal with their troubles. He has no training in child development nor as a counselor or social worker.

Many of the problems of the current fragmented system could be alleviated if the various professionals who work with children could be responsive to the wide range of problems that they confront day to day. However, the jobs of many professionals, such as Bill Davis, are simply not structured to enable them to be responsive even to some of the most glaring childhood problems.

Like teachers, school nurses, school guidance counselors, health-care providers, and police officers often simply lack the time to listen to a child's troubles, let alone to inquire into a parent's difficulties. At a typical health center, a pediatrician is likely to spend not more than ten minutes with a child. Even when professionals have time, they are usually not trained in child development or in listening empathically to children who are in crisis. And taking extra time with a child or parent is usually not rewarded and is sometimes discouraged by administrators. Sometimes bureaucratic regulations needlessly shorten the reach and squander the skills of professionals. Often social workers are unable to continue working with a child who moves to an adjacent neighborhood because that child is suddenly outside their jurisdiction.

As a result of these various obstacles, professionals may be effective only if they are willing to cut into their personal resources and time, if they are dogged and pestering with administrators, or if they are willing to bend or break rules.

Even when they have time and support, many professionals are not guided by any philosophy about how to work with families that have multiple problems. Some professionals try to respond to every problem that surfaces; they seek to scratch every itch. Yet care providers can quickly burn out if they seek solutions to all the needs and symptoms of some families. They may spend a great deal of time treating symptoms that continually reappear in different forms, rather than addressing the core problem.

Increasing the flexibility and responsiveness of professionals does not mean that teachers, health-care providers, and police officers should be expected to be social workers. It is important, in fact, for professionals not to regularly stray far from their primary roles, to stick to what they do best. But they should have the capacity to listen to and assess children's difficulties, they should know when to refer families to other professionals, and they should be supported by administrators in this broader, more meaningful role.

Services That Don't Work

Many of the problems with the system are even more fundamental than its fragmentation. Some areas of the country—especially rural areas—lack basic social, psychological, and health services, or have services of miserable quality. Large caseloads make effective work with any one child difficult if not impossible. Not uncommonly, guidance counselors in urban high schools are assigned as many as 250 children, all designated at risk. Sometimes care providers are confused about their mission and are inadequately trained and supervised. At a school outside Boston, a special education teacher supervises several children all day in a "behavior" trailer in the school playground. These children have been belligerent in regular classrooms, but this teacher has not been given explicit instruction as to her purpose. For hours every day these children play Nintendo. Some common problems are typically not addressed by any professional. For example, large numbers of children are undermined by hopelessness and disillusionment, yet professionals are rarely trained to respond to these troubles.

For countless families services are ineffective because of language and cultural barriers. A Boston pediatrician is reluctant to delve into the troubles of Cape Verdean families because she knows that there is no social worker available who speaks Crioulo. Misunderstandings of cultural norms and beliefs can wreak havoc. At a school in Massachusetts, several children from the Dominican Republic became involved in escalating conflicts with teachers. The children had been taught by their parents that maintaining eye contact while being reprimanded by adults is a sign of disrespect, but their teachers interpreted the *lack* of eye contact as disrespectful. The school principal and the school nurse in another school found themselves in a quandary after filing a neglect and abuse report on a Cambodian child who came to school with a large burn mark, in the form of a band, across his chest. The burn mark, it turned out, was the result of a religious ritual common in the child's community. Attempts to help families from some communities backfire because certain Western notions of treatment are entirely foreign and threatening to them: In Vietnamese, there is not even a word for *therapy*, and many Vietnamese adults, like adults from many cultures, consider seeing a mental health professional a clear sign that a person is crazy. Parents and children from different cultural groups may tend to enter the system at different times for different reasons with different treatment expectations, yet professionals often treat them based on a single, universal model. According to Will McMullen, an African-American psychologist in Cambridge, Massachusetts, working-class and poor African-American parents often seek help around "'this has got to stop now' issues. They want practical help in stopping a kid from using drugs, or staying out all night, or lying all the time," yet, "they are often treated based on a model developed by those who work with higher-income white parents—a social worker or therapist will try to help them understand the psychodynamics of the situation. They will try to promote insight." Even outsiders' attempts to help families out of poverty can be alienating: in some Native American communities, material poverty is very closely connected to purity of spirit.

In addition, services are commonly ineffective because professionals are unable to provide small aids to families that could stem problems early and make a large difference in their lives. Most families do not need months of psychotherapy, long-term support groups, or extensive medical attention. School administrators might go a long way toward solving a child's problem if they could pay the cost of transportation for a parent to attend a parent-teacher conference at school, for example, yet administrators often lack uncommitted funds. For Sheila, a foster mother, the stress of caring for a badly abused foster child with serious medical problems was increased many times because she couldn't afford to park twice a week at a children's hospital, yet the social worker assigned to the case couldn't pay for this expense. Large government programs, too, often make it difficult to do small, very meaningful things. For example, in Maryland, Medicaid pays for one pair of glasses per child per year. However, children frequently lose glasses, and school staff are deterred from the seemingly simple task of obtaining replacement glasses because the process requires extensive, time-consuming documentation. "As soon as it costs a nickel," says Barbara Ritter, a school consultant, "thousands of pages of documentation are required." Some crises could be averted if families could find someone to baby-sit in an emergency situation or if they could obtain a good job tip, yet commonly no one in the system has the leeway to provide this kind of help.

Only Human Caregivers

Families I have spoken with are bitter about services that can't be located, about being bounced from one program to another, about well-intentioned professionals who seem to have their hands tied by bureaucratic regulations. But families' primary concern about the system has to do with the qualities of the flesh-and-blood individuals with whom they interact. One study of an enhanced prenatal-care program in Washington, D.C., uncovered that the most important factor in keeping women in the program and utilizing health services properly was neither the program's cash incentives nor accessibility, but it was the "friendly support" of "someone to talk to about pregnancy and other life stresses."

Many efforts to help families backfire because parents never make a positive connection to a professional. It is hard to overstate how demeaned some parents feel in their contacts with state welfare workers and social workers. Images of themselves as deformed— "It's as if I'm a monster"; "I felt like I had six heads"—are common, as are sexually degrading images—feeling like "sluts" or "whores." Some families, such as the Morans, see themselves as buffeted by a long succession of insensitivities and degradations at the hands of many different professionals. Despite the differences in families' contacts with welfare workers, health-care workers, teachers, and other professionals, parents may feel with each a similar sense of helplessness and invisibility; they may feel at the mercy of professionals who treat them as "children," as "objects," or as "dumb," who bury them in labels or twist them to fit some easy classification or mental slot.

To be sure, some professionals are simply insensitive, and some professionals are bound by rules and regulations that are inherently degrading and perverse to families. To receive help, parents sometimes have to contort themselves into a pathetic shape; they sometimes have to dramatize their plight, for example, because state child protective service agencies only intercede when children are in extreme jeopardy. One mother living in a town outside Boston had to claim that she was suicidal to get help from a neighborhood social service agency because the agency only provided help to mothers in crisis. Often parents complain that simply asking for help can work against them: "It's a sign that you're strong enough to take care of your kids," one mother says.

When Michael Moran was two years old, Cora was interviewed by a nurse home visitor who determined that she was a solid mother and that Michael was not seriously imperiled. Cora beseeched the home visitor to "find something wrong" with her so that she could get help, overwhelmed as she was by the demands of raising two young boys when she was both poor and alone. Often parents suffer in their interactions with the social service system what psychologist Martin Seligman describes as learned helplessness, that is, a feeling that there is no connection between their actions and their consequences, that punishments and rewards are arbitrary and illogical.

Many families also feel degraded because they are defined solely by their deficits and problems. "A minimal test of a health care worker's effectiveness might be composed of these two questions," says Ron David, a Harvard health policy professor and pediatrician, "Can you list five of your patient's strengths? What is your plan for capitalizing on those strengths? I don't think many workers would pass."

Despite these serious problems, there is a more basic reason that families feel degraded by professionals. Large numbers of teachers, health-care workers, counselors, and social workers are themselves in circumstances that are draining and degrading, that erode their generosity and empathy, their willingness to learn from parents and children, and their tolerance of human foibles.

Take Brenda White. A teacher for many years, Brenda decided in 1987 to work as a state child welfare worker investigating child neglect and abuse. She had no formal training in social work, yet she was expected to conduct investigations after only three weeks on the job. A supervisor accompanied her on her first visit— a father and adolescent daughter had become embroiled in a fierce fistfight—but the supervisor vanished after asking the family a few preliminary questions. "Baptism by fire," Brenda recalls. Her supervisor also seemed far more concerned with adhering to bureaucratic procedures than with helping families. Long-range solutions especially were not part of this supervisor's vocabulary: She wanted to know that a threatening father was out of the house or that a child had obtained counseling, not how Brenda might help that father find a job or whether that child hated the counselor. Many administrators, involved in an elaborate game of duck and cover, were rarely available for help or guidance either: "Administrators had a kind of combat zone mentality," Brenda recalls. "They were looking not to be held accountable for some disaster. They were looking for shelter, a safe place."

There were for Brenda many other irritations and sources of drain; time-consuming, seemingly meaningless paperwork requirements spewed out by a bureaucracy that was itself daunting and incomprehensible, little recognition from superiors, no input into office procedures or into key management decisions that had a direct bearing on her. Several times she was shifted from job to job without her consultation. Moreover, although many families were grateful for her help, she had to contend constantly with others who were suspicious and distrustful, if not irate. Concerns about her physical safety loomed large in certain neighborhoods. On one occasion she was threatened with a knife after telling a mother that her child would have to be removed from the home.

For months on end Brenda struggled with depression. During these bouts, she was often impatient with families. Brenda believes that she was able to survive these periods only because she sought counseling herself, something that most social workers do not do.

Because of her skills and hard work, Brenda became a supervisor. But even as a supervisor she does not receive the support she needs, and she feels it is impossible to advocate effectively for her workers in a system that is not geared to their needs.

In discussions with professionals—social workers, teachers, health-care providers, police officers—the stresses described by Brenda are mentioned again and again. Staggering numbers of professionals feel unsupported, ill supervised, bolted to meaningless bureaucratic procedures, and as if they are tiny specks in huge, hulking institutions. Numerous professionals deal with wounded, volatile parents who are highly dependent on them yet recoil from precisely this dependency, parents with long histories of betrayal, rejection, and disillusionment. "There are parents who have only known neglect and exploitation," Diana Mullen, a New York social worker, observes. "They don't even have a model for forming a constructive relationship in their head."

Physical safety has become an increasingly serious concern. Richard Newman, a branch manager in Kentucky's Human Resources

Agency, described in the *New York Times* some of the daily slings and arrows absorbed by social workers on the front line: "Our people have been kicked with cowboy boots, threatened with Coke bottles, poked with umbrellas, bit on the ears, grabbed by the hair and smashed into desks." A California report documented 58 cases during 1990 in which social workers were hit, stabbed, beaten, or shot and 16 cases involving other types of assault. Teachers and health-care providers also increasingly fear the neighborhoods in which they work every day.

Many workers are strained in other ways, too. It is simply hard for some professionals to remain unjaded, to keep their faith in the human spirit, when they work with children who have been abandoned, betrayed, and emotionally and physically maimed. Many professionals not only feel in over their heads in the early phases of their work, but they deal with a chronic sense of failure. The realities of families' lives may make it hard to feel traction or progress on a daily basis. Often children can't be helped, for example, because parents simply can't be reached: they don't have phones or their phones have been disconnected. Plans carefully constructed over months end up in tatters because a child leaves school or moves to a new neighborhood. School counselors and teachers in particular note these embittering, Sisyphean aspects of their work. These failures can be devastating because work with children is typically not just a job to these professionals: it is work in which they invest their most cherished attributes and their fundamental ideals.

At the same time, professionals have huge expectations heaped on them—by administrators, by desperate families, by a public hungry for solutions to frightening problems—setting them up for a steep sense of failure. Both families and the public often look for immediate results, even though some families' complex problems require long-term attention.

Harvard social policy researcher Lisbeth Schorr observes that professionals who work with children are asked "to be some combination of Mother Teresa, Machiavelli and a CPA." They are asked to be saints and schemers and accountants; sometimes they are asked to be artists and social scientists and magical healers.

When people feel undervalued, defeated, and disappointing to themselves and others in work to which they have brought their souls, at some point it is fair to ask, Why wouldn't they become deaf? Why wouldn't they at times exercise excessive power and control? Why wouldn't they stop going the extra mile for families?

Today, many professionals are only effective if they have special qualities, such as unusual stamina and determination. If the typical family is to be helped by the caregiving system, we need to create a system that, instead of requiring professionals to be superhuman, supports them in being good enough.

PART II

In a dark time, the eye begins to see.
Theodore Roethke

9

HEALTHY STARTS

THREE-YEAR-OLD TOBIAS MONTOSE, ONE LONG braid sliding down his back, an earring in his left ear, is perched on an examining table, smiling beautifully, infectiously. This is his annual physical exam at Boston's South End Community Health Center, yet his pediatrician, Dr. Gerald Hass, is focused not on him, but on the boy's mother. "Have you enrolled him in Headstart? Are you planning to work when he goes to school? What kind of work are you interested in?" Tobias's mother says that she might enter a nursing program, but she is shy, tentative. "You know you're very smart," Dr. Hass adds, recognizing the need for encouragement. "You can do whatever you want to do."

At this moment, Tobias spies the otoscope, which Dr. Hass has in his hand, preparing to peer inside Tobias's ear. All the warmth and sun in Tobias's face disappear; large tears collect in the corner of his eyes and sprint down his cheeks. Without skipping a beat, Dr. Hass feigns pointing the otoscope into Tobias's mother's ear, and rousing Tobias's seven-year-old sister off a nearby chair, makes a big show of examining her ear. Now Tobias is smiling again, and as Dr. Hass conducts the ear exam, he continues to talk to Tobias and his mother in a whirl. He gives her a Headstart form. He asks her if her children have been exposed to lead. He tells her that she has beautiful children. He asks if she is having health problems. When she relates that she has recently had eye surgery, he tells her that her eye looks beautiful. He discovers that her

147

health is basically good. He then examines Tobias's sister, Lakeisha, asking her not only about physical concerns, but about friends and school. He tells both Tobias and Lakeisha that they are healthy, that they are wonderful.

In the course of this physical exam, Dr. Hass, a gray-bearded man whose eyes seem to dance, has identified and articulated, without a hint of condescension, something positive about every family member and has determined that each one is healthy and functioning in the important areas of their lives. Had he found that Tobias's mother wanted a job but was unable to find one or too frightened to look, he could have referred her to a social worker at the center. Had either of the children seemed distressed, he could have referred them to the mental health program. Dealing with housing problems, clothing problems, and food problems is part of the work of the South End Community Health Center, and the center serves as a kind of informal support network for scores of parents who spend part of their day here, chatting with each other and with receptionists. That people come here in droves, many from far outside the immediate area, is only one sign that this health center is strengthening families in many areas of their lives and is succeeding where many other efforts to provide health care to poor urban families have dismally failed.

———————□———————

Bitter and fatalistic as Americans have become about the nation's efforts to help children—and serious as the problems are with our current system of care—the reality is that there are institutions and programs across the country that are dramatically changing the prospects of vulnerable children and families. These institutions are taking prevention seriously—they are working to ensure that children receive the basic ingredients of sturdy growth—and they are keeping problems from spiraling out of control.

Moreover, these successes are occurring in many different types of institutions that care for children. The following chapters look at success in four critical child-serving institutions: health-care agencies, public schools, child protective service agencies, and police forces.

The health-care system has a special role to play in preventing childhood distress. Many children's problems have their roots in their mothers' pregnancies, and good prenatal care can profoundly affect every domain of a child's life. Mothers who fail to receive prenatal care are more likely to have low-birth-weight babies, and low birth weight is linked with several serious problems, including neurodevelopmental handicaps and various emotional and learning difficulties in childhood.

For the great majority of infants in the United States, the first and only professionals who will peer into the critical early years of their lives—the years that set the stage for so much of later development—are child-care providers and pediatricians. Pediatric visits are frequently the only way to reach families who are in jeopardy, because distressed mothers will often secure medical attention for their children even when they don't seek help for themselves. In addition, health-care services tend not to carry the stigma of other social services.

Pediatricians are provided a crucial opening for assisting parents. New mothers and fathers are typically highly motivated to launch their children well in the exhilarating, anxious swell surrounding pregnancy and childbirth; they are highly open to learning, interested in being positive role models, looking to better their family's condition. And pediatricians, unlike many other professionals, are offered an unusual opportunity to form a positive and lasting tie to parents—they can interact with families around positive milestones and share with families the great discoveries in a child's development.

Yet this unique opportunity is often squandered. Although the health-care system has developed astounding high-tech responses to certain health crises, such as caring for premature babies, and has made this technology available widely, it has been strangely ineffective in performing the more prosaic task of keeping mothers and infants well. In providing prenatal care, this nation is behind most other Western countries, with some poor American communities lagging behind developing countries.

In the United States, nearly 900,000 mothers do not receive prenatal care in the first trimester, and many more do not receive prenatal care that is sufficiently comprehensive, dealing with the basic ingredients of healthy growth. In their first contacts with children, health-care professionals commonly miss the opportunity to assess even such basic elements of a child's environment as whether a home and neighborhood are physically safe.

Yet throughout the country, initiatives such as the South End Community Health Center in Boston have demonstrated success in reaching families early and in helping families meet their children's basic needs. These clinics and initiatives are not governed by mysterious laws. It is possible to identify the principles and tools needed to engineer effective health-care responses early in children's lives. What are these tools? And what will it take for these principles and tools to be not the exception, but the rule?

The South End Community Health Center: Trying Something New

The effectiveness of the South End center is deeply rooted in the values and training of Hass himself. (If central casting had set out looking for a pediatrician, they could not have done better than this twinkle-eyed, hardy man with the slightly wild gray hair and beard.) Raised in London, Hass was trained at the prestigious Great Ormonde Street Hospital for Children. (This hospital was endowed by Charles Dickens and James Barry, author of *Peter Pan*, and treats the children of the royal family.) In 1966, he came to the United States, pursuing an attractive offer at Boston University Medical School. Within two years, he became the head of Boston City Hospital's pediatric ambulatory service.

Yet he was often pained by what he saw. Boston City Hospital was the primary health-care provider for numerous neighborhood families, many with serious needs—most families were poor and many were newly arrived immigrants. Children often waited for hours; they received virtually no preventive care, and little attention was given to their overall psychological and social functioning. Hass knew what high-quality pediatric care was, and he knew that this hospital at that time was not providing it.

Two coinciding events enabled Hass to launch something radically different, to test whether he could adapt the principles of care learned in London to the landscape of the urban United States. First, he met a shoe company executive, Mel Scovell, who was looking for a new career. The two men thought that by combining Scovell's business skills and Hass's medical skills they could start a new health center that was not driven by categorical funding, but responded instead to the broad range of children's and families' needs. Meanwhile, a group of South End residents, frustrated by the quality of their medical care, approached Boston City Hospital to sponsor a local health center, in part because they knew and trusted Hass. Hass and Scovell saw their moment.

But they knew that their center had to depart from the usual mold. To meet basic needs and to intercept problems early, Hass built the center on several fundamental principles, widely lauded in theory but rarely executed well in practice. He recognized early on the importance of respecting and working collaboratively with parents, and of respecting and working with parents from the many different cultural and ethnic communities in the neighborhood. He saw the importance of tending to the diverse psychological and social needs of families. This attention to whole children and families would mean moving beyond the usual clichés about comprehensiveness. Working with families effectively would also mean identifying root problems and leverage points, points of intervention that could have many positive reverberations in a family. Further, Hass recognized the need to draw continually on families' strengths, as opposed to focusing narrowly on problems and deficits, and he saw that to deliver services effectively, staff had to be flexible and improvisational. And Hass knew that it was critical for staff to maintain stable, continuous ties to parents. Such ties would make it possible to work with families on sustaining healthy environments for children over time and might help parents overcome the anxieties that typically keep them from seeking out a pediatrician when symptoms first appear. In every activity of the center, Hass was emphatic that clinicians should adhere to the highest medical standards.

Hass has worked hard to instill these principles in the center since its inception. For example, Hass recognized that parents and other community residents were typically bypassed in decisions regarding the location and design of children's health care. To ensure collaboration with parents on these decisions, he and Scovell created a board, primarily comprising community members, to work to fashion the center according to the needs of neighborhood families. To ensure that the center would be responsive to residents, Hass and Scovell also eschewed the usual grant funding mechanisms and elected to bill Medicaid for services to patients. Under this system, the health center revenue depends on the number of families seeking services, thus to keep families coming the center has to provide high-quality medical care that is genuinely responsive to family problems. In addition, staff maintain open channels to consumers so that they can swiftly respond to consumers' concerns.

According to Hass and Tristam Blake, the executive director for the last ten years, the key element in working with diverse families has been the creation of a staff that racially and ethnically mirrors the community—a rare achievement among agencies working with families today. Many staff members are community residents. The board also now mirrors the neighborhood; every major neighborhood ethnic group has a voice in shaping the direction of the center. In part because of this representation, attention to cultural differences informs all the activities of the center, but this attention, Hass emphasizes, is not self-conscious or high profile.

Hass has trained himself diligently in the subtle art of working with families' strengths, and he has helped other providers develop these skills. Issuing a steady stream of praise, as his work with Tobias's family shows, comes easily to him—"Perfecto," "Mucho contento," he says over and over again to his mostly Spanish-speaking patients—but Hass does far more than dole out compliments. He shows parents and children how to use their strengths. He reminds Tobias's mother that she has skills that make her a strong candidate for many types of jobs, including nursing. Similarly, he encourages children to pursue their talents. One girl was invited and gladly performed her first violin recital in the waiting room for parents and staff. Clinicians have also developed routines to enable children to witness their accomplishments. Dr. Gloria White-Hammond, a forty-five-year-old African-American woman who is another much-admired pediatrician at the center, has children sign their names for their files every year, and each year she shows them how their handwriting has progressed.

Going beyond clichés about comprehensiveness has been perhaps the most difficult challenge. For health-care professionals, treating families comprehensively does not represent a radical departure in ideology—the importance of comprehensive care and treating whole families has become a shibboleth in this field—but it does represent a marked shift in common practice. Working definitions of comprehensiveness vary wildly. In addition, many immediate pressures and constraints undercut the capacity of even the most sensitive and adroit health-care providers to understand and respond to problems that are not strictly medical in their causes or cures. Like other professionals, physicians not only lack time, but are often explicitly discouraged by cost-conscious administrators from listening carefully to families and responding to a wide range of children's and families' troubles. Nurses may be trained in providing comprehensive care, but both nurses and physicians tend to have little understanding of child development, of family patterns and dynamics, and of the interacting factors that cut children down. Other factors commonly undermine comprehensive care as well: Providers may lack knowledge of available services, or services may not exist, or providers may not have the time to help families navigate unwieldy bureaucracies, such as in housing or employment.

Some health-care providers, like other professionals, view comprehensive care as trying to respond to every problem that crops up. These providers thus squander huge amounts of time treating different kinds of symptoms that continually reappear in different forms rather than dealing effectively with root causes.

Hass and other pediatricians at the center sometimes fall short of real comprehensiveness as well. Simple fatigue can work against them. I was with Hass when, after seeing his usual long succession of patients one morning, he asked a mother how she was doing. She mumbled, while dropping her head and staring at the floor, that she was okay. Next to her name on his chart, he simply jotted down "O.K."

Significant as these lapses are, they appear to be the exception. Hass works hard to give real meaning to comprehensiveness. In the day I spent with Hass, he routinely asked several questions of parents that helped him uncover seeds of family distress. He asks single mothers if they are isolated, whether fathers visit and are supportive, and if they have plans for the future. He asks children about friendships and school. "What's your best subject?" "Are you playing sports?" Decades of practice also allow him—most of the time—to read body language and voice intonations and to scan children for signs of overall family functioning: "Every child is a kind of index of a families' strengths and weaknesses," Hass says. For example, psychosomatic symptoms and biting in young children are often indicators of marital troubles or other serious family difficulties.

Observing families enables Hass and other professionals to pick up many other kinds of information. Consciously and unconsciously, families reveal themselves. Hass learned about Tobias's family by their eager response to the otoscope trick. Sometimes families are in unmistakable chaos—a mother, for example, cannot stop her children from screaming in the waiting room. When red flags like these are raised, Hass and other pediatricians typically take the time to probe, even if it means working longer hours and keeping other families waiting. "People kid me here for being slow," White-Hammond says, "but you can't work effectively with families unless you're willing to stop the action and figure out what's happening."

Nurse practitioners play equally critical roles in creating a comprehensive picture of a family, inquiring about whether children are both safe and stimulated at home: Are books read? Are windows closed and safe? Are pipes exposed? Are toys available? Are seat belts and car seats used? Have you or your child been exposed to violence? Perhaps most important, pediatricians, nurse practitioners, and sometimes even receptionists work hard to pool their knowledge about families, piecing together what Hass calls a "composite picture" and developing coordinated treatment plans.

Once a full picture is developed, Hass and the center do not try to respond to every problem they uncover. They seek to ensure that children's basic needs are met, and they look for leverage points and make selective interventions that attempt to deal with core problems and may have many positive reverberations. Hass believes that helping a mother get from welfare to work can change the whole climate of a family, giving some mothers a kind of boost that can dramatically change their interactions with their children, so he regularly tries to propel welfare mothers toward work. When a low-income mother has three small children, Hass recognizes that a fourth child can break the family's back, making it impossible to parent effectively. He urges such mothers to seek family planning.

Aware of the many negative emotional and physical consequences of school failure for children, White-Hammond tends to focus on children's school performance and on making parents better advocates for their children at school. She tells parents about the importance of having high expectations of their children. She coaches parents in overcoming intimidation and establishing ties to teachers. She recommends reading materials on educational issues relevant to their children, and she explains the importance of being visible advocates, of consciously modeling activism for children. Recognizing the many risks to girls of becoming involved with reckless, self-involved boys—the risks of pregnancy, of sexually transmitted diseases, of establishing a pattern of destructive relationships that will be difficult to break—White-Hammond also talks directly to teenage girls about what real intimacy is, and she counsels girls not to tolerate boys who do not respect them.

Once core problems are identified, the center works hard to get families what they need. The mental health program provides individual, family, and group therapy. A social worker assists families in overcoming not only troubles related to housing, jobs, and food, but also in dealing with the seemingly minor problems that can create great stress. Flexibility and improvisation are fine arts here. For example, when it was discovered that many children in the neighborhood were developing infections because their ears were being pierced crudely at home, the center offered ear piercing as a service. The mental health program organized a crafts group for parents who make and sell their wares to the community. To deal with teen problems, the center instituted a teen night and has collaborated with police on reducing gang involvement. Flexibility has also meant providing transportation to the clinic and money for medication for some families and reviving a practice that now seems quaint—pediatricians occasionally make house calls. At times, White-Hammond has herself gone to a school to advocate for a child. "People are not accommodated as an afterthought here," she says.

Providing continuous care—seeing that every family has a lasting tie to a provider—has similarly required moving past rhetoric and deviating markedly from standard practice. Particularly in urban areas, families are likely to ricochet among health-care providers. In many health-care settings, staff appear and vanish virtually overnight. Many urban families receive health care at large, impersonal clinics or hospitals, where they see a shifting array of providers. Often these providers are stretched so thin that it is virtually impossible for solid relationships to take root. As Barry Zuckerman, the director of pediatrics at Boston City Hospital, describes it, "A mother calls into a hospital wanting prenatal care. She has to wait three to eight weeks for an appointment, she will meet briefly with three people—a receptionist, a nurse, a doctor—a couple of which, because they are so busy, will probably be curt and impatient. Why would we expect that mother to come back? We know good prenatal care depends on relationships, but we do so little to foster good relationships." Moreover, when a shifting array of providers interacts with families around immediate medical problems, information about preventive measures—such as stopping smoking, breast-feeding, or child proofing—is abbreviated or eliminated.

To reduce staff turnover, the center instituted several key administrative and hiring practices early on. The center selects providers who show commitment and who are less likely to move. Physicians are hired only part-time; Hass believes that full-time work with families in great distress can grind down the most vigorous and dedicated professionals. Hass himself works half-time at the center. Many bureaucratic burdens have been cleared away—unlike their counterparts in large, competitive, big-city hospitals, staff are relatively free of paperwork—and careful attention is given to creating a supportive, congenial climate. Hass and Tristam Blake are readily available to staff, and staff provide input to administrative decisions that affect them. At the same time, Blake points out that unlike other medical facilities, physicians are not asked to take on administrative responsibilities for which they have no training. Staff receive large doses of healthy, appropriate praise, and administrators stretch themselves to meet the staff's needs. Hass sees himself as a model for younger pediatricians and believes that his undiminished enthusiasm for his work has been a key factor in retaining these pediatricians. Hass looks for staff who have both the capacity to listen—to pull together the threads in a family's story—and the sensitivities out of which sturdy relationships are built. And he has worked to create a culture in which staff support and learn from each other. White-Hammond notes: "We check in with each other, we support each other, we press each other to make sure we're keeping up medically, we hold each other accountable. We've all raised our children together and we wish we could socialize more. We're like a family in the good sense of the word."

These efforts to maintain continuity have been resoundingly successful. Staff devotion runs deep. The center's first pediatrician stayed twenty-five years. The first nurse still practices there, and one of the first receptionists is now the patient-care director. Of the five currently practicing pediatricians, four have been at the center for more than ten years. Moreover, many staff have chosen to live in the community, including Tristam Blake and his assistant. They know residents, they have a handle on the neighborhood, and they feel a keen sense of responsibility.

Because administrators support and strengthen the staff, other benefits accrue to families as well. Being supported themselves makes it far easier for staff to stay in the fray with families and to meet families' needs. As White-Hammond puts it, "We go the extra mile for families and stretch ourselves because administrators stretch for us."

The South End Community Health Center is by no means perfect. Here, too, pediatricians, nurse practitioners, and social workers are often overburdened and do not have the time to identify or respond to signs of family stress. Here, too, most pediatricians and nurse practitioners are not trained to understand, let alone reverse, many of the interactions that undercut children. Here, too, outreach to bring in new families is insufficient. Hass recognizes that some hard-pressed families in the community receive inadequate preventive medical attention or none at all. White-Hammond points out that some male teenagers come to the center only when they have sexually transmitted diseases or gunshot wounds.

Yet on several key measures, Hass's approach to working with families has been powerfully validated. The center has managed both to keep patient satisfaction extraordinarily high and to serve more than five thousand patients a year—almost twice the number served by a typical health center of the same size—of every different stripe. A small but growing minority are young professionals, attracted by the center's reputation for high-quality care. And families land at the center doorstep not only when they are in desperation; they come regularly for physical exams and seek help for ailments when symptoms first surface.

In part because staff stay, families have become attached to the center. For many children and parents, it is an emotional oasis and a kind of sanctuary. One morning I asked the assistant director if I could talk with several mothers in the waiting room. One mother, who had been a center patient as a child, spoke of her and her mother's close ties to the staff; her mother had, in fact, named her after the daughter of a nurse at the center. Another parent had been coming to the center from several miles away for years because she felt so positive about it. She described herself as a friend of four receptionists and four pediatricians. A third mother, explaining why she would never seek health care elsewhere, recounted how moved she had been when a pediatrician called to inquire about her health because she had mentioned during the course of her daughter's checkup the day before that she had bronchitis.

Even some male teenagers have formed attachments. One young man, newly released from prison after serving four years, came to the center on his eighteenth birthday for a physical. "He came because I saw him as a boy," White-Hammond explains, "and he felt a connection to this place."

All the parents described high-quality medical care: none could recount a serious error or mishap. Pediatricians, too, attest to the high quality of medical care at this center. "Mediocrity is not accommodated here," says White-Hammond. Although concrete measures of success are hard to come by, one study suggests reduced hospitalizations because of the center's work.

———————□———————

In 1965, the Office of Economic Opportunity, a federal agency, launched the Neighborhood Health Center Program, which created hundreds of community health centers across the country. Although these clinics vary in quality, many share the goals and attributes of the South End Community Health Center, including the ability to adapt themselves to the needs of families and communities. This flexibility typifies the Jackson-Hinds Comprehensive Health Center in Mississippi, founded by Mississippi's first black pediatrician, Aaron Shirley. Concerned about contaminated water, this clinic purchased a truck that delivers clean water to families once a week.

One of the fiercest proponents of the neighborhood health initiative was H. Jack Geiger, a passionate and determined man who opened one of the first community health centers in the Mississippi Delta. Faced with the problem of combined malnutrition and infection of children, Geiger and his staff literally wrote prescriptions for food—so much meat, so much milk, so many vegetables. They made arrangements with local grocery stores to fill these prescriptions and send the bills to the pharmacy at the health center. When federal officials came to complain that this was an improper use of the health center pharmacy, Geiger responded, "The last time we looked it up, the specific therapy for malnutrition was food." With Ford Foundation support, Geiger and his colleagues also helped about a thousand families organize a 600-acre cooperative farm to grow vegetables instead of cotton.

The efforts of these various clinics appear to be bearing fruit. Research on community health centers throughout the United States indicates that this way of delivering health care is both cost-effective and far more humane, increasing the number of children immunized, decreasing incidences of low birth weight, infant mortality, and hearing difficulties, and reducing the number of children needing expensive hospital and emergency care.

Back in the South End of Boston, Hass, Blake, and the board are talking about additional steps to push their center further beyond the rhetoric about comprehensive care. They are considering an "all-day therapeutic day-care center," where parents can bring their children and receive parenting help and support. They are also considering a home-visiting program, which would allow center staff to check in regularly with mothers of newborns, linking these mothers with the center and providing them with information about safety, effective parenting, and other available community services. White-Hammond is seeking far closer collaboration with other Boston services and prevention efforts. Two days after the teenager released from prison came to see her at the center, he was shot and killed on a street in the South End, an agonizing reminder to her of the limitations of the South End center as a single institution acting alone.

Hospitals, too, are pioneering more comprehensive approaches to meeting the basic needs of children. Several hospitals now provide parents with child development and parenting information. For example, parents of newborns may be given information about how to deal with the jealousy of older siblings.

Boston City Hospital has come a long way since Hass departed twenty-five years ago. A seventeen-member nonmedical professional staff includes educators, psychologists, social workers, substance-abuse specialists, and a lawyer. The lawyer teaches the medical staff about how poor families can qualify for housing, food stamps, and other programs and provides legal advice to families whose health problems may be connected to toxic living conditions, such as unheated apartments or lead paint. An initiative called Pediatric Pathways to Success seeks to ensure that every child who comes to this hospital, no matter the reason, is ready for school. Parenting classes are provided, referrals are made to Headstart and other enrichment programs, and family advocates stretch themselves to obtain for families whatever other kinds of help they need. Barry Zuckerman, the hospital's director of pediatrics, wants to develop a two-generation model of health care, in which parents could obtain nutrition counseling and depression screening and their children receive checkups and immunizations at the same time and in the same place. "The best way to help children is to help their parents," he says.

Zuckerman has also created a literacy program for children called "Reach Out and Read." As journalist Anita Diamant reports, in creating this program Zuckerman took what appeared to be a problem and turned it into an opportunity. Five years ago, he was told that children's books left in the waiting room were "walking." Zuckerman realized that parents were desperate for books. Now, when children enter the Pediatric Primary Care center for checkups, volunteers look at picture books with the children and demonstrate book-sharing techniques. Pediatricians routinely tell parents during checkups about the importance of reading to children, even those children as young as six months old. And every parent receives a book at every visit. The "Reach Out and Read" program has distributed 20,000 books to more than three thousand children. "Getting parents to read books to their children is just as important as giving them information on nutrition," Zuckerman observes. He has also fostered programs that provide counseling and advocacy to children who are victims of violence and that train professionals, including police officers, doctors, and teachers, in responding effectively to victims of violence.

Hawaii's Experiment

The South End Community Health Center and Boston City Hospital are unusual in terms of their level of involvement with families, yet other health-care efforts have gone to even greater lengths with certain populations of children to assess families' needs and to coordinate interventions to respond to those needs. The Healthy Start program, run by Hawaii's Department of Health, is an early intervention program focused on preventing child abuse. This program provides the kind of very early intervention and extensive home visiting envisioned by Hass. Providers do not begin asking questions after abuse occurs; they identify overburdened families at high risk for abuse immediately after a child is born. Mothers are interviewed in hospitals during the prenatal period or after delivery. About 85 to 90 percent of mothers identified as overburdened at the hospital elect to obtain the primary service of Healthy Start—regular visits by a home visitor.

Although preventing abuse is the main mission of this program, home visitors work with families across many domains to provide the ingredients of sturdy growth. They offer parenting information, hook children up with needed programs, assist parents in landing educational and employment opportunities, and link every family to a medical home, a clinic or private practitioner who is available to the family on an ongoing basis so that patients are not shuffled among pediatricians.

Home visitors also serve as ongoing resources, counselors, and advocates for a small number of families—caseloads vary from fifteen to twenty-five. No family is written off as too time-consuming or too costly to help. Healthy Start workers, in fact, take great pride in helping families in the most difficult straits and in counteracting the stigmatizing tendencies of communities. "Healthy Start serves families that communities often want to forget about," one Healthy Start worker says. "They're not the ones people want to befriend."

Among the various home-visiting programs that have emerged across the country, this one is unusual both in its degree of involvement with families and in the utter tenacity of its workers. Visitors work hard to gain the trust of families, to support parents, and to understand and reverse the negative interactions that imperil children by building positive interactions right from the beginning.

Consider the work of Healthy Start visitor Evelyn Moore. Evelyn went to a home once a week for three months, even though she was not allowed in the door. On the basis of a hospital assessment, this family was deemed at risk, largely because the mother, Jane Redding, had a history of drug abuse, was isolated, was living in an overcrowded apartment, and had just given birth to twins, leaving her with four children under three years of age. At the hospital, Jane had said that she wanted a home visitor and had signed a consent form for this service. When Evelyn knocked on the door, she typically heard Jane and her partner shouting and yelling and children sobbing and screaming. Yet Jane still did not open the door.

Three months later, Jane opened the door for the first time, and before long Evelyn became a welcome presence in the home. Early on, Jane told Evelyn that although she was too afraid to let this strange woman into her chaotic household, somehow she felt soothed just knowing that Evelyn was outside her door.

The creation of an alliance between Jane and Evelyn was only a beginning. Like Dr. Hass, Evelyn sought to identify root problems and leverage points. The family had no medical home and no concept of what ongoing, preventive health care meant. Evelyn discovered that Jane had used the drug ice and that extended family members sold the drug on the streets. Two months after giving birth to the twins, Jane was pregnant with a fifth child. In another ten months, she would be pregnant again.

Evelyn did not seek to tackle every problem at once, or to foist on Jane her notions about what Jane needed. She and Jane created goals for their work together, including finding an acceptable means of birth control, getting her children a decent start in school and a medical home, and finding Jane a serious substance-abuse treatment program.

After three years of weekly home visits, the family has taken large steps toward achieving these goals. The older children have been enrolled in kindergarten and Headstart; the twins have entered a special program for developmental delays; and the newest baby has received consistent medical care since birth and shows no signs of delay. Just as significant, Jane's thinking about her children's health and development has changed dramatically. Rather than seeking health care only in response to emergencies, all six of the children receive regular health exams.

The tenacity and flexibility of Healthy Start workers in supporting parents and dealing with families' needs were similarly key in eliminating the great perils faced by Annie, the two-year-old daughter of a blind mother. Healthy Start first came into contact with the family when Annie was eight months old. (Typically a family is enrolled immediately following the birth of a child, but in this case the family was referred to Healthy Start later.) When a Healthy Start worker entered this home, she found Annie in a gated area with no toys. Her diaper was almost entirely ripped off, and a bell hung from her ankle—the bell enabled her mother to track Annie's movements. Annie's mother was having difficulty preparing food for herself and Annie. She usually served whatever food could be easily grasped and opened. Annie's mother was terrified that her daughter would be taken away from her. Yet over time the worker was able to develop a strong, trusting alliance with Annie's mother and has provided various kinds of ongoing, practical assistance, including labeling all the food, knives, and kitchenware with Braille and arranging for a caretaker to monitor Annie during the day and assist her mother.

Healthy Start workers are trained to deal with many other types of family problems. They are trained to identify sibling and marriage problems. They are taught to understand the family patterns and communication styles that drag children down. Services are carefully customized to family needs. At one site, for example, a male home visitor specializes in reaching and assisting male spouses or partners of mothers, because father absence was identified as such a pervasive and serious problem. Workers understand how community problems also undermine children, and they have strong and extensive ties to community institutions, such as Headstart and the schools.

These services are possible because Healthy Start administrators, like Dr. Hass, have worked hard to find and keep able and committed caregivers and because Healthy Start workers are guided by highly trained supervisors. In addition, workers form teams in which they support, coach, teach, and cheer for one another. "We do in the office what we do out," a Healthy Start worker says. "We nurture each other, along with our clients." At many sites, small successes are celebrated and trumpeted. Because worker caseloads are kept reasonably low and because of the effectiveness of this program, workers are also able to witness improvement—the kind of feedback that is perhaps most critical in maintaining high morale.

Like the South End Community Health Center, the Healthy Start program has its problems and limitations. Like other home visiting programs, this program raises questions about intrusiveness, about violating a family's privacy. In the Healthy Start program, because of its tenacious outreach efforts, this risk is especially high. Important as it was for Evelyn to be persistent with Jane, Evelyn's intuitions could have been incorrect: Jane could have resented this persistence, and this resentment might have diminished her willingness to receive help at some later point.

Healthy Start, however, works aggressively to avoid intrusiveness. In both orientation training and individual and group supervision, home visitors deal directly with family boundaries and with reading conflicting or murky signals about whether they are welcome.

And the program's successes have been impressive. Incidences of neglect and abuse have dropped markedly. Immunization rates have increased, and there is evidence that participating children are starting school more prepared to learn. Further, many of the principles and practices of Healthy Start have been validated by the successes of other home-visiting programs around the country. Evaluations indicate that home visiting can reduce the number of children suffering cognitive and developmental delays and improve mother-child interactions and various health outcomes.

Resource Mothers

The Healthy Start program intervenes with families right after birth. Other innovative programs begin working with families even earlier: by working with pregnant mothers, these programs try to ensure that children receive the key ingredients of healthy growth. Operated by South Carolina's Division of Maternal Health, the Resource Mothers program links older, experienced mothers—called resource mothers—with teenage girls during pregnancy. Resource mothers—who are carefully recruited, trained, and supervised—meet with teens at least once a month during pregnancy, usually in the teens' own homes. They also meet with teen mothers in the hospital at the time of delivery and at regular intervals throughout the first year of life. This program is located in three counties in a poor, rural area in the northern edge of the state—an area called the Pee Dee. Prior to the inception of this program in 1980, the Pee Dee had the highest rate of teen pregnancy in the state and the highest rate of infant mortality in the nation.

At the heart of this program is the notion that a mother who has a strong, caring tie to another adult has a much greater capacity to develop a supportive, caring tie to her infant. Older community mothers are deemed to have the best chance of creating trusting, mature relationships with teenage mothers, and within this relationship resource mothers are able to transmit crucial knowledge and skills. Resource mothers supplement traditional prenatal care by providing information on such topics as family planning, labor and delivery, infant safety, and nutrition. Resource mothers give practical advice about how to nourish children with a limited budget, for example, suggesting that children eat a peanut butter and jelly sandwich and drink milk every day. Safety and self-care, too, are stressed. Resource mothers take a hard line on alcohol and drugs; some resource mothers demonstrate to teen mothers the adverse effects of substance abuse by showing them pictures of damaged newborns. Ensuring that pregnant teens keep their prenatal-care appointments, clarifying doctors' instructions, connecting teen parents with needed community resources, and helping teens obtain Medicaid, WIC, and other benefits are other key aspects of the job; so is working with teens closely in their development as adults and as parents, including assisting them with education and employment plans.

For resource mothers, half the battle is identifying pregnant teens, which can require a good deal of initiative and creativity. For example, one resource mother follows up on rumors that she hears in church or on the street. Told by a boy that several girls in his school were pregnant, she did an in-service training at that school, urging girls to seek prenatal care.

The other half of the battle is establishing a tie with a teen early on. Resource mothers emphasize that a key is moving slowly, taking baby steps, not forcing themselves on teens. "I tell girls that I'm there to be their friend," Mary Otis, another resource mother, says. "I also tell them that it's okay to tell me they don't want me to come some days, and to ask me to come back." She emphasizes, too, her ongoing availability—"I'm with you as long as you want me to be."

These strategies appear to be having the desired effect. Resource mothers often become mentors and confidantes. "Once these kids trust you, they'll pour out their hearts," Otis says. Otis often finds herself, rather than working to draw teen mothers out, having to make clear the limits of her availability because the teens come to depend on her enormously.

Many other health initiatives are improving on traditional means of providing health care to vulnerable families and are sparing families the distress of queueing up at large urban hospitals. Some cities have coordinated multiple agencies and interests in tackling serious community health problems. In Hartford, Connecticut, businesses, hospitals, public agencies, and service providers, among other groups, successfully banded together to drive down a high rate of premature births by developing a new teen pregnancy program, reaching deeply into communities to find expectant mothers, and providing specialized prenatal care for women at risk for premature births.

Because each of these initiatives has strengths and flaws, and because each is customized to its particular community, it does not make sense to attempt to graft any one model onto communities across the country. But these initiatives do suggest certain principles and day-to-day practices that should form the core of health care services for vulnerable families.

These initiatives are committed to overcoming the stubborn realities that stand in the way of reaching families early, as opposed to basking in the rhetoric of prevention and comprehensiveness. They take comprehensiveness seriously, working with children in the context of their families, and families in the context of communities. Rather than seeking to solve every problem simultaneously, these initiatives tend to look for interventions that will reverse negative interactions and positively reverberate through many domains of families' lives. Providers in these programs not only identify, but also develop plans for utilizing the strengths of children and parents. They do not make unilateral decisions or adhere rigidly to formulaic treatment plans, but collaborate with families to solve problems. Providers accept as a crucial challenge reaching the most resistant and difficult families, they understand that trust is often painstakingly earned, they refuse to give up on families, and they communicate to families this commitment—they work to convince families that they are there for the long haul. Providers tend to attribute problems to things that can be changed, rather than to intractable aspects of a child or parent. Administrators devote concerted attention to supporting providers and to creating a culture in which providers support one another. Providers and programs judge themselves by important small steps that families have taken, rather than by how far families have to go. Just as important, each of these programs has been willing to take risks, to innovate, to tolerate failure, and to change direction in midstream.

The challenge over the next decade will be to implement these principles and practices widely to ensure that every family in every community has access to high-quality health care. Getting from here to there is no simple matter. Towering bureaucratic and financial barriers stand in the way. Many families lack adequate insurance. In particular, preventive services and services that are not strictly medical are inadequately covered. Financial incentives, such as those Dr. Hass strained to avoid, can work against effective services. Health expert and Carnegie Corporation president David Hamburg argues that "success is often modest… because good programs that work are a rarity in a complicated, fragmented nonsystem of maternity services crippled by pervasive financial and institutional obstacles to care." Further, health-care providers are distributed highly unevenly across the country—in many communities, pediatricians and family practitioners are scarce.

Health-care leaders can disseminate knowledge about good principles and practices, however, just as they effectively distributed knowledge and technology that is now sustaining life in very premature babies. Advocacy groups and families, too, need knowledge of good principles and practices to fight effectively for reforms.

Principles of Effective Health Care
for Vulnerable Children

1. Providers take comprehensiveness seriously, which includes understanding how children's health is related to attributes of their families and communities.

2. Instead of treating every symptom, providers respond to root problems and look for leverage points that can set in motion positive cycles of success.

3. Providers work respectfully and collaboratively with families in identifying and responding to problems.

4. Providers identify and work with families' strengths.

5. Providers are willing to work with the most difficult and resistant families, they don't give up, and they communicate to families this commitment.

6. Providers have the skills to build trust and understand that trust-building can be a lengthy process with many setbacks.

7. Providers work with families in creating clear, rational goals and judge themselves by important small steps.

8. Administrators support providers and create a culture that enables providers to strengthen one another.

9. Administrators and providers are flexible and innovative and are responsive to the changing needs of families.

10. Administrators and providers adhere to the highest medical standards.

Sources of funding can be redesigned to support effective principles and practices. Rather than piecing together a patchwork of interventions for hundreds of specific illnesses, such as diabetes, hospitals and clinics should have available to them more discretionary funds, so that they can allocate dollars and fashion services in ways that make sense in their communities.

Far too much is known about how to provide effective health care to vulnerable families to remain passive, to acquiesce to the status quo. Too many children are undermined early in life by physical, emotional, and social ailments that are entirely curable; too many lives are being wrecked that needn't be wrecked.

10

SCHOOLS
THAT WORK

I T IS THREE O'CLOCK IN THE AFTERNOON, THE
second-to-last week of the school year, a time when most
elementary school students clatter down halls or sit in class
and drift, their minds already lost to summer. Yet at the Lincoln-
Basset Elementary School in New Haven, children quietly glide
down halls in lines that quiver only slightly, and in class they are
devotedly engaged: reading, drawing, listening. When Kevin Miller
asks a question of his eighteen fourth graders—"What happens
when you grow up if you don't have any skills?"—pleasant, fresh-
faced children, their arms flat on their desks or angled into pyramids,
are all eyes and ears. Not one or two, but eleven hands spring up.
"If you don't have skills, you can't do anything," a handsome boy
pipes up, displaying the earnestness that is typical of students here.
"If you don't have skills, you can't even work a grill at McDonald's."

This kind of serenity and industriousness is not easy to find,
even in affluent suburban classrooms. But Lincoln-Basset is not
well-heeled, and children here are not driven to school in Range
Rovers. Many carefully pick their way through streets that are
minefields of broken glass, dodging street corners clogged with
drug dealers. In this almost entirely African-American area of New
Haven, longtime homeowners are pitted against encroaching gangs
and crime. Poverty is pervasive; more than 70 percent of Lincoln-
Basset children are from poor families. What is different here is
that children are soundly overcoming these hardships. Since a

series of novel reforms based on the work of Dr. James Comer, a Yale psychiatrist, were implemented under the deft direction of Verdell Roberts, the school's principal, school staff have dealt effectively with the troubles that choke children's ability to learn, and achievement test scores have rocketed. Reading and math scores are well above the statewide average, and serious behavior problems have nearly disappeared.

Early in children's lives health-care institutions and child-care programs serve as a front line—the institutions where young children are most likely to see a responsive professional. As children grow older, this front line becomes the schools. Nearly 90 percent of the nation's school-age children spend more than one third of their waking lives in public school buildings.

Perhaps no other institution that works with children is now more cynically viewed than the public school. Once upon a time, public schools were seen as a great escalator for disadvantaged children. Today, shaken by horror stories and grim statistics, Americans are more apt to see public schools as yet another obstacle for these children to overcome. Embittered and disillusioned by cycles of reform that end in finger-pointing and frustration, many Americans are ready to hand responsibility for educating these children over to the private sector.

There are good reasons for despair. Most of the horror stories and grim statistics are real, and numerous educational reforms in the last few decades have done little to help the great majority of vulnerable children. Many of these reforms have had little impact because they have not targeted vulnerable children directly, yet many that have focused on these children have failed.

But this despair is also rooted in misconceptions. Disheartened as people are by failed reforms, caring for vulnerable children has only recently been considered the responsibility of public schools. Before World War II, children who had difficulty learning because of poverty, family troubles, or learning disabilities often simply drifted out of school or were tacitly encouraged to take up another pursuit. Disabled children, before 1960, were routinely shunted into special institutions. About 19 percent of children drop out of school today—a staggering number—but more than 90 percent of children failed to complete high school in the late 1800s.

In 1940, 60 percent of young adults did not finish high school, yet these high drop-out rates hardly incited panic. As late as the early 1960s, 40 percent of young adults failed to finish high school and, as the former superintendent of New York's schools Joseph Fernandez points out, "no one blinked an eye." Fernandez who dropped out of school, came close to killing a person, overdosed and nearly lost his life, was a victim of this neglect. He recalls, "The public school might just as well have been on Mars for all it meant to a neighborhood kid's survival problems."

And schools were never the great escalator they are imagined to have been. Although some schools have vaulted children out of blight and into prosperity—poor white children such as Abe Lincoln as well as poor black children such as Thurgood Marshall and Colin Powell, education historians now recognize that many schools have reinforced or even cemented racial and class barriers.

Most important, the fact is that there are schools that directly contradict this deepening pessimism. Just as there are health-care programs that help provide children with the basic ingredients of growth, there are schools, such as Lincoln-Basset in New Haven, that demonstrate that it is quite possible to meet the basic needs of vulnerable children and that disadvantaged children are as capable of learning as are their better-off peers. At the same time that confidence in public schools appears to have hit rock bottom, it has become clear that certain public schools do work. If the typical public school is ever to become an escalator for vulnerable children, it is vital to understand why and how these model schools work — and, crucially, what can be done to ferry these principles and practices to schools in every community in the country.

Effective Schools

During the past decade, educators have proposed a panoply of reforms designed to assist vulnerable children. Many have argued for new teaching methods, for example, arranging chairs in circles, rather than in rows, and having teachers circulate around a classroom, rather than lecture from the front, to help involve disengaged students. Others have called for new and better curricula, especially curricula relevant to minority students. A growing chorus of educators is calling for higher pay for teachers; new research has established a direct correlation between teacher pay and student achievement.

These individual proposals are important, but by themselves are not likely to reverse the prospects of vulnerable students. Over the past twenty years, various educators have begun independently to engineer new types of schools, taking into account the many dimensions and tangled nature of school problems. Although they have different visions, these reformers nevertheless share an assumption: the problems of schools cannot be fixed by reforming just one piece of a school. Responding to struggling children is not simply a matter of acquiring better teachers, better teaching methods, or more culturally relevant curricula. It is a matter of markedly changing the fundamental structure—and at times even the function—of schools. Because of the diversity and ambition of the reforms, and because these schools deal with large numbers of children with very serious troubles, it is these schools that offer the most valuable lessons for educators in the United States.

The oldest and most prominent of these model schools was started in 1968 by James Comer, who dramatically restructured two New Haven schools mired in chaos and despair. The Comer process, as it is called, has since been adopted by more than 200 schools in twenty-eight states. Over the last several years, the New Haven school system has adopted the process in all of its forty-two schools, including Lincoln-Basset Elementary.

At the heart of these schools is a set of principles championed by their founder, a soft-spoken African-American psychiatrist and educator. Perhaps foremost, Comer believes that teaching children effectively means addressing all the elements that children need to grow, rather than focusing on education in the narrow sense. Paying attention to the needs of whole children and families means, in part, creating a school that is a kind of model home. Comer set out to overturn the entire school environment, to create a climate that is orderly and structured, that includes and supports parents, and that promotes the kind of values and habits that he believes are essential to function effectively in mainstream America. Comer also recognized early on that children come to school with very different kinds of problems as a result of diverse family and community circumstances and that schools need structures that allow staff to be flexible, to craft their work according to each child's and family's specific needs.

To realize these principles, Comer instituted two chief structural reforms, disarmingly simple at first blush. He created a school-based management team, comprising a principal, parents, and teachers, who jointly run each school. This gives both parents and teachers far more say in school governance. Comer believes that school staff typically become demoralized because schools lack structures or mechanisms that encourage them to collaborate, to offer input into how their school is run, and to use their creativity and intelligence. He also instituted a mental health team, comprising a social worker, a psychologist, a special education teacher, and a school counselor. This team provides child-development guidance to the management team and to teachers, seeks to prevent problems by improving school procedures, and assists teachers in dealing with problems in the classroom. Frequently the mental health team helps teachers interpret possible signs of neglect or abuse. This team also works with teachers in hooking kids up to community services and activities.

At Lincoln-Basset these reforms, carried out daily by a school principal who not only subscribes to the rhetoric of sharing power and supporting staff but who has an intuitive understanding of what this sharing and this support actually mean, have clearly had the intended effect. The Comer model works there at full throttle. School staff bustle with commitment and enthusiasm. "For children to feel positive, staff have to feel positive," says Mary Freeman, who works on curriculum and social development, "so projects are planned for staff, including custodial staff, such as trips to the museum. People feel this is a special place."

The commitment of the staff makes the realization of Comer's other principles possible. School staff pride themselves on their ability to accommodate and improvise. They talk frequently about their willingness "to go the extra yard," to "pitch in," to "do anything" to help children and families. When children miss school, a teacher or administrator often treks to their homes to uncover the problem and work with parents in solving it. Confronted with the persistent fighting of a group of girls, one group of teachers instituted a cooking class to bring them together regularly. When students expressed interest in learning the martial arts, the school principal persuaded the fire inspector, who had a black belt in karate, to teach a class. No child is deemed unsalvageable. Teachers seem to exude what Boston principal Kim Marshall calls "a serene, sometimes irrational confidence that an effective classroom and school can and will overcome entering disadvantages."

This enormous energy and flexibility are also at the heart of what may be the Comer schools' most noted accomplishment: their ability to engage parents. A good deal of research now points to the importance of parent involvement in children's education. Yet although many parents are extremely involved in schools, many others, because of cultural barriers or because they were victims of bad school experiences themselves, among other reasons, are hostile and estranged. Often parents' involvement in schools is superficial.

At the Comer schools, parents are not only on the school management team, they work as tutors and teacher aides. They attend classes on such topics as child development and career opportunities, plan social activities and school events, such as potluck suppers and book fairs, and are involved in many other aspects of school functioning. Staff and parents believe that because the school is a friendly, supportive place—a place where, as one parent says, "you are always confronted with a warm, smiling face at the door, instead of a sign that says 'Sign in at the office'"—parents *want* to be in the building, and the usual resistances break down.

Staff and parents also work very hard, and exercise a great deal of imagination, to build bridges between alienated parents and the school. One group of involved parents held an evening beauty salon at school for other Lincoln-Basset parents—especially those parents who typically shunned the school building. While parents got free haircuts, Yale University students volunteered as baby-sitters for their children. School staff also arranged free memberships for some parents at the YMCA. If a parent does not attend meetings at school because of a serious problem, such as a drug addiction, an involved parent who has suffered from a similar problem works to help the parent and involve him or her in school activities, according to Mildred Mabry, a school parent and the head of Lincoln-Basset's parent-teacher organization. And when parents simply can't be involved, school staff reach out for substitutes—an uncle, a grandparent—who will take an active interest in a child's education.

The Comer process recognizes that the values, attitudes, and skills of many disadvantaged children may not mesh with the mainstream values and expectations of schools. As Comer points out, a child who is punished for fighting back in school may be punished at home for *not* fighting back. Staff and parents thus have devised a broad curriculum designed to familiarize students with mainstream values and skills. Students learn about business, politics, and health; they also learn practical strokes that will help them swim in the mainstream, such as how to write invitations, thank you notes, and checks. In addition, the importance of adults' sending consistent moral messages is stressed. "Children hear all kinds of crazy things out there on the street," Lincoln-Basset's school principal says. "In here we all sing from the same hymn book, we all strike the same chord."

Whether the Comer model can be replicated successfully throughout the United States remains to be seen. For one, high turnover among staff can torpedo the best-laid plans. "Often teachers leave before they fully understand the model," says James Braun, who works with Comer. Yet in several schools around the country, the Comer process has increased achievement while markedly reducing behavior and attendance problems. By 1986, the two original New Haven schools, once the worst of the district's thirty-three schools in terms of achievement and attendance, were among the best. The Comer schools also appear to reduce transience; some parents find ways *not* to move so that their children can stay in a Comer school.

Further, these schools help not just one generation but two. In part this is true because the Comer schools, unlike other public schools, create *positive* dynamics. Children believe they can succeed when they see their parents being active and effective, and parents feel better about themselves when they see their children learning. And when teachers and administrators see both children and parents thriving, they are far less likely to burn out or to move on to another school; they continue to provide the energy and stability that starts the positive cycle.

Although other model schools are less well-established than the Comer schools, they show early signs of success. The Accelerated Schools model, developed by a team of researchers at Stanford University and first implemented in the late 1980s at two schools in California, draws on many of the same principles espoused by the Comer schools to meet children's basic needs, including responding to whole children and strengthening and involving parents. This model seeks to realize these principles through similar methods also, such as giving teachers and parents more authority and enlisting community resources and services. Yet the Accelerated Schools model departs from the Comer schools in a crucial respect: the Accelerated Schools try to upgrade the prospects of disadvantaged students in large part by changing what goes on inside classrooms. The Accelerated Schools model focuses on one key element of healthy growth; it seeks to ensure that disadvantaged children have frequent and meaningful achievements at school. Whereas the Comer schools typically employ standard teaching methods, the Accelerated Schools use highly innovative teaching methods and an enriched curriculum intended to speed the acquisition of knowledge and skills. "When kids fall behind in most schools they are typically taken out of class and put in remedial classrooms where they do basic drills all day—they are taught to crawl before they can walk," notes Wendy Hopfenburg, the associate director of the Accelerated Schools Project. "We believe all kids can walk and even run, so Accelerated Schools communities—and that includes teachers, parents and support staff—work with kids in classrooms. They do hands-on learning with kids, they teach kids how to solve problems, they help them with higher order concepts. They utilize the different strengths that kids have.... They let sparks fly."

Other commonly used instructional strategies include cooperative learning, which assigns students to groups and rewards them for group proficiency. These cooperative exercises often emphasize accomplishments that are concrete and tied to meaningful adult roles. At one Accelerated School—the Holibrook School in Houston—a third-grade class established its own popcorn-selling enterprise. This project entailed problem solving, higher-order concepts, cooperative learning, and the development of skills with real-world significance. A stockbroker helped the class incorporate, and the children sold shares, held a stockholders' meeting, and established a franchise with fifth graders. They then planned a trip to the National Aeronautics and Space Administration in Houston, financed by a portion of their profits.

Like the Comer schools, the Accelerated Schools model is a philosophy and a process, not a packaged program. While each school is designed to undo the expectation of failure that drags down vulnerable children, each school is also encouraged to develop its own goals, projects, curriculum changes, and teaching methods.

Seven hundred schools in thirty-seven states are now transforming themselves into Accelerated Schools. While many schools have not been carefully evaluated, numerous schools show improvements in student achievement and attendance and fewer discipline problems. Parent involvement has increased in several schools, and at one school the student mobility rate has decreased by 50 percent in two years. Two factors appear to be key to the success of these schools: a principal who is highly committed to the model, and the allotment of sufficient time for staff to plan and develop curricula.

The Success-for-All model was developed jointly by Johns Hopkins University researchers and Baltimore school department officials and was first implemented in five Baltimore schools in 1987 and 1988. This model draws on some Comer principles, including responding to children's diverse psychological and social needs, and focuses on meaningful accomplishment by promoting major changes in instructional methods and content. Yet unlike the Comer schools or the Accelerated Schools, which give school staff wide latitude in shaping school activities, the Success-for-All model gives schools a specific, tightly focused goal and a detailed plan for achieving it.

Based on research that shows that children are far more likely to fail in school if they are not reading at grade level by third grade, Success-for-All aims to bring all children to this level by this crucial juncture. Parents become partners in reaching this goal. Many strategies are employed to improve children's reading capacity, including intensive tutoring, newly proven reading methods—for example, children read to each other a good deal—and preschool and kindergarten programs that focus on reading and language development. Perhaps most important, schools don't give up on any child: The job is not done until every child is reading successfully. When reading problems can't be handled in a classroom, extensive efforts are made to involve parents, and in some cases a family support team is called in. These teams, which comprise a Success-for-All facilitator, a school administrator, a parent liaison, and sometimes a social worker or counselor, work with families mainly on problems that undermine reading, rather than, as at the Comer schools and the Accelerated Schools, attempting to deal with whatever family problem crops up. Family support teams try to replace lost eyeglasses, for example, for the many children who lose the glasses that they need in order to read. Teams provide toiletries to children who come to school with unkempt hair, in part because these children are ridiculed by other children, and the ridicule makes it difficult for them to pay attention to reading. According to Robert Slavin, the principal founder of this model, these family support teams are relentless, sticking with students and doing whatever it takes to manage or solve their problems. One team, after trying various strategies without success to comfort a boy who cried and screamed in kindergarten every day, obtained an old coat of his mother's and hung it on the wall. This coat became an emotional oasis for the boy, providing a needed link between home and school. Family support teams also provide activities intended to engage children in reading early on. A Books and Breakfast program provides all children from prekindergarten to second grade with forty books a year and encourages parents to read to their children.

The Success-for-All program, which has been replicated in twenty-four states and more than three hundred schools, has been repeatedly and rigorously evaluated. Compared with similar students from other schools, Success-for-All students do significantly better on reading tests by the third grade. Moreover, the highest gains are among the lowest-achieving quarter of students. At two of the original pilot schools, not a single student scored two years below grade level by the third grade, a common criterion for tagging a child learning disabled. Because of this improved achievement, placements in special education classes and retentions have dropped sharply.

Although by different means, the Success-for-All schools may accomplish many of the far-reaching aims of the Comer schools. When children achieve in school, they function more effectively in other areas of their lives—behavior problems have diminished at many Success-for-All schools. Because of their school success, children may also be less vulnerable in later childhood to a host of problems, including delinquency and dropping out of school. Seeing their children read instills great pride in some parents, and many parents, in part because of the Books and Breakfast program, become more interested in books and in reading to their children. Many parents become more involved with schools, and some take positive steps in their own lives, such as learning how to read or enrolling in GED courses.

Other model schools also appear promising at this early stage. The School of the 21st Century program, implemented in more than four hundred schools in fourteen states, has gone to impressive lengths to support families. All-day, year-round child care is offered for children from age three until they enter kindergarten, for example, and every family in a school district is visited after a child is born by a parent educator who offers information about child development and who lends support. Preliminary evaluations of indicators ranging from achievement test scores to family satisfaction to stress in the household have shown positive gains.

Other schools are experimenting with exciting instructional strategies and working out new ways of involving parents and families. The Central Park East schools in New York, developed by education reformer Deborah Meier, arrange family-teacher conferences, rather than parent-teacher conferences, which all family members are asked to attend—including at times, aunts and uncles, grandparents, or even baby-sitters—to discuss any number of family problems. Efforts are frequently made to address sibling problems that interfere with learning, such as an older child's mocking a younger sibling who has a learning problem. Parents are encouraged to work with teachers in developing goals for students and in creating meaningful ways of measuring student progress. In addition, these schools routinely give homework assignments that require students to engage their parents—for example, elementary school students are asked to bake a cake at home.

Each of these models has strengths—and weaknesses. Whether the Comer model sails depends a good deal on having a strong and agile principal, such as Verdell Roberts, at the helm—a principal who is able to share authority with teachers and parents. The Comer schools have also been criticized for not drawing on the knowledge of parents in educating children, for excluding parents from decisions on curricula and teaching methods.

The Success-for-All model is effective in improving reading. It is unclear, however, whether this model can generate changes in families' psychological and social functioning as wide-ranging as those generated by the Comer schools, which aim explicitly at developing the whole child and family. The Success-for-All program has a distinct advantage in terms of replication because it is more prescriptive and mechanical, it depends less than the Comer schools on a single, talented leader, on staff continuity, or on many different people working together effectively to create a positive climate. "Principals don't have to be charismatic," Slavin says. "They simply have to be willing to use the model."

It is too early for a blanket endorsement of any one model school, but these schools—as well as the literature on effective schools—suggest certain principles that should become the backbone of public education. Schools that are effective with vulnerable children strongly emphasize academics. Yet they help meet children's basic needs and respond to the multiple, messy troubles of children, rather than, as Ramon Cortines, New York's former chancellor of schools, says, "simply screwing off the tops of children's heads and trying to pour in knowledge." They make school an exciting place to learn, and they create a safe and orderly—but not severe—school environment. These schools aggressively combat the disease of low expectations, imbuing with high expectations all school policies and activities and the actions of all school staff, and they pay attention to academic achievements, to results. Instead of dealing with children and parents as clusters of risk factors, these schools work with parents and children respectfully and collaboratively and as individuals. They examine the various roles of school, child, family, and community when a child is having difficulty, and they devise strategies for individual children that interrupt negative interactions and set in motion positive cycles of success. These schools understand the importance of giving parents authority and a sense of belonging, they reach out to parents of all races and classes, and they provide a variety of opportunities for parents to become involved in school—from volunteering in classrooms to serving on governance committees to fund-raising. These schools work to engage fathers and to involve adults other than parents who play crucial roles in children's lives. They recognize the importance of mining teachers' wisdom and of giving teachers the time, support, and resources they need to work with a wide range of struggling students. Sometimes teachers' jobs are restructured to give them more time to prepare for class and to talk informally with students. These schools continually promote teachers' learning and professional development. Guidance counselors, school nurses, and other school staff have clearly delineated roles and are similarly supported, and school staff are encouraged to work in teams. These schools also break down the boundaries that usually divide schools and communities, drawing on community services and resources, including businesses, universities, and senior citizens. School-community partnerships are not haphazard: They are designed to achieve specific goals that further students' academic achievements.

**Principles of Schools that Are Effective
with Vulnerable Children**

1. Staff emphasize academics and pay careful attention to results, to academic achievements.
2. Staff have the capacity to respond to the emotional and social troubles and material needs of children.
3. Staff create a safe and orderly but not severe school environment.
4. Staff imbue high expectations for children in every aspect of school functioning.
5. Staff work with parents and children respectfully and collaboratively. When a child has a problem, staff examine the child's role, the family's role, the community's role, and the school's role.
6. Staff seek to identify root problems and to turn negative interactions into cycles of success.
7. Staff give parents authority and a sense of belonging; they reach out to all parents and provide a variety of opportunities for parents to become involved in school.
8. Staff work to engage noncustodial parents and other adults of great importance to a child.
9. Administrators mine teachers' wisdom, seek to provide teachers the time, support, and resources they need to work with struggling students and continually promote teachers' learning and professional development.
10. Guidance counselors, school nurses, and other school staff are similarly supported, and school staff are enabled to support and strengthen one another.
11. Staff form effective partnerships with community services, businesses, and other community resources. These partnerships are designed to achieve specific goals that further children's academic achievements.

Talking to teachers in these and other schools reveals the critical attributes that enable teachers to work effectively with vulnerable children. Effective teachers focus on results and operationalize high expectations for every child, in part by attributing failure to things about a classroom or child that can be influenced, rather than to intractable aspects of a child or family or community. These teachers don't use poverty, "broken homes," or a pervasive community drug problem as a pretext for giving up on children. Rather than simply touting the importance of self-esteem and engaging in superficial praise and cheerleading—a fad in many schools today—these teachers seek to provide every student with the elements from which real and durable self-esteem is built, including specific, tangible skills and achievements, progressively increased responsibilities, and opportunities to give to others. Rather than seeing a vulnerable child only in terms of weaknesses, these teachers view children as having complex constellations of strengths and weaknesses, and they are able to communicate this understanding to parents. These teachers show children how to use their strengths, and they work to develop children's adaptive capacities, their ability to manage disappoint-ment, frustration, and conflict. Effective teachers pick up on the less visible, more prosaic problems that undermine children in school, such as mild hunger or wearing the same clothes day after day, and respond flexibly and aggressively to these problems. They view the classroom and the school as a complex culture and system, and they seek to understand the difficulties of a child in terms of the interactions between children and that culture or system. They are aware, for example, when a child is scapegoated or rigidly typecast in a classroom, and they work to give the child a variety of opportunities and roles both within the classroom and within the school. These teachers have the skills to engage parents proactively as well as to work with parents when a child is in crisis.

Effective teachers also look for ideas and feedback from both colleagues and children—they see children as active partners in their education—and are self-observing and alert to the possibility that they may be contributing to a child's difficulty. This capacity for self-observation includes knowing when to provide services themselves—when to advise a child, for example—and when a child needs to see a professional with specialized training. Perhaps most important, effective schools and teachers tolerate failure and take risks, continually shaping and reshaping their activities based on close attention to results, to what does and does not work.

Attributes of Effective Teachers Working with Vulnerable Children

1. Effective teachers operationalize high expectations for every child and focus on academic results.
2. Effective teachers attribute failure to aspects of a child or classroom that can be positively influenced, rather than to intractable aspects of a child, family, or community.
3. Effective teachers provide every student with the elements from which real and durable self-esteem is built, including specific, tangible skills and achievements, progressively increased responsibilities, and opportunities to give to others.
4. Effective teachers view children as having complex constellations of strengths and weaknesses and communicate this understanding to parents.
5. Effective teachers work to develop children's adaptive capacities, their ability to manage disappointment and conflict.
6. Effective teachers pick up on the quiet troubles that undermine children in school, such as mild hunger or wearing the same clothes day after day and respond aggressively to these problems.
7. Effective teachers view the classroom and school as a complex culture and system and seek to understand the difficulties of a child in terms of the interactions between a particular child and a particular culture and system.
8. Effective teachers engage parents proactively and have the skills to work with parents when a child is in crisis.
9. Effective teachers are self-observing and are responsive to feedback and ideas from both other school staff and children—they see children as active partners in their education.
10. Effective teachers know when to respond to a child's problem themselves and when a child needs to see another professional who has specialized training.
11. Effective teachers innovate, take risks, and reshape their activities based on close attention to results.

Making the Exceptional Typical

The great challenge over the next decade will be to realize these principles in schools across the country and to piece together the strengths of these model schools in an effective way. Many educators set various reform ideas against one another. Some argue for new teaching methods, others for more parent involvement, still others for higher teacher pay. But these reforms are not incompatible. James Comer, Ted Sizer, the founder of the Coalition of Essential Schools, another broad school reform initiative (though not a reform effort focused on vulnerable children), Harvard educator Howard Gardner, and others combined their models in response to President Bush's America 2000 plan, which offered financial support to school innovators. Ed Zigler, the founder of the 21st Century schools, points out that combining aspects of these various model schools can have "very positive synergistic effects."

The problem is that replicating model schools, whether alone or in combination, is not likely to touch the great majority of American schoolchildren. Those promoting model schools report that they receive more requests for assistance from other schools than they are equipped to handle, yet replication is not likely to lead to changes in most of the 83,000 public schools in the United States. Innovative models tend to drum up excitement and to be replicated in a small number of schools, and then to evaporate over time. Obviously, embracing a whole new vision of how to function is daunting for many teachers and administrators. There is also an unhappy history in education of innovations being oversold, touted so highly at first that even modest accomplishments are met with disappointment and then discarded.

But even if entire models cannot be easily transplanted, many of the basic principles and practices that energize them can be successfully replicated. At least three states—Kentucky, California, and Vermont—are now experimenting with statewide education reforms that could dramatically alter the education landscape for vulnerable children. These innovations are built around new assessment instruments. Rather than relying solely on standardized tests, these schools are seeking to improve accountability by relying on performance assessment or a mixture of performance assessment and standardized tests, which indicate student progress across many intellectual domains. While these measures are in their infancy and questions have been raised about their validity, these measures can potentially offer a richer and more accurate picture of a student's constellation of strengths and weaknesses.

Such reforms also enable state and district education offices to work with schools in implementing effective principles and practices for working with vulnerable children. District education offices are typically busy policing individual schools to ensure that they comply with regulations. These monitoring functions use up large amounts of time and money, and sometimes become ridiculously extreme. Local schools sometimes have to file reams of forms with district or state education offices before they can fix a broken window or change the school menu. In Kentucky and Vermont, state education offices are seeking instead to hold schools accountable by monitoring student progress—according to new performance assessment methods—which enables state and district offices to redeploy their energies into assisting schools in the implementation of effective principles and practices. Rather than merely disseminating information, state and district education staff work closely with schools in absorbing these principles and in managing a complex transition.

In addition, these three states provide technical assistance that directly boosts schools' capacities to meet the needs of vulnerable children and families. In Kentucky, schools are funded and given technical help in developing family support centers, which address a wide range of family difficulties. In Vermont, the Department of Education and the Agency of Human Services are creating local collaborations among schools and human service agencies and developing comprehensive early childhood service systems and early intervention teams that have as one goal smoothing children's transitions to school. Making these collaborations and programs work is no simple matter, but each of these states is taking serious steps to bring schools more closely into line with the realities of students' lives and to strengthen schools' capacities to respond to students' needs.

Widely realizing the principles of these model schools will also require paying attention to the conditions that enable innovations to take root. These new principles and practices will have difficulty taking root if teachers lack basic skills—teacher training institutions tend to give teachers little or no skills in working with parents, for example—if teachers are teaching out of their fields, if they are repeatedly shuffled among schools, if they constantly have to cope with inadequate materials, or if substitutes are doing a large amount of teaching. Nor can these principles take root if administrators lack adequate training or if schools lack basic staff, such as a school counselor, or if these staff have impossibly large caseloads. Especially in schools attended by low-income students, such problems are pervasive and persistent. Promoting the principles of model schools needs to be combined with continued attention to improving these dimensions of school functioning.

For such principles to become standard practice will require help from many other sectors of society as well. Armed with knowledge about good principles and practices, parents can better fight for reforms. The Right Question Project, started in Somerville, Massachusetts, is an exciting effort to give parents, especially low-income parents, information about model schools and other tools that can help them advocate for their children and for school change. Parent are learning how to monitor and hold schools accountable for their children's progress. Education reformers can do more to increase public awareness about good public schools, setting aside their differences long enough to promote their large areas of agreement. Businesses have a role to play as well, not only in funding high-profile school interventions, but also in disseminating information about effective principles and practices and in helping schools implement and manage innovations.

The challenge ahead is to figure out not so much what should go on inside a school building than how to change entire school systems. As Michael Timpane, former president of Columbia University Teachers' College, wrote in a critique of the America 2000 plan: "There are many good ideas already in practice, including those championed by... James Comer, Bob Slavin, and many others. Our problem is learning how to shepherd these ideas through unwieldy bureaucracies to principals and teachers in every school, people who are just beginning to believe they can take charge." The danger is that cynicism and skittishness, based on the mistaken notion that public schools cannot be fixed, will undermine these large-scale reforms, especially because early evaluations may show failures that confirm this cynicism. There is a tendency in education reform to pull up the plant every ten minutes to make sure that it is still growing. Yet the challenges ahead, large as they are, are no greater than the challenges that have already been met.

11

EVEN IF THE BOAT GOES DOWN: CHILD PROTECTIVE SERVICES

BOUT NINE O'CLOCK ON A FRIDAY EVENING, the Massachusetts Department of Social Services child abuse prevention hot line received a call from a thirteen-year-old girl named Marge Walker. Marge was calling from a pay phone. She had missed her curfew and reported that if she went home her father would beat her with his belt; he had done this, she said, many times before. The hot-line worker called the police, and a police officer, Mark Daniels, was dispatched to bring both Marge and her parents, Dwight and Beverly, to the police station for a conference.

The hot-line worker met the family at the police station and thought a conference might settle the matter fairly quickly. Because serious abuse was not involved, she would issue a stern warning to Dwight, and keep close tabs on Marge. Yet Dwight and Beverly denied the beatings and told the worker that the real problem was that Marge was out of control. She had "fallen into the wrong crowd." She was regularly coming home at one or even two in the morning. Dwight thought she was using drugs. The next day Dwight and Beverly filed a CHINS petition requesting assistance from the state because they no longer believed they could effectively exercise their guardianship. Dwight and Beverly, in effect, threw up their hands. That day, a judge granted custody of Marge to the Department of Social Services.

Phyllis Chesterton is a social worker at the Parkside office, an area office of the Massachusetts Department of Social Services that covers a few largely middle-class and affluent towns. When she received the order giving custody of Marge to the state, she followed standard procedure. She called Dwight and Beverly to arrange a home visit, but the call did not go smoothly. Beverly flat-out rejected the idea of a home visit. With her husband eavesdropping on another phone, she said that the family was "private and religious." Dwight interrupted to elaborate: "state people," or what he repeatedly called "socialists," would never enter their home and try to "cast out" their religious beliefs. Eventually, Phyllis suggested a meeting at her office, and Dwight and Beverly agreed.

During the meeting Dwight talked almost incessantly, and Phyllis recalls that he was a strange mixture of gracious, chatty, and intimidating. A thin man with a grizzled beard, he repeatedly laid down his two laws: he would not be told what to do, and he would not let anyone working for the state enter his home. Phyllis listened carefully, and several times tried to shift the focus of the discussion to what might be helpful to them in managing Marge. When Dwight at last registered the question that Phyllis was asking, he became interested and engaged. He confessed his helplessness in getting Marge to comply with his wishes, and he and Beverly agreed to attend weekly meetings to discuss better strategies for overcoming Marge's resistance.

The following week, Phyllis received a call from a school counselor about another child in the Walker family, their eleven-year-old son, James. She was told by the counselor that James was threatening to kill other students and himself—he wanted, he said, to be put out of his misery. He had drawn two pictures of children impaled with knives, and he had recently curled into a fetal position in the corner of the school parking lot. The counselor thought that part of the problem was that James was badly ostracized in school because he espoused strange religious beliefs and sometimes acted bizarrely. School staff's request for assistance from Dwight and Beverly had not cut through the ice. Dwight was outright belligerent and kept repeating that the problem was not James, but was the school's persecuting him. Persuaded that James was not safe, the school decided to file a "Care and Protection" petition on him—a claim that he was not receiving proper care and protection at home.

This petition would be reviewed in court, after which action could be taken to place James, too, in the custody of the Department of Social Services. But Dwight loudly put his foot down. They could take Marge away from him, he told the school principal, but not his boy. He added that he would not be coerced, that he had guns in his house and he knew about his "Second Amendment rights."

When Phyllis heard about these threats, she consulted her supervisor, Ruth Rettig. Ruth's first reflex was to file with the local court a writ that would allow Phyllis—or preferably a police officer—to enter the home. As she put it: "This guy had rotten teeth, he was unshaven, he wore combat fatigues, and he looked furious. He intimidated the hell out of people. It was just around the time when David Koresh was holing himself up in Waco, Texas, and people who saw this guy—the rotten teeth, the combat fatigues—thought of Koresh. At first I thought: We have to get the kids out of there."

But Ruth also knew that taking this step would shatter the tenuous relationship that Phyllis had created with Dwight and Beverly and could become an utter nightmare—a mini-Waco. Phyllis or a police officer might be hurt, one of the children might be badly hurt, and the prospects of working out a solution that would allow the family to stay together would vanish entirely.

After consulting with other supervisors and workers, Ruth and Phyllis took another tack. They decided to step up the meetings. Dwight and Beverly came in twice a week, and together with Phyllis they set a goal: developing concrete strategies that they might use to avoid escalating conflicts with all the children. Dwight would describe a confrontation in which he found himself boiling over, and Phyllis would suggest to him another route. Phyllis quickly discerned something signal: so long as Dwight did not perceive that he was being threatened or challenged or that someone was claiming authority over him, he was quite eager to get help. To be sure, he was still extremely distrustful and occasionally angry and outright paranoid. Phyllis could not warm up to him. But he was not David Koresh, and he wanted to learn.

Within a few weeks, Dwight and Beverly had joined a parenting group and agreed to have a counselor come to their house. The counselor continues to work with them on dealing with the difficulties of their children. Marge is in the home, generally complies with her parents' wishes, and reports that she does not feel threatened. Although James is not having an easy time with school, he is not threatening to hurt other children or himself. Police never had to enter the home; there was no armed standoff, and the children were not shunted into the foster-care system. By almost any measure, this social service office's intervention with this family was a success.

------------□------------

When health-care institutions, schools, and other services are unable to detect or protect children vulnerable to neglect and abuse, children have one last line of defense: the child protective service system. Yet child protective service agencies have come to epitomize to many Americans everything that is wrong with government and all that is futile about the nation's attempts to improve the lot of children. These agencies are routinely guilty, according to weekly headlines, of mind-boggling incompetence, recklessly ripping some children out of the womb of their families while allowing others to languish in homes where they are in terrible peril. For weeks in the spring and summer of 1993, a major Chicago newspaper carried a story about the failure of a child protective service agency, after an investigation had uncovered signs of abuse, to extract from a home a three-year-old who was later hanged by his mother. People who interact with these agencies regularly, including teachers, police officers, and health-care providers, are typically no less harsh in their assessments. These professionals look to these agencies for help with endangered children, yet their pleas are often met with deafening silence or with responses so bureaucratic as to be worthy of Orwell or Kafka. In Massachusetts, professionals who go to great lengths to document a case of neglect and abuse may receive in response a slip of paper that reads, "The injury reported does not constitute neglect/abuse as defined by departmental regulations."

Such criticisms are reactions to very real problems, yet they obscure a wholly different story about these same agencies. Child protective workers are faced every day with muddy, complex moral decisions that will have staggering consequences for children and their families—decisions that are usually left to biology or to God. Who should a child's parents be? When should children be taken from their parents, and when should they be returned? When should a child be permanently placed with another family? When should children be separated from their siblings? Who, in fact, should constitute a child's family? In making these decisions, workers inevitably make tragic errors, and the number of these errors is often multiplied because workers are burdened by large caseloads and sluggish, encrusted bureaucracies.

At the same time some offices—such as the Parkside office—typically make decent and humane decisions that achieve the best possible outcomes for children. These offices pay attention to the range of things that all children need to grow and to the many interacting family and community circumstances that undermine individual children. Children are rarely provided with an ideal solution, but they are generally placed in environments that maximize their chances of safety and of receiving support, stimulation, and moral guidance. Workers are also able to sustain attention on families over time, so that children are less likely to be victims of repetitive cycles of neglect and abuse. And these agencies work because of clearly identifiable principles and practices, principles and practices that, like those in health-care and education reform, should form the backbone of the typical child protective agency.

The Parkside Office

To understand the success of the Parkside office, it is important to understand the failures elsewhere. Some of these failures are illuminated by contrasting the response of the Parkside office to the Walker family with the likely response of a typical office. Although few families investigated for neglect or abuse are religious extremists, the Walker case is illustrative of the most difficult child protective cases—those in which workers have to make swift decisions with deficient information about whether a parent on the edge is capable of a collaboration with a worker that will ensure the safety of a child.

Phyllis developed an alliance with Dwight Walker that enabled her to work with him constructively and that gave her confidence that during their work his children would not be hurt. Just as important, she was able to confirm her judgment about the safety of the children with a highly trained, experienced supervisor. Lacking time, experience, and clinical skills, most workers would be unable to get past the fear and anger that Dwight Walker provoked. A large percentage of workers are inexperienced and young—in their mid-twenties—and often unable to confirm their judgments with supervisors, many of whom are overburdened and lack clinical training. Without such consultation, a prudent worker would have no choice but to shift responsibility for the Walker children to the police.

Furthermore, child protective services workers are especially likely to suffer bitterness and cynicism that makes it hard to get past fear and anger and to summon patience and empathy for such families as the Walkers. Of all the professionals who work with children, it may be that those in child protective services suffer the most degradation and danger and receive the fewest rewards. Perhaps no other professionals deal more regularly with hopeless, desperate families whose problems will never be cured; and few workers deal so routinely with parents who seem to have lost their basic humanity. Recently, workers at the Parkside office came across two children, abandoned by their parents, who were eating wallpaper to survive and investigated other parents who were leaving their dog to baby-sit for their two-year-old. Another parent sought help for her three-year-old because, she explained, he was waking up in the middle of the night and wrecking the house. It turned out that he was foraging for food.

Child protective services workers are also like referees in sports in that their successes are hardly noticed and their mistakes can bring massive, highly public humiliation. Lacking training and supervision and set up for failure, many workers simply protect themselves by focusing on how effectively they've fulfilled their bureaucratic requirements—how many home visits they've made, for example—rather than on whether they've made a positive difference in a child's life.

That workers in the Parkside office do not feel snowed under or beaten down, that they do not act reflexively or out of fear, that they tend to provide the best possible environment for a child almost everyone attributes to the leadership of Elaine Lake, the office director for the past twelve years. A fiftyish woman with light blue eyes, freckles, and reddish brown hair, Lake took over the office with the commitment to making it radically *unlike* the office where she had first worked as a social worker, where she was isolated and felt "like a cog in a very large wheel." Over time, she came to see the workings of the state Department of Social Services from other outposts; she assisted the state commissioner of social services in writing policy, and she was a deputy administrator of a local office. When Lake was put in charge of her own area office, she knew that she had to create a new model, starting in certain places from scratch.

At the core of the Lake revolution are several key principles and practices. Lake believes that every worker needs a guiding philosophy, a clear sense of mission. As workers commonly judge themselves by how effectively they've fulfilled bureaucratic requirements, Lake sees the necessity of keeping them focused on meeting children's basic needs.

Lake recognizes, too, that to deal with many different children and families with very serious and complex problems, staff have to be constantly supported and strengthened. Although workers at the Parkside office do not have to deal with certain kinds of complex problems suffered by ghetto families or with the hazards of working in ghetto neighborhoods, every worker there confronts difficult and demanding problems every day. Regulations prohibit any office from taking on so-called filler cases, cases in which a child is not imminently and seriously at risk. Moreover, well-heeled communities pose their own particular threats. Liability fears haunt workers at the Parkside office. "In a ghetto neighborhood you worry about opening a door and having a gun pointed at your head," a worker at the Parkside office quips. "Around here you worry about opening a door and facing a lawyer."

To ensure that children's basic needs are met, Lake believes that workers need not only support, but also quality supervision and basic knowledge and skills. She views knowledge about child development and family patterns as especially critical. One of her workers recently failed to recognize that an infant who was not crawling at one and a half years old was developmentally delayed. Lake also recognizes that to work effectively with families, staff need to be flexible and creative, they need to closely collaborate with a wide range of community agencies and services, and they need to be able to sustain attention on families over time rather than jumping from case to case.

Lake did not attempt to sweep these principles into the office in one broad stroke. Supporting and strengthening workers in particular requires not broad strokes, but small gestures day to day. Lake and other administrators constantly seek to make work meaningful and manageable; they rationalize office procedures and give workers clear, achievable goals. They have streamlined bureaucratic requirements and go out of their way to explain how each article of paperwork is connected to the child-focused mission of the agency, so that workers don't view paperwork as an exercise in futility and alienation. Nor do Lake and other administrators allow disappointment and frustration to fester. "I like a lot of people yelling at me," Lake says. "I'd rather have them yelling up the hierarchy than me yelling down it. Workers feel enough blame without my yelling at them."

No worker is deemed marginal or without need of support. Administrators train receptionists and include them in the team, in part because they recognize that if family problems are to be stemmed early, then families' initial contacts with the office must be positive.

Lake is convinced, too, that the way in which administrators treat workers is directly reflected in the way in which workers treat families. In responding to workers she takes as a starting point *their* perception of their needs. Recently, workers requested a major overhaul of the office's intake procedures, and Lake accommodated their request even though she didn't believe that the new system would be an improvement: "The reform didn't make any sense to me, but because all the workers believed in it, they *made* it work. We now do the best assessments in the state." At the same time, staff respect Lake because she doesn't approve requests blithely, because she is willing to make unpopular decisions, and because she makes decisions quickly: children are not left in limbo.

Lake not only seeks to strengthen workers directly; she knows the crucial importance of creating a climate in which workers strengthen one another. She has labored to get workers to walk the walk—and not just talk the talk—about collaboration: "Everyone talks about a team approach as if a team approach is simply a lot of meetings," Lake says. "But a team approach means creating an environment where there is bottom line respect, but where people actually use one another and feel free to speak their minds." Especially when the stakes are high, Lake insists that workers challenge one another relentlessly.

To ensure that workers acquire basic knowledge and skills, Lake encourages younger workers to consult regularly with more experienced workers and has developed training for workers in child development, in family patterns and dynamics, and in working with families' strengths. Like Dr. Hass, Lake realizes that she is a model for her workers and sees her behavior as transmitting crucial information and skills. Lake conveys the priority of staying focused on children by example. When a worker is faced with a difficult case and a supervisor is unavailable, Lake drops everything to help out "because it's a way of showing that the most important thing, always, is to care for the child."

To enable workers to respond flexibly to a wide range of family needs, Lake employs several concerted strategies. Workers are openly encouraged to meet families where they are and to shift gears accordingly. Lake is not averse to workers' stretching bureaucratic procedures or ignoring the job manual when it can make a large difference to a family, so long as she is consulted. And workers are provided with the small amounts of flexible funds needed to do the small things that can make a large difference, such as paying for transportation so that families can receive a desperately needed service.

At the Parkside office, the Lake principles have taken deep hold. Workers say over and over that Lake listens to them and genuinely respects their suggestions. "You don't feel like a victim in this agency," is how one worker puts it, "like you're just floating on a tide that you can't do anything about." Workers here do not relish paperwork, but, unlike those in other offices who complain about it fiercely, they tend to *defend* it. They see documentation of their activities as improving the quality of care they provide to families—they have an ongoing record to which they can refer—and as protecting themselves from lawsuits. Staff pride themselves both on their respect for one another and on their ability to speak their minds. Arguments can at times seem frenzied, out of control—"it can be like a food fight," one worker says—but all agree that better decisions emerge from these storms. Recently staff were polarized about whether an infant should be taken from a mother who had already badly abused two of her children, even though she had not hurt the newborn. A decision was made to remove the child— it was not a consensus decision, but no staff member left wounded or questioned the integrity of the process. Other differences are predictably wide and deep. Staff members differ in their willingness to be intrusive and to violate parents' rights when a child may be in jeopardy; they differ about how much treatment should be required for a sexual-offending parent before a child is returned to a home; they differ because of their varied perspectives as biological parents, as foster parents, as stepparents—but all these differences are viewed as part of a healthy and necessary struggle.

This kind of close collaboration yields many benefits. Because decisions are made by teams, no worker has to shoulder responsibility alone. "We're all in the boat together," Margaret Henderson, a supervisor, says, "even if the boat goes down." When agonizing, wrenching decisions are made—such as a recent decision to separate two extremely close biological brothers because the foster parents could not handle both of them—workers support and counsel one another. Working in teams that are focused clearly on what is best for children, staff members point out, causes the degradations of traditional hierarchies and pecking orders to evaporate. "The most powerful person in the office is the most knowledgeable," a worker says, "the person who has the information about how to get things done."

Because staff at the Parkside office are supported and believe in the office, they stay far longer than is typical of such workers, increasing the continuity of care to families. Almost the entire supervisory team has been at the office for at least ten years, a staggeringly low rate of turnover, and turnover among caseworkers and receptionists is far lower than it is at other offices.

It is hard to attach hard outcome data to the work of the Parkside office, but signs of success abound. Workers in child protective services offices often appear edgy and despondent, yet workers here radiate enthusiasm for the place. Families feel the difference in every contact they have with the office, starting with the crucial first contact. Receptionists are warm, responsive, unbureaucratic. The manner in which administrators treat workers is strikingly reflected in the manner in which workers treat families. Workers such as Phyllis give families such as the Walkers achievable goals; they justify their actions; they listen carefully and respectfully; they try to turn parents' passivity and helplessness into useful activity. Some families maintain relationships with workers at this office for many years—long after their cases have been officially terminated. Tragic errors occur, but rarely, and they are always plumbed for lessons.

Because the office is run efficiently and because workers are responsive to a wide range of troubles, Parkside takes on families that other offices stiff-arm. Many agencies turn away parents who seek help voluntarily because these parents are deemed less desperate, but the Parkside office sees some voluntary families, and working with voluntary families often becomes a boon rather than a burden. Ruth Rettig notes, "Voluntary families are often the most gratifying to work with because they want help and often they don't require a lot of time—a single intervention can go a long way. Voluntary families rejuvenate workers."

The Parkside office is not the only area office to embody these principles—they characterize the efforts of several successful state child protective area offices around the country. The key element appears to be a strong administrator—not necessarily an administrator with special qualities, with great intelligence, or great charisma, but an administrator with the skills to support and strengthen workers.

Creating more child protective services offices such as the Parkside office will not be simple, and it will not happen without many concerted interventions and strategies. Minimally, state agencies have a role to play not only in disseminating effective principles and practices, but also in supporting and strengthening, rather than dragging down, area directors such as Elaine Lake. Like workers, administrators need resources and clear, achievable goals. In addition, the kinds of principles and practices that Lake intuits need to become part of standard training for administrators. States also need to focus on recruiting and training the supervisors who are so critical to providing quality services.

Family Preservation

Even the best offices often lack the resources they need to stabilize families. In the last decade, a promising movement has emerged to buttress the work of child protective agencies. Called family preservation, this movement seeks to provide intensive services to families when neglect or abuse is first reported. These programs are a vital resource and a crucial last line of defense for families.

The first such program, called Homebuilders, was initiated by the Catholic Family Services Agency in Tacoma, Washington. From the start, Homebuilders ran against the grain. Service providers worked with only three families at a time—as opposed to about thirty at a typical agency—and they devoted up to twenty hours a week per family initially, with continued intensive work for six to eight weeks. Families typically became stable after the eight-week period. Meanwhile, they were hooked up to a variety of other supports and services, such as parenting groups or substance-abuse programs.

Much of what underlies the Homebuilders model resembles the principles and practices of the Parkside office. Children's safety is the overriding concern of this program, but understanding children requires understanding complex family systems. Like Dr. Hass at the South End Community Health Center, workers at Homebuilders do not seek to address every family symptom, but to find leverage points—targets of change that will ameliorate core family problems and have many positive reverberations within families. A high premium is placed on the deceptively complex goal of understanding and respecting families, even families who, like the Walkers, seem bent on alienating and provoking workers. "It is relatively easy to hold these beliefs about respect and liking with articulate, cooperative middle-class clients," reads a Homebuilders' report. "It is more challenging to hold them with people who smell bad, go after each other with butcher knives, leave fingernail tracks in their kids' faces, and swear at counselors. We try hard to maintain the position that inside every frantic, overwhelmed, unpleasant client, there is a decent person struggling to get out."

One concrete way in which workers respect families is by seeking to maximize parental control and authority in their routine interactions with families. The time and place of meetings is determined by families. Looking for the "decent person struggling to get out" also means rejecting the deficit model. Workers are trained not simply to tally up pathologies but to identify and actively engage families' strengths. Family preservation programs also operate under the assumption that crises are opportunities for change. At such times, families are more motivated to change in part because parents can plainly see that their usual coping mechanisms have broken down.

These goals, once again, are accomplished by workers who are trained in flexibility, in improvisation, in doing whatever it takes. "Trouble has no timetable," a Homebuilders' report says. At Homebuilders, workers carry beepers—they're on call twenty-four hours a day, seven days a week—a practice nearly unheard of among social service agencies.

Although evaluations of family preservation programs have been plagued by methodological problems, the evidence suggests that these programs are enabling some children to live safely with their own families rather than bouncing among foster homes.

In recent years, the Edna McConnell Clark Foundation has sought to spread this model far beyond Tacoma by using the principles of family preservation to induce reforms in states' child welfare, juvenile justice, and mental health programs. Today, approximately one-half million children live outside their homes in foster care, group homes, and juvenile justice and psychiatric institutions. In part because of the Clark Foundation's prodding and assistance, fourteen states are planning to make family preservation services available statewide to families within the next two years to avoid inappropriate institutional placements. The Clark Foundation is also joining with social work programs to immerse students in the principles of family preservation.

Good child protective services agencies, such as Parkside, and family preservation, are only two pieces of what needs to be a far more comprehensive, integrated approach to preventing neglect and abuse. Teachers, police officers, health-care providers, and other professionals need better skills in assessing neglect and abuse. Sometimes parents are falsely accused because professionals lack basic assessment abilities, and many cases of neglect and abuse are never reported. It is often difficult for professionals to know what to do, for example, when a child recants or refuses to confirm an initial report of neglect or abuse. A great deal of attention needs to be given as well to fixing the broken lines of communication between these professionals and child protective services agencies. Child protective services agencies might also function more effectively if nonsevere cases of neglect and abuse could be routinely dealt with by community agencies, such as family support centers, designed to strengthen families and prevent problems. This idea is now being seriously considered in a few states. Although many knotted legal and practical issues need to be worked through in creating such a preventive system, such a system could dramatically lighten the load of child protective services agencies, making the work of these agencies far more manageable. Even some of the serious problems routinely handled by child protective services agencies might be better handled by other institutions. Child protective services agencies are required to investigate cases of babies who are exposed to drugs, even though many of these children are not neglected or abused. A health-care institution that employs social workers may be better positioned to obtain drug-treatment programs for parents and good pediatric care for children, as well as other kinds of help that these families typically need. Many aspects of the foster care and adoption systems—other important systems within child protective services—are also badly in need of reform.

Several sectors of society can advance these prevention efforts. For example, the media, rather than focusing on tragic failure, could highlight successful child protective services interventions and analyze the underlying elements that produce them. Businesses, universities, and other community services and agencies clearly have a role not only in strengthening families but in educating the public about signs of neglect and abuse, and in encouraging parents to seek help before abuse occurs.

These various strategies, effectively combined, can produce what all Americans want: smaller, less costly, more humane child protective services agencies and fewer children who are neglected or abused.

12

THE POLICE

I
T IS NINE O'CLOCK ON A WEDNESDAY NIGHT, AND
Sergeant Tom Flanagan is playing his part in the war to spare
families crime and disorder in an ethnically and economically
mixed neighborhood in the Dorchester area of Boston. He is not
barreling down a rain-slicked street, sirens wailing, or slogging
through the motions of reading some dazed drug dealer the Miranda
rights, or busting down the door of a suspected rapist. This is not
Cops or *Kojak* or even *NYPD Blue*. This police officer is in the
basement of a school building talking to a group of some thirty
residents about how he had a truck removed that was illegally
parked. He is sharing his strategies and eliciting ideas for
eradicating neighborhood graffiti and stopping teenagers from
drinking in the park. (The solutions to these problems are linked.
He has proposed legislation that would enable judges to sentence
children to thirty hours of community service as a penalty for their
first public drinking offense, and the community service can include
painting over, under his supervision, neighborhood graffiti.) After
this meeting, Officer Flanagan is buttonholed by his cousin, who
gives him the latest update about a family that is creating an
uproar in her neighborhood. The mother openly berates her children
and neighbors on the street and can be heard howling at her
children at four o'clock in the morning.

Earlier that same evening, at another neighborhood meeting,
Flanagan also plotted solutions with residents to the problem of
graffiti and strategized about how to deal with a group of neighborhood teenagers whose partying had become too loud. In the last

decade this neighborhood has, in fact, become a community, rather than a collection of houses bound only by common tenancy on a piece of earth. According to residents, Flanagan's brand of policing has played a critical part. They have a palpable feeling of order in the neighborhood and a sense that they control the streets, rather than the streets' controlling them. Flanagan's different activities, what he calls the "many little, boring things" that he does, may be doing more than all the firepower and technology in the world to create safe and healthy environments for children.

———————□———————

When policy makers discuss ways of better caring for children, when advocates seek to mobilize children's campaigns, when academics write papers about how to break the cycle of childhood disadvantage, one large group of professionals is almost always absent: the police. Yet when families are in crisis, police officers are often the first ones called. Police officers are summoned when violence erupts in a family, violence commonly witnessed by children, and they are often summoned when children are victims of serious neglect or abuse. How police intervene in these situations can determine whether a problem is stemmed early or explodes. Moreover, hundreds of police forces throughout the United States are now engaged in Sergeant Flanagan's brand of police work, called community policing, which seeks in part to prevent problems in childhood by creating safe environments and by reducing stress on parents.

Creating Trust

For most of this century, police reforms have had the effect of distancing police from families and eroding the capacity of officers to avert childhood problems. Reforms have been almost single-mindedly designed to strengthen the capacity of police to deal with serious crime by motorizing patrols and increasing the speed of response to crime. Special attention has been given to creating technologies to reduce response time to 911 emergency calls.

Although important, these aims have made police officers strangers to families and communities. Officers spend the bulk of their time in cars, dispatched to neighborhoods where they are unknown. Once they arrive at a crime scene, their sole purpose is to document an incident and, if necessary, to make arrests. Interactions with neighborhood residents are formal and brief. New York Police Commissioner William Bratton has remarked that police have been trained to operate like the character Jack Webb in the old television show *Dragnet*. Webb frequently interrupted his witnesses to keep them on the point: "Just the facts, Ma'am." Bent on responding to serious crime, police in many communities have simply stopped responding to minor annoyances, such as graffiti and rowdy teenagers, even though the vast majority of calls received by police stations—often termed garbage calls—are about these seemingly trivial troubles.

This distance between residents and police officers has created unforeseen problems. Police have lost almost all capacity to prevent problems or to detect them early, and residents feel less safe without personal ties. Moreover, the failure of police to respond to problems such as graffiti appears to have been the first step down a very slippery slope for many neighborhoods. In a landmark article entitled "Broken Windows," crime experts James Q. Wilson and George Kelling argue that when small violations of public space and civility are left untended, residents begin to feel that the police are ineffective and that their neighborhoods are spiraling out of control. Residents then retreat into their own homes, and when they do venture out they keep to themselves. As residents become more remote and less vigilant, a neighborhood becomes far more hospitable to crime—to drug dealing, to vandalism, to panhandling—which increases the remoteness of residents, in an escalating cycle. Eventually, many residents abandon a neighborhood altogether, and neighborhoods become places where no parent would elect to raise a child. In addition, when police officers are strangers and episodes of police corruption or brutality surface in a community, negative stereotypes of officers quickly spread and balloon. Flanagan believes that in some communities police officers have become so alien that small children would not approach them for help even if they were lost.

Community policing does not reject the aims of traditional reforms: it seeks to remedy their serious deficiencies. Major strategies of community policing include giving greater authority and discretion to local police stations, basing officers within neighborhoods, giving these officers the authority and latitude they need to deal creatively and effectively with a wide array of community problems, and inculcating a proactive, problem-solving approach that draws on a wide range of tactics and resources.

Simple as these goals and strategies may sound, they are not at all simple to achieve, which makes the work of officers such as Tom Flanagan of the C11 area office in Dorchester so crucial to understand. Forty-eight years old, Flanagan is a burly, affable, perceptive man with white hair and warm, ocean-blue eyes. He grew up in this neighborhood and is a third-generation police officer. Flanagan remembers when he was a boy in the 1950s riding in a police car with his father, who bantered easily with almost everyone.

Flanagan's partner is Paul Johnston, fifty-two years old, a bearded, thoughtful man who has a merry, slightly elfin quality. He also carries images in his head of a different era in policing, of times in the 1950s and early 1960s when police officers were widely respected and trusted. These images drew these men to join the force, yet over the years these images began to clash with the realities of the day-to-day job. In the late 1960s and the 1970s, these men worked together on riot squads—"we spent so much time at Boston University and Harvard we should have gotten degrees," Johnston says—and were hated. In later years, both worked out of patrol cars.

When offered the opportunity to spearhead C11's experiment in community policing, Flanagan and Johnston were enticed, in part, by nostalgic memories. But they knew quite well that the old model of police work could not simply be grafted onto modern communities. The challenge would be to blend old ideas with new in a community that had become extremely diverse and far more complex along many dimensions.

Although these officers are guided by several principles and practices, they see earning the trust of families—a means to an end in many programs—as the heart of their work and as a crucial end in itself. In their view, the ability to meet children's basic needs and to prevent problems depends on trust.

Early on, these officers grasped that to earn trust in a neighborhood they had to dramatically alter the way in which they were perceived. Two years ago their unit instituted a "cop card" program: children collect a forty-nine-card set with pictures of police officers at the Dorchester station. On Wednesday, officers autograph children's cards at the station. Children with enough cards receive certificates for free merchandise at neighborhood stores.

Flanagan and Johnston believe that this kind of high-profile strategy may help crack icy perceptions of police officers. But they emphasize that this is the showy part of their work, that the deeper kinds of trust are won an inch at a time with far less glamour. Much of their time is spent at community meetings, such as the two evening meetings at which Tom Flanagan spoke, at churches, schools, and community centers, listening to the concerns of parents and other residents, gathering suggestions, describing what the police can and cannot do, guiding people to other possible sources of help, offering safety tips, and, not insignificantly or accidentally, gently threading themselves into a neighborhood and into families' lives. A large part of their time is spent on the phone. If Flanagan had to identify a single key to their success in earning trust it would be that he and Johnston purchased an answering machine that enables them to return phone calls promptly, "That answering machine is like a great pipeline for this neighborhood." Johnston adds, "People are so appreciative that you call them back promptly, and that you actually talk to them. They're not used to that with police officers." Flanagan and Johnston also make a special effort to lodge positive images of police officers in children's heads. They visit schools, where they teach children about safety and answer any questions children have (kids are chiefly interested in all their paraphernalia— "What's the radio for?" "When do you use that stick?"—and in how much money they make).

Special attention is given to reaching out to immigrant populations. A Vietnamese liaison, Tram Tran, helps to create bridges between the police and the Vietnamese community, a community suspicious of the police. Tran helps police avoid the cultural chasm into which officers frequently plunge. Tran has explained, for example, that some Vietnamese parents who don't speak English don't like police officers, in the course of an investigation, to ask children to be translators; parents view this translator role as a challenge to their authority and may punish their children for accepting the role.

Guiding all their activities is a set of basic assumptions about *how* trust is earned. Early on, these officers recognized that in order to win resident's respect and confidence, they had to see the neighborhood as residents see it. Even though they had lived and worked in this community for many years, they recognized that what was important to residents and what was important to police officers were not always the same. Johnston recalls an episode that brought this perception gap home. At a Dunkin Donuts shop just down the street from the police station, a disheveled, dirty man with long, scraggly hair and a lobster-red face—"He looked like a mass murderer," Johnston says—leaned on a trash can all day, frightening children and shaking down customers, threatening to kill them if they refused to give him money. The police did not interfere, because they knew that this man was harmless. "He was just a drunk," Johnston points out. "If we had pulled out that trash can he would have fallen over." Residents, it turned out, viewed the police as ignoring a glaring menace, and so Johnston arrested the man for disorderly conduct. These officers learned that the chronic irritants that are typically low priorities for police officers—speeding cars, graffiti, disruptive tenants, overgrown trees blocking streetlights—are not minor to residents. As Flanagan says: "When a homicide occurs in a neighborhood, people are interested on Monday and they read about it in the paper on Tuesday but it's out of their minds by Wednesday. The barking dog is there every day."

To understand residents' perceptions, these officers spend much of their time listening, and they mine residents' wisdom about solutions to problems. Listening carefully to residents itself builds trust, and residents are able to see results, that their concerns are being addressed—perhaps the most important element in building trust. As these officers address the minor irritants, as Wilson and Kelling predict, they are reinforced each step of the way—people feel more trust in the police and more in command of their environment. "These kinds of successes register," Flanagan says. "People believe that if you can't get the little things done you'll never successfully get the big things done. We're showing them that we can do the little things, and they treat us like the second coming."

There is another main component to breaking through distrust. Flanagan and Johnston believe that residents view the police as indifferent or antagonistic in part because they don't understand police work. These officers go out of their way to explain to residents the nature of their work and the work of officers in other divisions, and they are brutally frank about their own limitations and the limitations of the system. They explain that certain kinds of problems—like high rates of homicide—often can't be remedied in the short run. They tell parents that officers can't respond to certain complaints because it exposes them to lawsuits—they can't put a child in a police car or look in a child's pockets, for example, unless there is tangible evidence of a crime. They openly share with residents their view that aspects of the system stink—and they coach residents about how to work the system. The C11 area office also runs a citizens' academy where residents, including many parents, are run through a mini-police-training course. Flanagan and Johnston don't see this academy as simply a fantasy camp for cop wanna-bes. They believe that if run with a modicum of intelligence, it can help dispel harmful misconceptions about police officers. At the academy, residents are provided with myth-dispelling information about various aspects of police work; information about how 911 calls are prioritized, for example, may help them understand why officers are late responding to some calls. Residents also try their hands at a high-stress, simulated firing range: potential assailants appear on a screen, and residents are forced to make choices about when to shoot. Flanagan thinks that this simulator can give citizens a much deeper understanding of the kinds of impossible choices that police officers confront and may generate empathy for officers who make mistakes.

Important as their ties to residents are, these officers know that to safeguard children and strengthen families it is even more important for residents to form ties to one another. The officers use the trust they have earned to help build these ties. Community policing is predicated on the notion that the community itself is the front line against crime and disorder, and a good deal of this type of police work focuses on, as Flanagan says, "teaching people how to be neighbors." Flanagan and Johnston demonstrate for residents how to help one another and the strengths of a unified neighborhood. They explain how crime plummets when residents are willing to call the police or tell each other when a stranger is seen in a neighbor's backyard. They describe the successes of neighborhood crimewatch efforts, and they go to great lengths to explain to residents the nuts and bolts of putting together an effective crime watch. They teach people how to solve various problems on their own and how to access needed government services.

At the same time, these officers work against the destructive aspects of neighborhoods and communities. In some neighborhoods, crime watch efforts take as their implicit or explicit purpose protecting one group of residents from another group of residents of a different class or ethnicity or protecting residents from immigrants or "outsiders." Flanagan and Johnston challenge residents who blame neighborhood problems on any particular group; they point out that crime is not perpetrated by any one group alone. They also state explicitly that they are not asking residents to be friends, but to collaborate because it will stop crime, a goal that is obviously in everyone's interest. "We're being totally mercenary about it in a sense," says Tom Lembo, another community police officer who works with Flanagan and Johnston. "We're telling people it's in your self-interest to get along. Don't do it because you like each other, do it because it works."

Like other professionals—perhaps even more so than other professionals—these officers' effectiveness depends on their willingness to be tenacious, flexible, and improvisational. Flanagan and Johnston work doggedly—every bit as aggressively as police chasing criminals—in responding to chronic neighborhood irritants. They are outcome oriented, doing whatever it takes to solve problems. Often they work closely with other city agencies—the health department and the sanitation department, for example. They also work with the mayor's office, which recently created a neighborhood liaison, who frequently helps community police officers track down and access a needed city service ("Lights get fixed quickly now," Flanagan says).

Improvisation is at the heart of their jobs. In a broad sense, so much of what these officers do has never been tried before that they feel that they are creating their jobs as they go along: "We're like the first space shuttle," Flanagan says. Instead of incarcerating teenagers for public drunkenness, these officers have proposed that they be required not only to paint over neighborhood graffiti, but also to write a 300-word essay on what the police can do to stop public drunkenness. Individual cases often require flexibility and complex problem-solving skills. For example, Flanagan took the time to talk to an obstreperous twelve-year-old boy who was disturbing residents and found out that the boy had been sexually molested by two older children in a vacant lot. Flanagan emphasized to the boy the importance of talking about this experience and gave the boy his name and the names of counselors (Flanagan did not report this incident to the state child protective services agency because the boy would not reveal his name). These officers are also aggressive about snaring any resource that comes to their attention. After interviewing them periodically for a few weeks, I was asked to help them develop a counseling program for Vietnamese parents whose teenage children had run away.

Because Flanagan and Johnston have created these strong ties, because they have helped neighbors ally with one another, because they are flexible and improvisational, they are able to weed out certain kinds of problems that threaten children and families before they take root. Often they receive calls notifying them that a drug dealer has entered a neighborhood. They know that the sudden appearance of a highly visible drug dealer can shatter families' sense of security. Typically in these situations, police officers try to catch a dealer in the act—a time-consuming process—and then must engage in the lengthy, exhausting process of documenting a case, only to find that dealers often serve little or no time. Flanagan and Johnston take another route. Because they have strong neighborhood ties, they are able to collect detailed information from residents about a drug dealer's activity; then they pay a visit. "We'll tell the dealer, 'everybody's watching you and so are we,'" Flanagan says. "We tell them that we know exactly what they are doing. We document for them the drug deals they have made. We destroy their anonymity." Almost always, the dealers vanish.

Because of their strong ties and because they go out of their way to explain to residents that they're not looking for witnesses in court, but for information that they can use to build a case, these officers are able to make use of residents in investigations. They take seriously the notion that the community is the front line against crime. Although careful not to endanger civilians, these officers are not shy about cashing in on residents' eagerness, for a few thrilling moments, to slip into the high drama of police work. Flanagan and Johnston tell residents what to do when they spot a drug deal—do not confront the dealer, but take down the license plate number. "We tell them we *want* you to get sneaky," Flanagan says. "They love it." Some residents, perhaps motivated by the videotaping of the beating of Rodney King, have used their own camcorders to document deals.

As in other organizations, the effectiveness of these officers depends on an administrator who is able to give them the support and resources they need. Robert Dunford, the captain of C11, is adamant about giving officers latitude, about "getting people what they need to do the job," and about keeping lines of communication wide open: "Many officers feel like they're mushrooms, kept in the dark and fed nothing but bullshit," Dunford says. "Here I tell them what is going on and they tell me what is going on."

New York is now engaging in a major community policing effort, and Chief Bratton, who is extremely popular among the rank and file, is focusing on supporting officers on the front line. He regularly visits officers on the street—not to monitor their activities, as many commissioners do, but to ask at least these questions: What are the problems out there? What do you need to do the job?

At C11 other officers and programs reinforce the work of Johnston and Flanagan. A few officers read to children in schools for forty-five minutes every two weeks. C11 has helped develop a law-enforcement curriculum for schools, jointly taught by the police and the Bar Association. C11 has developed an original course of instruction for officers investigating child neglect and abuse, in which they are taught to identify bruises, to distinguish accidents from intentional injuries, and to date bruises by coloration. Monthly seminars provide parents with safety information, such as how to prevent childhood injuries. One C11 officer has created a safe house, a sanctuary for children in his neighborhood, and Dunford hopes to create a safe house in every neighborhood in this district. Dunford also has ambitious plans for better preparing officers to work in the changing and diverse communities of the modern, urban United States. He is looking for recruits who have taken courses in psychology, sociology, and anthropology, and he actively advocates for the police academy to take up these subjects.

Although these officers consider their work to be in its infancy, signs of success are bubbling to the surface. In several neighborhoods, drug dealing has been reduced or eliminated. The C11 police station has become a friendly, inviting place for children—800 children dropped by for Halloween. A wide range of parents contact these officers with concerns—about children who are breaking curfews or who have run away from home for brief periods—that enable the officers to become involved in a child's life before an arrest is necessary. Parents report to the officers that they and their children feel safer and more in control in their communities.

These officers are discovering that responding to minor problems can be key not only to building trust and to increasing residents' sense of safety, but also to relieving stress on parents. Johnston likens these problems to toothaches for parents, toothaches for which these parents have not been getting any medicine. Domestic violence also has been significantly reduced in this area of Dorchester, and Flanagan and Johnston's brand of policing may have played a part. Perhaps most important, these officers have become an integral part of rebuilding certain neighborhoods, something that has defied, for decades, the best-laid plans of politicians, community development experts, and urban planners.

Other police stations are embarking on promising community policing strategies. Although bound by common principles, individual stations and individual officers are adapting community policing to local needs, their own resources, and their own proclivities and values. At another area office not far from C11, officers have developed a variety of activities explicitly designed to support and to create meaningful opportunities for children. Their activities have included a female police officer mentor program for neighborhood girls, a flag football league for teenagers, co-running a day camp in the summer, taking children on day trips to amusement parks and on cruises, and teaching teenage gang members CPR and other life-saving techniques. Officers in other parts of the country are heavily involved with individual schools. Kevin Jett, a community police officer profiled by Michael Norman in the *New York Times Magazine*, has become a kind of patron of a particular elementary school: "He's told the bad element in the street, 'You don't come into my school and mess with my teachers and my kids,'" the school principal says. "I feel like he's part of the staff."

In North Camden, New Jersey, a community with a long history of hostility toward the police, almost half the population is under age eighteen. When diminishing funds threatened to curtail a police bike patrol that had been established by a community policing program to bring police deeper into communities, children from a neighborhood school protested to the chief of police (and the chief changed his mind). In this same community, two children dressed up as police officers for Halloween, a gesture of admiration, according to Richard Malloy, a local journalist, that would have been unheard of ten years earlier.

Other community police officers are effectively cooling racial and ethnic antagonism. For example, community police officers in Pittsfield, Massachusetts, were confronted with a group of residents suspicious of residents from an adjacent, high-crime neighborhood. The officers managed to elicit sympathy for these neighbors and to create alliances between the two neighborhoods in part by explaining that residents of the high-crime neighborhood were not perpetrators; the high crime was the result of outsiders preying on this community. Officers in Pittsfield have also quelled fears of immigrants by explaining that historically every new immigrant group in the area has been distrusted and feared.

Community policing has significant problems and limitations, and no one is more keenly aware of them than police officers themselves, many of whom are distinctly hostile to this new trend. Some officers say that this type of policing depletes the capacity of the police to respond effectively to serious crime and that it's simply too hard to turn around entrenched hostility and hatred of police officers in some neighborhoods. Some officers liken this police work to social work, work they did not sign up for and work they are convinced won't make a dent in hard-core crime. "Community policing works," a New York officer told reporter Michael Norman, "if you live in Mayberry R.F.D." Older police officers, such as Flanagan and Johnston, frequently complain that pumped up, young-buck police officers are ill suited for this kind of work—they are far more interested in high-tech gadgetry, high-profile drug busts, and adrenaline-boosting car chases than in performing the small, invisible deeds that win trust in a community. Flanagan and Johnston have had to weather the open disdain of some officers, both young and old. Still others worry that community policing leaves police out on the street alone, where they are more vulnerable not only to assault but also to the seduction of corruption. A long-standing incentive and reward structure runs against community policing as well. In the great majority of police forces, Norman observes, people don't earn a detective shield, sergeant's stripes, bonuses, or accolades for dealing with petty annoyances (although community policing does offer the reward of being appreciated, rather than hated, by the public). Still others argue that it is futile to change one gear in a broken, bureaucratic machine: how can police officers be effective problem solvers when the other wheels of government—the transportation department, the parks department, the health department—remain in narrow ruts and adhere to the old rigid and self-protective ways?

Finally, there's a danger that officers will imbibe the rhetoric of community policing without embodying its subtler, deeper meanings, a danger heightened by the fact that many community police officers receive very little supervision and training. For example, field officers in New York receive just two days of training in community policing.

These criticisms need to be taken seriously. Community policing surely cannot fly solo—it depends on support from and reforms in other city agencies. It is crucial to enrich the training and supervision of community police officers. But these criticisms also need to be responsive to results. Community policing, as officers such as Flanagan and Johnston state over and over, is an experiment, and whether or not police officers should do this kind of work depends in large measure on evidence of its effectiveness, on whether children and families both *feel* safer and *are* safer in their communities, on whether the problems of children and families are intercepted at early stages, on whether serious crimes are reduced. Early signs of success warrant expanding and further testing of community policing, but the answers to these questions are not yet clear, and it is on these answers that the future of community policing should rest.

Listening to Children

It is one o'clock in the afternoon, and seven men and two women are seated around two tables that have been pushed together in a conference room in Boston City Hospital. What this group is discussing at the moment is the presence of a group of teenage boys who are hanging around and disturbing pedestrians on the corner by a police station. The police regularly tell these boys to disperse, yet within hours the boys reappear.

These men and women are not searching, at least yet, for some solution to the problems created by these boys. They are trying to get inside these boys' heads. Various hypotheses emerge. Might the boys be hanging around near the police station because at some unconscious level they recognize that the police will protect them and that their proximity to the police will keep their disruptiveness from careening out of control? Isn't this the normal testing of authority that adolescents do?

Other topics discussed by the group include how children's disappointment with and distrust of their own fathers is transferred to the police and how children's views of authority and of the police as authority figures change at different developmental stages. The group agrees that many nine- and ten-year-old children idealize police officers, but that this idealism crashes and burns into antagonism by the time children reach their teens. This group has also considered how to create sources of self-esteem other than gang involvement for adolescents. Recognizing that the police often unwittingly subject adolescents to public shame by berating and arresting them in front of their friends, the group has struggled with ways to confront teenagers that do not destroy any possibility of their developing positive ties to officers.

Trying to understand the psychology of adolescents is not a typical pastime in a health-care setting, but even more unusual is the profession of most of the members of this group. One is a psychologist, one is an internist, and five are police officers from C11.

———————□———————

Although community policing can be effective in weaving officers into the lives of children and families, officers still lack the skills to be responsive to a wide range of children's and families' troubles. Neither community policing nor academic preparation for police work—typically comprising four months of academy training and two years of supervised on-the-job training—provide officers with rudimentary knowledge about child development or family dynamics or with basic skills for working with families in distress.

Yet some officers are faced with children and families in anguish nearly every day. Police investigating incidents of spousal abuse are frequently confronted with women and children reeling from the violence, yet they often have no training in listening empathically or in obtaining needed services. Many officers do not receive training in listening to and supporting families who are victims of crime, or families suffering the deaths of family members. Officers typically do not receive specific training in adolescents' developmental needs and in working effectively with adolescents, despite their frequent contact with police. Lacking these skills, officers miss numerous opportunities to respond to basic needs and to stem problems before they explode.

Moreover, of all the professionals who work with families, police are among the most likely to experience debilitating stresses and self-doubts. Many police officers suffer from some form of post-traumatic stress disorder—large numbers of police witness gruesome violence on the job and many are war veterans. Officers who deal with children are frequently confronted with the human condition in its most debased forms. An officer in Maryland says that child injuries and abuse "are the number one stressor for law-enforcement

officers...it's overwhelming even for the most macho cop." Like
child protective services workers, police officers must often make
agonizing moral decisions, too, that have profound consequences
for children—such as whether to arrest a battering husband who
has a close tie to his child—and they must endure the consequences
of their errors. Many officers are openly hated by the people they
serve. Officers are especially demoralized by the fear and hatred
of children, including children who see the police as taking a parent
away, as breaking up their families.

Officers' own emotional needs are rarely addressed in their
training or supervision. It is too simple to say that officers, like
soldiers, are uniformly trained to avoid self-reflection—some
supervisors encourage officers to deal openly with their worries
and self-doubts—yet it remains true that many officers inhabit
cultures that support the notion that this kind of reflection, in any
circumstance, is a risk to themselves and to others. And many
officers are dangerously isolated, unable to share their frailties
with colleagues or superiors in cultures that champion imper-
viousness to vulnerability and unwilling to frighten or burden their
families with their troubles. Perhaps because of this toxic mix of
stress and isolation, suicides in some departments are high: between
1985 and 1994, fifty-two police officers committed suicide in New
York City alone.

Recognizing that officers can be vital in identifying children in
trouble—and learning that officers lack both coping capacities and
basic tools to deal with families in crisis—spurred Betsy McAlister
Groves, a warm, perceptive social worker, to design a program at
Boston City Hospital to supply police officers with basic knowledge
about child development, skills in working with families in turmoil,
and strategies for coping with the everyday lacerations and downs
of police work. To create an alliance between police officers and
psychologists and social workers, Groves had to bridge a wide
chasm. Police officers and social workers have a long and ugly
history. (As one officer remarked, "When we used to get together
with social workers it was like Sumo wrestling: we see them as
sixties flower children, and they see us as gorillas.") Some officers
resent being used as "errand boys," rather than as important
resources in solving problems, by psychologists and social workers.
In the view of these officers, social workers and psychologists call
them only to arrest a parent when a family problem is completely
out of hand.

Yet when Groves approached Captain Dunford, he grasped immediately the value of this program. Despite some skepticism, most officers at C11 are keenly aware of their own limitations in dealing with children and families. More than thirty C11 officers have voluntarily taken this ten-week seminar, and their participation has been enthusiastic. Officers Tom Flanagan and Paul Johnston were among the first group. (Groves also initiated the Child Witness to Violence Project at Boston City Hospital, which provides counseling to children who have been exposed to serious violence, and officers at C11 now routinely refer children there.)

Topics of the seminars include children's responses to violence, children's moral development, common family dynamics and effective family interventions, ethnicity and family violence in Vietnamese families, and improving the ability of officers to work with the child protective services system and the criminal justice system.

The session on working with Vietnamese families has proved especially helpful. Officers have been able to diminish problems that they had previously aggravated. For example, they learn the importance in some cases of involving extended family members— a Vietnamese tradition—in containing spousal abuse, as a first intervention before making arrests that publicly shame husbands and often lead to worse abuse. Officers also learn the importance of courtesies, such as always asking permission before entering a home, with Vietnamese families. The session on violence may be helpful in stemming problems early in part by making officers aware of the amount of stress that neighborhood violence creates for parents and of the importance of obtaining help for parents as well as for children in these circumstances.

This program provides officers with crucial information about when and how to talk to a child. They learn that sometimes a child has to be asked to repeat a story many times before a clear and true picture of an event emerges. During the course of the seminar, officers develop guidelines about whether and when to intervene with different kinds of families suffering different kinds of crises, for example, for determining when a parent's hitting a child constitutes abuse.

Just as important, this seminar helps officers deal with on-the-job stress. The expression of vulnerability, once taboo, is given some legitimacy. Officers talk freely about the distress of being feared and hated by children. In the session on moral development, Groves explains that children may demonize officers because all children between four and ten years old divide the world into good and evil—this kind of splitting is an inevitable aspect of development—and over time, if children encounter officers who are responsive, their views of police may become less hostile and more nuanced. According to Groves, this type of insight into child development greatly relieves officers who face this kind of hostility.

The effectiveness of this program, even newer than community policing, is not yet reflected in any dramatic results. But there are early, concrete signs of success. Most striking, some officers say that they are paying attention to children for the first time. "My eyes now see children" is how one officer summed up his gains from this program. Many officers are mindful of problems that never used to enter their consciousness: "A child recently asked me whether he should call the police when people are shooting at his mother," C11 officer Dennis Rorie reports. "Normally, I would investigate the shooting, but I wouldn't realize that both this child and his mother might be having emotional troubles. I spent some time talking to this kid and I got him to talk to the school counselor and I'm planning to get the mother some help." Officers are now far more likely to stay in contact with children who have been traumatized. One police officer has maintained contact for over a year with a three-year-old boy who found the body of his murdered mother. The referral sources have made a large difference, too. "When I came across a kid who's upset I never even knew there was a place I could send them," says Johnston, who now routinely refers children to the Child Witness to Violence Project as well as to other counseling and social service agencies.

The New Haven Experiment

C11 is not the only police station where officers are entering the academic worlds of child development and psychology. The New Haven Police Department and the Yale Child Study Center established the first such collaboration. The New Haven and Boston projects have similar goals, if somewhat different emphases. Whereas the Boston collaboration focuses mainly on domestic violence, the New Haven collaboration gives greater emphasis to community violence. And whereas the Boston collaboration emphasizes how the police can work more effectively with health-care providers and hospital-based programs, the New Haven collaboration emphasizes making connections with a wide variety of community-based organizations.

Moreover, the New Haven collaboration is far more ambitious in many respects. This collaboration not only gives officers psychological tools, but it seeks to change the tone of police interactions with children and the entire atmosphere of police departments in relation to children. According to psychoanalyst Steven Marans, one of the founders of this collaboration, the purpose of these reforms is to raise officers' awareness of how they are perceived by children and to provide them with strategies for working with children that increase the chances of children's viewing the police not as indifferent, but as positive authority figures, as adults worthy of emulation, and as anchors of stability and security. The New Haven program recognizes the powerful psychological meanings that police officers have for children, that police are potent symbols of adult authority and responsibility and even of the moral nature of government and society. (Recall, for example, that in Kotlowitz's *There Are No Children Here*, a key factor in Lafeyette's growing disaffection with the world was the abuse he suffered at the hands of a police officer.)

To accomplish its aims, this collaboration has five main components. First, a seminar created by senior officers and the faculty of the Child Study Center provides rookie police officers with basic information about child development, attunes them to the impact of their own interventions on children and families, and increases their awareness of how they are perceived by children of different ages. Officers become versed in how the phases of child development and children's sense of self are influenced by various family and community experiences. Seminars are built around discussion of actual cases as well as scenarios from films such as *Boyz 'n' the Hood*.

Second, a fellowship program within the Child Study Center supplies sergeants and lieutenants, the primary supervisors of community police officers, with special expertise in child development. Police supervisors spend several hours a week over the course of eight to twelve weeks in the Child Study Center, where they are familiarized, much as residents in psychiatry are, with developmental concepts, patterns of psychological disturbance, methods of clinical intervention, and settings for mental health treatment and care. The program includes observation of evaluations of children with emotional troubles and meetings with the Family Support Service program to discuss families in crisis because of AIDS, cocaine, or family violence. Fellows also visit schools with a consultation team, with an eye to how various emotional difficulties undercut children in school, and they are introduced to the Comer model as an approach to dealing with children's school troubles.

Third, a fellowship for clinicians introduces them to the basic principles of police work. Clinicians ride with police officers and observe investigative activities and drug interdictions. This fellowship not only exposes clinicians to the culture and work of policing, but it also helps build ties between clinicians and officers.

Fourth, police fellows and a team of Child Study Center faculty, including psychologists, social workers, and lawyers, attend weekly seminars. The ongoing discussions allow families to be seen from many angles as interventions are developed. Strong emphasis is placed on understanding the meaning that events have for children and the nexus of feelings that children arouse in police officers and clinicians, ranging from intense sympathy to rage, and how these emotional reactions might inform and enhance rather than undermine interventions. Attention is also given to dealing with parents and children who demonize and displace rage on police officers.

The final component of the collaboration is perhaps both most important and most unusual. The Child Study Center provides a twenty-four hour consultation service to the police—clinicians carry beepers—to enable officers to work more effectively in the heat of a child's or family's crisis. Officers recently consulted this service when a mother of five stabbed her estranged boyfriend in the middle of the night. Clinicians arrived within ten minutes.

Like the Boston collaboration, this marriage of police and psychologists appears to be fruitful. Children whose emotional needs were previously ignored are receiving counseling. A sixteen-year-old gang member was recently referred by the police to a clinician after suffering a full-blown panic attack while being arraigned for the shooting death of a close friend. Despite having spent two years in a correctional facility, this boy had never been evaluated by mental health professionals. Children who are shot, including very small children, are now routinely referred to clinicians. Officers pay attention to healing minds as well as bodies. Rather than following the typical course of action and letting the courts deal with a teenage girl arrested repeatedly for fighting, officers decided to first help her obtain mental health care.

Officers are also mindful that the effects of trauma are often delayed and that children need continuous ties to adults. Some officers are more effective with families because their interventions are informed by a more complex awareness of the problems of children and families. As Marans points out, an officer's typical reflex when a child has been abused is to express anger at a parent and to seek to rescue the child. As a result of this program, however, officers are more apt to recognize the complex and intense ties that a child has to an abusive parent and the danger of alienating a child by lashing out at the parent.

Increased effectiveness has relieved some of the job stress for officers: "There used to be a time when we would walk into a home where there was a battering situation and kids would not even be in the picture," a New Haven officer observes. "It was very depressing, because we knew we would be seeing these kids in a few years. I'd say to myself, 'I'm not a social worker or psychiatrist, I've got nothing in my bag of tricks. I can't do anything here.' But now we can become a bridge for some of these kids. I don't walk away from these homes now with a big pit in my stomach."

Whether the New Haven or the Boston collaborations will ultimately have a great impact on children remains to be seen. These programs have problems and limitations. Although it is clear that these collaborations increase officers' awareness of children's needs and that some officers are able to translate this awareness into useful interventions, it is unclear how regularly officers are able to use their child development knowledge to create effective interventions. It is one thing to understand that some rowdy teenagers are hanging out by the police station in an unconscious effort to keep themselves in check, but it is quite another to form a strategy that both addresses the rambunctious behavior and preserves for these teens some sense of security. Even highly trained child psychologists sometimes strain to make the leap from theory to effective practice. When I asked several officers what they had learned from these programs about concrete strategies for dealing with children and families in crises, a few drew a complete blank.

Another significant drawback of these programs is that they raise serious moral dilemmas for police officers. One officer points out that sometimes it is entirely inappropriate for officers to focus on building children's self-esteem; it is the child with low self-esteem who may be the weak link in a gang, the child who needs to be broken down and exploited for information. Other officers relate that if they do not "come down hard" on certain kids they run the risk of being perceived as weak—and to be perceived as weak not only destroys their effectiveness, but can jeopardize their lives. But Marans notes, the challenge is for officers and clinicians to recognize that they play divergent roles. It may be entirely appropriate for an officer but inappropriate for a clinician to come down hard on a gang member, and under certain circumstances it is important to a child psychologically for an officer to play a strong, authoritative role.

Despite the downsides, the potential benefits of these experimental programs are great—a far better understanding of children and families and a far greater capacity to prevent a wide range of troubles. Such collaborations are also important models, examples of how professionals can traverse the usual bureaucratic barriers. These collaborations demonstrate how a small group of disparate, committed individuals can topple the walls that separate vastly different and even openly antagonistic professions.

The Dorchester and New Haven divisions are not alone in piloting ways to prevent problems in childhood. Among its many interwoven and novel police interventions, Norfolk, Virginia, has established family assessment service teams, comprising representatives of the police, the schools, the department of public health, the parks and recreation department, and other agencies, that provide comprehensive responses to multiproblem families, in addition to needs assessment, problem solving, and advocacy for all families within certain neighborhoods. A high premium is placed on involving residents in fashioning solutions to neighborhood troubles. Many police departments are developing far better skills in investigating child neglect and abuse. In Maryland, the Montgomery County Police Department works with elementary school teachers and students as well as with hospital staff to identify signs of neglect and abuse. Several departments are piloting new ways of collaborating with child protective services agencies and are forming teams that join police officers with child protective services workers and others which greatly improve the officers' responsiveness to families.

The verdict on these efforts is still out, but impressive gains have been made. Crucial corners have been turned in children's perceptions of police officers: "Kids see us almost like human beings," a community police officer told me. In some communities where police were once seen as uncaring or even hostile, police are trusted and respected—not simply as responsible authorities, but as empathic and compassionate human beings. And police are becoming part of and sometimes leading real and substantial collaborations—collaborations with communities and with other city agencies and services—that hold the highest promise for sparing children sorrow. We can piece together strategies that enable children to clear the obstacles before them, but only if we recognize and strengthen the vital work of police officers.

13

Beyond the Edifice Complex: What Cities Can Do

MICHAEL MORAN IS NOW 16 YEARS OLD. SOME awkwardness and agitation are still with him. But the ways in which he has changed are more evident than the ways in which he has stayed the same. He knows when he is rambling—he is, in fact, acutely sensitive to whether he is holding others' attention. He is less prone to lacerate himself for his failings or to tangle himself in contrition for some harmless remark. When he speaks with adults his eyes no longer swim out of focus. He is not a child who moves through life fluidly. There is little of the jaunty confidence of adolescence. But one senses in him a solidity. It is easy to imagine him as an adult as a valued employee, a good, trustworthy friend, a decent and caring human being.

No single event explains Michael's improvement, just as no single event explained the agonies that he endured. Michael was eventually placed in a school for learning disabled students, and he gradually found his footing there. He came to trust a counselor who, Cora emphasizes, clearly understood both his special qualities and his anguish. Michael credits group counseling, where he was given help in reading social cues, for boosting his confidence with other children. With the support of the counselor and the group and with a teacher who paid close attention to his learning difficulties, Michael's school performance improved. He even became something of a star. He has won several awards for student achievement and considers himself among the most popular children in his class—an unusual and highly credible claim for this deeply modest child. Because of these gains, Michael is now taking classes for half the day at a public high school, and he plans to enroll full-time next year.

The point, however, is not that Michael is a success story or a tribute to the effectiveness of our system of care for children. His gains are fragile, and he has a whole life in front of him, a life that is likely to defy easy categorization. This is not a story about an ugly duckling turning into a swan. Like many of us—perhaps most of us—Michael is likely to thrive in certain areas of adult life and struggle in others, and he is likely to find some stretches of adulthood gratifying and others painful and difficult.

Moreover, no matter how much Michael prospers as an adult, it is hard to think of the system as successful when Michael spent hardly a day of his childhood feeling easy with himself or anything like at home in the world, when he experienced so little innocence, so few moments of self-forgetfulness, of pure abandonment. Too often childhood is seen as simply a prelude to adulthood—children, as the popular rhetoric now has it, are "an investment"—as if well-being in the first eighteen years of life is trivial in its own right.

If our efforts to help children are to be successful, they need both to prepare children for adulthood and to spare them agonies in childhood. Health-care agencies, schools, child protective agencies, and police forces that work to meet children's basic needs are part of the answer. But a single effective school or health-care agency will not spare a child such as Michael serious troubles. Children need continuous support throughout childhood and support that changes as their developmental needs and capacities change and interact with a changing environment. To prevent the serious troubles of Michael and other children, we need a wholly different way of thinking about children and a fundamental shift in policy and practice. We need a caregiving system that provides continuous attention to children. We need communities that launch all children well and that nurture their development throughout childhood, that seek to ensure that every child at every stage of development receives the basic ingredients of sturdy growth.

Providing this kind of scaffolding involves every level of government and nearly every sector of society, but most important, it requires the serious attention of local government officials. Good local officials understand the needs of families in their communities and know the lay of the land for families—the activities and services on which children and parents depend, the vital informal networks, the visible and invisible neighborhood boundaries. Good city and county officials recognize the levers that shape parents' and children's social connections, and they understand the various funding streams and programs that can respond to children and families' needs. Local government officials, because they understand local needs and can shape a wide range of services, are uniquely positioned to promote children's development.

Yet if local governments are to provide such a scaffolding, they need to fundamentally redefine the nature of their responsibilities for families. They need to pay attention to areas of family life that they have traditionally ignored and to adapt to the dramatic changes that have occurred in families in the past thirty years. Local officials need to take up the following goals. They need to work actively to reduce stress for all parents, and in so doing they must adapt services and activities to the needs of single parents. They need to engage fathers and other men in children's lives. They need to help parents maintain positive ties to other neighborhood parents, and they need to facilitate parents' access to various social networks or communities. They need to supply information about effective parenting. They need to furnish ongoing opportunities for children and parents to talk about difficulties in their lives, and they need to create systems that respond to these difficulties swiftly. Local leaders need to bring children into contact with an array of caring adults and help children form diverse friendships. They need to ensure that children with persistent troubles receive continuous care over time. Officials need to provide children with a variety of opportunities for achievement and to ensure that they reach certain cognitive, academic, and developmental milestones. Further, city leaders need to work aggressively to bridge the racial, ethnic, and class divisions that are so poisonous to community and family life. Obvious as these goals may appear, only a few municipalities in the United States come anywhere near attaining them.

Yet the means to achieve these goals are clearly available. Their attainment does not require creating vast and costly new programs; it does require creating or expanding relatively inexpensive programs that strengthen parents, in particular, family support programs. It requires educating city officials about basic principles of child development and focusing on the critical junctures in childhood where concerted interventions can make a huge difference.

It means utilizing strategies to increase the capacity of professionals to work with children over sustained periods. It means encouraging a wide array of public and private administrators to pay attention to their institutions' influence on children's environments and enabling a wide array of citizens to play more active and positive roles in children's lives. And it means creating a culture of responsibility for children that supports all these activities, a culture that inspires all citizens to recognize their responsibility for children's well-being.

Family Support Centers

Recognizing that the best way to meet the basic needs of young children is to strengthen their parents and recognizing the importance of early intervention in children's lives, numerous cities are now developing family centers to provide parents with support and skills. These centers are not simply another community service center. They are guided by a philosophy about how to engage and strengthen families that radically departs from traditional services. Family centers are deliberately different from typical bureaucracies, with their tendency to slice up families into discrete problems. The goal of these centers is to understand and meet the needs of whole children and to understand both parents' developmental needs and the interrelated needs of children and parents. These centers seek to meaningfully integrate services for families. They often become the hub of neighborhood services. Unlike traditional bureaucracies, family centers also pride themselves on their elasticity, on their ability to stretch themselves to meet the needs of families. Further, they explicitly seek to avoid the degrading and stigmatizing tendencies of traditional bureaucracies. Family center staff, instead of assuming that they hold the answers to families' troubles, work collaboratively with families in defining and responding to problems.

Parents do not drop their children off at these centers; they come with their children. The centers provide activities for children as well as activities and services for parents, such as parent support classes, adult literacy classes, and job information classes. Parents commonly obtain information about home and community safety and child development. At some centers, caseworkers are intensively involved with hard-pressed families, helping them obtain needed services and deal with root problems. Much attention is given to spotting the problems of children early in their lives. Some centers employ home visitors, who check in with mothers during pregnancy or soon after the birth of a child.

Perhaps most crucial, family centers are fashioned to provide the kinds of ongoing support that prevent problems altogether. These centers create vehicles through which parents can strengthen one another. At such a center, Cora Moran could have received information about parenting during Michael's early years, and she could have talked about her anxieties with parents with kindred concerns, rather than relying solely on books or feeling as though she was constantly badgering her pediatrician. She could have received both informal and formal counseling to deal with her marital troubles. Some centers now work specifically with fathers, too, helping them overcome the various inner and outer obstacles that drive them away from their children.

Further, these centers do not simply re-create traditional communities, with all their divisive and scapegoating tendencies. Guided by a moral vision, they seek to bridge cultural, racial, and economic divides and to actively challenge prejudices.

Although promising, these programs are scattered across the country. Families in every neighborhood—and especially parents of children in the early years of life—are marooned. Parents in every neighborhood need basic parenting information and help in times of crisis. These needs are often most pressing for single mothers and mothers in the workforce. Every state and city government needs to assume responsiblity for giving parents this kind of help. And family centers may be cost-effective, given their potential to prevent many of the serious childhood problems that require costly crisis intervention and long-term care.

Cities reluctant to create whole new centers can facilitate many of the functions of these programs in other ways. Numerous schools, churches, health-care agencies, public libraries, and other community institutions promote parents' development by providing activities that bring parents together informally as well as adult literacy, parent education, and other classes. Cities can support and expand these efforts.

Focusing on Crucial Junctures

There is now substantial evidence that there are crucial junctures in childhood. At these points children are vulnerable to problems and setbacks that are difficult to overcome, and interventions at these points can make a huge difference in promoting children's cognitive and social development. Birth and entry into kindergarten are two such crucial junctures. Problems that are untreated during pregnancy and in the first months of a child's life can be highly destructive in the long term. Similarly, long-term education prospects are significantly better for children who are prepared for kindergarten than for children who suffer delays as their school career commences. Family support programs are one important strategy for ensuring that children are not markedly impaired at birth or delayed at kindergarten entry. The capacity to read at grade level at third grade is another crucial juncture. At third grade children's educational pathways commonly diverge, with good readers progressing and delayed readers falling farther and farther behind. Recall that the Success-for-All model elementary schools are based on the importance of all children reading at grade level by third grade. For older children, entry into high school and the transition from high school to work are critical junctures. At these times many children have difficulty taking the next step and fall behind in ways that make it very difficult for them to catch up with their peers.

Cities should focus their energies on and coordinate public and private agencies around meeting the needs of children at these key junctures. Many collaborations of city agencies, businesses, foundations, and universities have little long-term, positive impact because they respond to the latest problem flagged by the media. Focusing on specific junctures can help the major services and institutions that care for children work toward common and critical prevention objectives. In reaching these objectives, it is vital to create specific numerical goals that are simple and vivid, such as increasing the number of children who can read at grade level by third grade. Clear benchmarks of success can counteract pervasive despair about solving children's problems and serve as rallying points for a community. Specific goals at these junctures are also an important management tool, enabling cities to meaningfully track children's progress and to redirect services and activities if targets are not met.

Several cities have formed collaborations to help children at these crucial junctures. Recall that in Hartford, Connecticut, business leaders, hospitals, public agencies, and service providers successfully banded together to prevent problems at the crucial juncture of a child's birth by developing a teen pregnancy program, reaching deeply into communities to locate pregnant women who were not receiving health services, and providing specialized prenatal care for women at risk for premature births. This project reached a specific goal: it markedly reduced the number of low-birth-weight babies. Several small cities have successfully united various community agencies and institutions in heading off some of the troubles that undermine children as they enter kindergarten.

Public and private leaders in Boston are launching a major, citywide effort designed to get every child to read at grade level by the third grade by the year 2005. Among many concerted strategies, businesses and universities would be expected to supply tutors and books to schools and continuing education classes and literacy classes for parents. The *Boston Globe*, one of the city's two major newspapers, intends to regularly monitor and publish the progress of schools in meeting this objective, publish information on literacy for parents, elicit volunteers from businesses and other community institutions to tutor children, and run a series of articles on successful literacy programs around the country. In addition, the paper may publish a paragraph that every child should be able to read by the third grade, along with instructions as to what parents should do if their children cannot read the paragraph. Little Rock, Arkansas, and Savannah, Georgia, are among several cities in which businesses, foundations, schools, and city agencies have been working together to help children make the transition from school to work, focusing primarily on driving down school dropout rates.

Most of these projects are too new to evaluate systematically, and they will each surely require many midcourse corrections and refinements along the way. Yet these projects are worth pursuing, given their potential to spare large numbers of children great misery at relatively little cost.

Continuous Care for Children

Developing family support programs for young children and focusing on crucial junctures only makes sense if cities simultaneously work to ensure that the gains that children make are not lost. Cities can take several steps to greatly increase the continuity of care for children.

One step is to hook programs together so that children have contact with some professionals over long periods of time and are handed off smoothly from one program to another. Michael's life might have taken a different course if a family coordinator working from a school-based family center had conducted a home visit with his family soon after his birth and had continued working with his family throughout Michael's elementary school years. Cities might encourage and enable programs to work with children for longer periods of time and to adapt to the needs of children as children grow, rather than limiting their work to children within a certain narrow age range. Many early childhood programs for children with special needs, for example, should continue to work with children and parents through the early grades of elementary school, rather than cutting off services for children at this difficult transition. Mentoring programs should connect adults to children in early rather than late adolescence and should ensure that adults are able to make long-term commitments to children. Such programs for teenagers might also expand at least a few years into adulthood to help children through this perilous transition.

Continuity also means following up with children after they leave programs and checking in with children periodically so that problems that have delayed effects, such as divorce or exposure to violence, are detected by professionals. Teachers, health-care providers, police officers, and others who interact with children need to be attuned to the signs of post-traumatic stress disorder and other forms of delayed distress. In addition, cities might formalize one or two check-in points with all city children, for example, at nine years old and at fifteen years old, when a teacher or other involved adult would conduct a simple assessment designed to uncover emotional or social difficulties. At such a check-in point, parents could be interviewed about any concerns they have beyond the narrow academic concerns that typically emerge in a parent-teacher conference. Parents and children would also be given the opportunity to specifically identify types of assistance they need. Key to this type of assessment would be the capacity of professionals to respond swiftly and effectively to any troubles that surface.

To ensure continuous care for large numbers of children cities must tackle the many circumstances that force children out of valuable relationships with professionals prematurely, including repeated residential moves and high turnover among professionals working with children. Cities not only can help families stay in one place through housing, zoning, and employment policies; they can help professionals stay in one place by providing city employees with decent compensation, resources, training, and supervision. Cities also need to advocate for decent compensation and training for private professionals and to routinely recognize and celebrate the work of caregiving professionals.

Reorganizing services so that they focus on critical junctures and are more continuous requires changes in the structure of local government and compatible changes in state and federal governments. At the city level new structures are needed so that different agencies can work together routinely and more closely than ever before. Cities, in turn, need the right kind of support and encouragement from federal and state governments. The federal government should provide states and cities with more discretionary funds so that they can develop more fine-grained policies and reorganize services to meet the needs of their particular vulnerable families. Flexible funding does not mean large-scale federal block grants—now a popular idea—that simply pass the buck to states for meeting the needs of vulnerable children. The federal government needs to give states and cities assistance in utilizing these funds effectively. More important, these funds need to be tied to high program standards and to measurable outcomes for children. Because so little is known about the capacity of states and cities to manage such a change effectively, this flexibility needs to be increased at a careful pace.

Family-Friendly Cities

When Charles Royer became mayor of Seattle in 1986, large numbers of families were leaving. According to Royer, "The city was bleeding kids." To stem this exodus, Royer knew that he had to overcome the "edifice complex," the tendency of city planners to think only in terms of buildings and services. He needed to create a city that paid serious attention to children's basic needs and that fostered a climate that supported all children. He didn't tinker on the margins. He redrew the responsibilities of city government, requiring every city agency, from the health department to the water department, to include an item in its budget that benefited children. During his tenure the first policy plan for children and youth was created as well as a children and youth commission.

He embarked on a major marketing campaign; he declared Seattle "Kids Place," and he enlisted various sectors of the city in supporting children. Numerous commercial businesses post Kids Place logos in their windows, a signal of their willingness to give various kinds of help to children, such as use of a phone or bathroom, or directions. He initiated the development of Seattle's first family support centers. These various activities had at least one desired effect: they have slowed and perhaps stemmed entirely the tide of families leaving the city.

Prevention is more than providing good health, social, and education services for families. It is creating environments that ease the task of parenting and that provide stimulation and support to children at every stage of development.

Seattle appears to be far ahead of other cities in creating such environments. When Norman Rice replaced Royer in 1990, he picked up where Royer left off. Rice has actively promoted multicultural environments, educated citizens on the changing needs of families, and adapted the city to these changing needs. He has focused on meeting the needs of employed parents by encouraging family-friendly workplaces and by creating the city's Comprehensive Child Development Program. This program subsidizes child care for low-income working families, advocates for high-quality child care, and helps parents complete training programs and find jobs. Recognizing the burdens that elders can place on families, Rice has advocated for decent elder care. Building and land-use codes encourage housing development with families in mind, and Seattle now has a consolidated planning department that takes as its specific purpose promoting community. This department's citizens' guide says that "investment in the city's 'social infrastructure' for neighborhood planning is as important as its investment in physical infrastructure." Along with this attention to the environment, Seattle has concentrated on providing good services. In addition to developing family centers in several neighborhoods, the city has initiated the Family Support Worker program: forty-eight workers assist children in elementary schools with food, clothing, housing, after-school care, and access to health and social services. Rice also gained voter approval for a "Families and Education Levy" which provides $8.5 million a year in new dollars specifically for services to support and assist children and families so kids can succeed in school. Services include teen health centers and before- and after-school care and activities.

Other cities are seeking to provide a climate in which children will prosper. San Francisco, San Diego, Austin, Minneapolis, and St. Louis have identified children as a policy priority and have taken up activities that explicitly value and support children. In San Francisco, an approved ballot initiative guarantees children's programs a fixed percentage of the city's budget—more than $10 million a year above current funding levels. A few cities now have several local city halls that are designed to be more responsive to the particular needs of diverse communities. Planning, zoning, and building inspection departments in some cities now pay serious attention to their impacts on the availability and quality of child care. Several cities are working hard to create not only ample and safe parks and playgrounds, but decent indoor play spaces as well.

These efforts are impressive, yet there are other pieces vital to any comprehensive strategy to create environments that nurture children's development. Although some cities provide an array of athletic, academic, and artistic opportunities after school and in the summer, most cities need to greatly expand these opportunities, especially evening opportunities for teenagers. Few cities give children adequate opportunities for community service, to give to others. Yet children need to feel that they are not simply a burden or a threat to adults—they need to experience themselves as useful to a neighborhood, even as essential to the health of neighborhood life. The ATLAS project, a school-reform effort based in part on the Comer model, sees this role for children as critical to school reform. It plans to deputize children to recruit parents and other community adults who can participate in school projects and activities.

Nor do cities commonly create multiple opportunities for parents to make connections to other parents, especially to parents who are not their immediate neighbors. They can create these opportunities, though, in the concrete physical planning of neighborhoods, as well as by encouraging child-care agencies, schools, health-care agencies, churches, and other community organizations to create settings that enable parents to form these ties.

In forming healthy environments for children, cities need to pay attention to another basic need: the need of many children for a lasting, close tie to an adult other than a parent. Demographic trends may help cities forge these ties. Because the birthrate has declined, there are fewer children in most neighborhoods. (The "boomlet," the large numbers of children born recently to baby boomers, will only temporarily offset this trend.) Meanwhile, neighborhoods have more adults. The number of households comprising nonparent families and empty nesters has steadily increased in the last few decades, and this trend is expected to continue.

Despite the potential serious downsides for children—for example, the danger that services for children, such as public education, will increasingly lose in city budget battles to services that are primarily for the elderly, such as health care—communities can use these demographic trends to their advantage. Cities can help create the mentor-rich environment that Marc Freedman envisions. Fewer children and more adults mean more adults per child. Rather than laying off teachers, schools could reduce classroom size. More children might be brought into contact with a wider variety of neighborhood adults.

Key to linking neighborhood adults with children is overcoming certain basic obstacles. Many adults devote little time to children, not because they are narcissistic or disinterested, as is commonly imagined, but because of job stress and time constraints. Many adults also simply do not know how to involve themselves with children; they often have no way to utilize their particular talents to meaningfully contribute to children's lives. The idea that adults are simply disinterested in children is betrayed by visiting any fire station in this country. Firefighters clearly enjoy describing to young children the nature of their equipment, entrancing children with fire-fighting stories, and supervising young children as they play on the fire trucks. Fire fighters differ from most other professionals in that they have job security, time, and a way of contributing their particular skills and knowledge.

If larger numbers of adults are to be involved with children, both public and private institutions must make time for adults to volunteer, and cities must create varied and visible opportunities that tap adults' different skills in working with children. Citizen Schools, an exciting, pioneering after-school program in Boston, is attempting to create precisely these opportunities through an apprenticeship program in which diverse professionals—including carpenters, journalists, graphic designers, and writers—teach children their particular trades.

Underlying all these efforts to create healthy environments for children should be the principle that cities' doing for families and communities is less important than cities' working *with* families and communities and building on families' and communities' natural strengths and resources. Minimally, this means that cities need to give community leaders and parents a strong voice in developing and implementing programs and to find ways to tap the strengths of natural helpers—such as adults on the block whom children respect and look to for advice, adults who watch children play outside and care enough to tell them what they should and should not do, or senior citizens who are apt to be especially concerned about neighborhood safety.

Creating a Culture of Community Responsibility for Children

To propel cities to take on these activities, to encourage citizens who are not parents to take on expanded responsibilities for children, to generate more extensive informal networks and activities that support kids, to encourage parents to care about children who are not their own, we need communities whose norms and cultures support the notion that adults are responsible for children—and for all children.

Many circumstances are combining to force Americans to pay attention to children and to see that the fates of troubled children and their own lives are entwined. If the prospect of millions of children skidding out of school, abusing drugs, and landing in jail has not evoked Americans' compassion, it has provoked their self-concerns and fears. Business leaders fret about fielding a competitive workforce when huge numbers of young people lack basic skills. Social and political observers warn of the costs to democracy of legions of uneducated and illiterate adults. Many Americans now recognize the importance of early childhood—not only Bill Clinton, but also Ross Perot in the 1992 presidential debates raised the importance of strong support for children in the first years of their lives.

Community leadership and media attention can capitalize on these concerns. Some cities have created children's councils that take as a central purpose raising awareness of children's issues and developing meaningful responses. Many cities and states report publicly indicators of children's well-being, including infant mortality, school dropout, and teenage pregnancy rates. These indicators not only raise awareness, but help cities discern problem areas and prioritize their efforts to help children. Public forums on children's issues and public celebrations of professionals who work with children can be used to mobilize communities and generate specific ideas for public and private strategies to help children.

Perhaps more important, the public will be responsive to what works. To earn the kind of public confidence and sense of responsibility that sustains efforts to help children, city programs must be accountable to the public: they need to provide quality services, they need to provide these services at reasonable costs, and they need to actively demonstrate that they are providing effective—and cost-effective—services. This demonstration requires monitoring both community-wide indicators of children's well-being—such as infant mortality rates and the number of children who can read at grade level by third grade—and the effectiveness of individual programs. Programs should develop outcome measures for assessing many different aspects of their performance as well as relatively simple outcome measures for which the community can hold them accountable. Because outcome measures can create perverse incentives—teachers keenly aware that their school will be evaluated by the achievement test scores of its students, for example, may simply teach to the test—these measures must be selected with great care. And if outcome measures are to be meaningful, they need to reflect widely shared values. Not only adminstrators but professionals, community leaders, parents, and sometimes children themselves should be intimately involved in developing outcome measures.

It is tempting, in conclusion, to point to a grand strategy or single solution. Yet what improving the prospects of children requires is many different strategies that are fashioned to meet the needs of many different types of children at different stages of development and that continually demonstrate their effectiveness, building public confidence. I have tried to make the case that these strategies are more likely to be effective if they strengthen parents, if they create meaningful opportunities for children, if they build on families' strengths and recognize the many pathways to healthy development, if they respond to the needs of all vulnerable children—creating constituencies across race and class lines—if they increase the capacity of professionals to identify root problems and to respond to the complex, interacting factors that shape children's fates, and if they enable professionals to sustain attention on children's difficulties over time. Children cannot afford to wait as adults wage great ideological battles about their state. They need adults who do something obvious in conception but rare in reality: who actually listen to them and see them clearly and who understand how their lives are affected by their families, schools, and communities. It is out of such clear visions that we can make childhood gratifying and help children develop the strengths and trust they'll need as adults for productive work, enthusiastic friendship, and lasting love.

NOTES

PART I

p. 1, Tillie Olsen quote. Tillie Olsen, "I Stand Here Ironing," *Tell Me a Riddle*, (New York: Delta), 1961, p. 12.

Chapter 1

p. 10, percent of children in poverty in 1993. "Current Population Survey, 1993," U.S. Bureau of the Census, Washington, D.C., March 1994, press release tables and other unpublished data.

p. 10, statistics on length of time children spend in poverty. Naomi Goldstein, "Why Poverty Is Bad for Children," Ph.D. dissertation, John F. Kennedy School of Government, Harvard University, 1991, p. 81.

p. 11, effects of sudden "downward mobility" on parents. Katherine Newman, *Falling from Grace: The Experience of Downward Mobility in the American Middle Class* (New York: The Free Press), 1988.

p. 11, percent of poor children with working parents. M. J. Bane et al., "Childhood Poverty and Disadvantage," unpublished paper, John F. Kennedy School of Government, 1991, p. 7.

p. 11, health care statistics for children of poor working parents. Nicholas Zill et al., "The Life Circumstances and Development of Children in Welfare Families: A Profile Based on National Survey Data," working paper, Child Trends, Inc., October 1991.

p. 11, Katherine. Sylvia Ann Hewlett, *When the Bough Breaks: The Cost of Neglecting Our Children* (New York: HarperCollins Publishers), 1991, p. 48.

p. 12, for a description of poor children in the hollows of eastern Kentucky, see Robert Coles, *Children of Crisis*, vol. 2, *Migrants, Sharecroppers, and Mountaineers* (Boston: Little, Brown & Co.), 1967.

p. 12, 17.5 percent of poor kids reside in ghettos. See 1995 tabulations by Paul A. Jargowsky, University of Texas, Dallas. Tabulations based on U.S. Census Summary Tape File 3A (CD-ROM Version). Poor children are distributed evenly. Based on 1989 data, about 30 percent of poor children live in nonghetto urban areas, about 30 percent live in suburbs, and about 30 percent live in nonmetropolitan areas. M. J. Bane and D. Ellwood, "One Fifth of the Nation's Children: Why Are They Poor?" *Science*, vol. 245, September 8, 1989, p. 1048.

p. 12, percent of African-American children living in ghettos. 1995 tabulations by Paul A. Jargowsky, University of Texas, Dallas. Tabulations based on U.S. Census Summary Tape File 3A (CD-ROM Version).

p. 13, children missing school to take care of family members or close friends. *New Futures Surveys: Dayton, Little Rock, Pittsburgh, and Savannah, 1990–1993*, Institute for Survey Research, Temple University, Philadelphia. (Note: Statistics are averages computed from a series of 16 reports, one for each city for each year.)

p. 14, statistics on high school dropouts with family responsibilities. National Center for Education Statistics, *Dropout Rates in the United States: 1992*, p. 36, table 20. Cited in Arloc Sherman, *Wasting America's Future*, The Children's Defense Fund Report on the Costs of Child Poverty, Boston, Beacon Press, 1994, p. 28.

p. 14, health problems of poor children. Sherman, *Wasting America's Future*, p. 70, 74–75. See also Steven Parker, Steven Greer, and Barry Zuckerman, "Double Jeopardy: The Impact of Poverty on Early Child Development," *Pediatric Clinics of North America*, vol. 35, no. 6, December 1988, p. 1227–1237.

p. 14, hearing and vision difficulties connected to delinquency. Lisbeth Schorr, *Within Our Reach* (New York: Doubleday), 1988, p. 87.

p. 14, poor families less likely to have working smoke detectors. Andrea L. Piani and Charlotte A. Schoenborn, "Health Promotion and Disease Prevention: United States, 1990," *Vital and Health Statistics*, series 10, no. 185, National Center for Health Statistics, 1993. Cited in Sherman, *Wasting America's Future*, p. 45.

p.14, poor families keeping milk cold in Newark. Speech by Reverend Monsignor William J. Linder, Founder, New Community Corporation of Newark, NJ, Villanova University, March 5, 1992.

p. 15, small problems that interfere with learning. For a description of these problems see Sherman, *Wasting America's Future*, p. 26-28.

p. 16, description of poor children. The description quoted appears on the inside jacket cover of Robert Coles and Maria Piers, *Wages of Neglect: New Solutions for the Children of the Poor* (Chicago: Quadrangle Books), 1969.

p. 16, physicians more likely to diagnose abuse when told children are from poor families. Turbett and O'Toole study cited in Vonnie C. McLoyd, "The Impact of Economic Hardship on Black Families and Children: Psychological Distress, Parenting, and Socioemotional Development," *Child Development*, vol. 61, 1990, p. 325.

pp. 16–17, teachers' stereotypes of poor children and parents. Valerie Polakow, *Lives on the Edge: Single Mothers and Their Children in the Other America* (Chicago: University of Chicago Press), 1993, pp. 131–147.

p. 17, over 90 percent of poor children ages 3–5 have never experienced a serious delay or learning disability. This percentage is derived from data reported by N. Zill and C. Schoenborn, for "Advanced Data," *Vital and Health Statistics*, National Center for Health Statistics, no. 190, November 16, 1990, pp. 12–13, tables 1 and 2. Assertion that a majority of children 3–5 who suffer delays and learning disabilities are not poor is derived from the same table.

p. 17, over 75 percent of poor children ages 6–11 have never experienced significant developmental delays, emotional troubles, or a learning disability in childhood. This percentage is derived from data reported in Zill and Schoenborn, ibid., table 4.

p. 17, 14 percent of teenagers reported using drugs in previous year. 86 percent of 12–17 year olds in families with incomes below $20,000 reported no illicit drug use in the previous year. Data computed from 1993 National Household Survey on Drug Abuse, U.S. Department of Health and Human Services, Public Health Service, DHHS publication no. (SMA) 95-3020.

p. 18, data on teen pregnancy. M. J. Bane et. al., "Childhood Poverty and Disadvantage," 1991, p. 21. Goldstein, ibid., p.109. I define briefly poor as 1–2 years.

p. 18, decline in rate of teen pregnancies. Christopher Jencks, *Rethinking Social Policy: Race, Poverty, and the American Underclass* (Cambridge, MA: Harvard University Press), 1992, p. 191.

p. 18, study shows that 6 percent of children in Illinois born in 1988 to parents who are on welfare at some point in the first five years of their children's lives are neglected or abused. "Longitudinal Analysis of Public Aid and Child Welfare Experience of Illinois Families with Children," working paper, Chapin Hall Center for Children, November 1993.

p. 18, 10–18 percent of poor children neglected or abused by their parents at some point in childhood. According to the Illinois study (previous note), approximately 6 percent of poor parents neglect or abuse their children during their first five years. If this were the only "cohort" of parents to abuse their children, then 6 percent of poor children would be neglected or abused by their parents during some point in childhood. If, on the opposite end of the spectrum, the same 6 percent of parents continued their abuse and a new "cohort" of parents began to abuse their children each five years, then the high estimate would be that 21 percent (6×3.5) of children would be neglected or abused by their parents at some point during childhood. The 10–18 percent figure assumes that the real number falls somewhere between these two extremes.

p. 18, socioeconomic status a very weak indicator of sexual abuse. *The Future of Children*, Packard Foundation, Summer/Fall 1994, p. 48.

p. 18, for information on Home Inventory, see R. Bradley and B. Caldwell, "174 Children: A Study of the Relationship between Home Environment and Cognitive Development during the First Five Years," in *Home Environment and Early Cognitive Development: Longitudinal Research* (Orlando, FL: Academic Press), 1984.

p. 19, about 11 percent of three- to-five-year-olds live in "deficient" home environments and about 25 percent of poor children live in deficient home environments. Data tabulated from Nicholas Zill and Kristen Moore, "Progress Report and Summary of Findings: Adult Welfare Recipients as Potential Employees and the Quality of the Home Environments Experienced by Welfare Children," Child Trends, Inc., 1990.

p. 19, poor parents buy foods that are more nutritional. Studies cited by Sherman, *Wasting America's Future*, p. 13.

p. 19, ethnographic research shows that a majority of ghetto families provide healthy home environments. See, for example, E. Anderson, *Atlantic Monthly*, "Code of the Streets," May 1994.

p. 19, black children are three times as likely as white children to be poor. Calculations based on 1993 Current Population Survey press release tables, Octobeer 1994, and other unpublished data publicized by the U.S. Bureau of the Census.

p. 19, black children nearly six times as likely as nonblack children to be poor at least 11 years of their childhood. Personal communication with Jean Yeung and Greg Duncan, May 1995.

p. 19, black child's chances of spending at least some part of their childhood in a single-parent home. In 1991, almost 70 percent of black births were to unmarried mothers. "Statistical Abstract of the U.S.: 1994," U.S. Bureau of the Census, Washington, D.C., 1994, table 100, p. 80. Approximately 55 percent of the remaining 30 percent are likely to suffer their parents' divorce during their childhood. Thus, approximately 85 percent [70 percent + .55 (30 percent)] will spend at least part of their childhood in a single-parent home.

p. 20, white poverty seen as "atypical." Andrew Hacker, *Two Nations* (New York: Ballantine Books), 1992, p. 100.

p. 20, stereotypes of white poverty. Randall Kenan, "Sorrow's Child," *The Nation*, December 28, 1992, p. 815.

p. 20, percents and numbers of children in poverty, by race. Poverty data for related children under 18, from the 1993 Current Population Survey press release tables, October 1994, and other unpublished data publicized from the U.S. Bureau of the Census.

p. 20, U.S. child poverty rate, excluding blacks. Calculations based upon 1993 Current Population Survey press release tables, October 1994, and other unpublished data publicized from the U.S. Bureau of the Census. Data on European poverty rates, L. Rainwater and T. Smeeding, "Doing Poorly: The Real Income of American Children in a Comparative Perspective," Luxembourg Income Study, Working Paper no. 127, Walferdange, Luxembourg, August 1995. Although the authors use a definition of "poverty" that differs from the U.S. definition, they arrive at a comparable U.S. child poverty rate.

p. 20, Hispanics are the fastest growing poverty population. "Poverty in the United States: 1992," U.S. Bureau of the Census, Current Population Reports, Consumer Income, Series P-60-185, table B, p. xi.

p. 20, white children's chances of spending at least part of their childhood in a single-parent family. In 1991, 22 percent of white births were to unmarried mothers. "Statistical Abstract of the U.S.: 1994," U.S. Bureau of the Census, Washington, D.C., 1994, table 100, p. 80. Of the remaining 78 percent of white births, approximately 40 percent will suffer their parents' divorce during their childhood, and a negligible number will suffer the death of a parent. This means that roughly 50 percent of white children [22 percent + .4 (78 percent)] are likely to spend at least part of their childhood in a single-parent home.

p. 20, Charles Murray, "The Coming White Underclass," *Wall Street Journal*, October 29, 1993.

p. 21, poor African-American children are no more likely to drop out than poor white children. Marily M. McMillen et al., *Dropout Rates in the United States: 1993*, U.S. Department of Education, Office of Educational Research and Improvement, 1994. Data indicate statistically insignificant differences in poor black/poor white dropout rates.

p. 21, white teens account for about 67 percent of today's teen dropouts. *The Challenge of Change: What the 1990 Census Tells Us about Children*, Center for the Study of Social Policy, Washington, D.C., September, 1992, p. 64.

p. 21, dropout rates for blacks fell from 28 percent in 1970 to 15 percent in 1988. Jencks, *Rethinking Social Policy*, p. 173. Dropout rates declined even in ghettos. Ibid., p. 177.

p. 21, Jencks quote. Ibid., p. 173.

p. 21, poor blacks more likely to attend college than poor whites. C. Manski and D. Wise, *College Choice in America* (Cambridge, MA: Harvard University Press), 1983, p. 9.

p. 21, basic reading levels for blacks have increased. Jencks, *Rethinking Social Policy*, p. 177.

p. 21, gap between black and white teen pregnancies narrowing. Ibid, p. 191.

p. 21, controlling for social class, no difference between blacks and whites in divorce rates, proportion of births to unmarried mothers, proportions of children living in female-headed families, etc. David A. Hamburg, *Today's Children: Creating a Future for a Generation in Crisis* (New York: Times Books), 1992, p. 40.

p. 21, parents' race and likelihood of physical abuse, controlling for economic class. McLoyd, "Impact of Economic Hardship" p. 326. Parents' race and likelihood of sexual abuse, *The Future of Children: Sexual Abuse of Children,* Packard Foundation, p. 48.

p. 21, poor white children more likely than nonpoor children to commit violent crimes. American Psychological Association, *Violence and Youth: Psychology's Response*, 1993. Reported in Sherman, *Wasting America's Future*, p. 38.

p. 22, Atlanta study. A Centers for Disease Control study found that the domestic homicide rate of poor whites who live in overcrowded urban conditions was the same as the domestic homicide rate of overcrowded poor blacks and was higher than the rate of less crowded, more economically advantaged blacks. "NMA Seeks Prescription to End Violence," *Journal of the American Medical Association*, vol. 270, no. 11, September 15, 1993, p. 1283. Original study by Brandon Centerwall, "Race, Socioeconomic Status, and Domestic Homicide: Atlanta, 1971–1972," *American Journal of Public Health*, 74, 1984, pp. 813–815.

p. 22, homicide rate for young white males is twice as high in the United States than in any other industrialized nation. Deborah Prothrow-Stith with Michaele Weissman, *Deadly Consequences: How Violence Is Destroying Our Teenage Population and a Plan to Begin Solving the Problem* (New York: HarperCollins Publishers), 1991, p. 14.

p. 23, about 65 percent of children who drop out are not poor at the time of dropping out. "Dropout Rates in the United States, 1993," U.S. Department of Education, OERI, National Center for Education Statistics, NCES 94-669, p. 6, table 2. 55 percent of children who drop out of school have never been poor. Bane et al., "Childhood Poverty" p. 21.

p. 23, Robert F. Kennedy quote. Mickey Kaus, *New Republic*, June 29, 1992, p. 14.

p. 24, talking or singing with young children important to children's brain development. *Starting Points: Meeting the Needs of Our Youngest Children*, The Carnegie Corporation of New York, 1994. Cited by Albert Shanker, "Where We Stand," *New York Times*, November 27, 1994.

p. 24, description of decent environments for children's development. Drawn in part from Jerome Kagan, *The Nature of the Child* (New York: Basic Books), 1984, and Mussen et al., *Child Development and Personality* (New York: Harper & Row), 1989.

p. 24, "good enough" parenting. D.W. Winnicott, *Playing and Reality* (New York: Routledge), 1989.

p. 24, more than half of children who grow up in a deficient home environment are not poor. Data tabulated from Zill and Moore, "Progress Report and Summary of Findings," 1990.

pp. 24–25, chances of a preschool child living in a home with unsafe play areas are far greater for poor children, but the majority who live in such homes are not poor. Data tabulated from Zill et al., "The Life Circumstances and Development of Children in Welfare Families," 1991, table 10. Cited in Sherman, *Wasting America's Future*, p. 46. To estimate the percent of children in unsafe home environments who are not poor, I used data on the number of nonpoor 3–5 year olds in 1986 (the year the rates were calculated). "Poverty in the United States, 1986," Census Bureau, Current Population Reports, Consumer Income, Series P-60, no. 160, p. 27, table 7.

p. 25, overlap between poor parents and uneducated parents. These data are derived from calculations by David Ellwood on the March 1988 Current Population Survey. Cited in M. J. Bane et al., "Childhood Poverty and Disadvantage," p. 15.

p. 25, children with nonpoor, uneducated parents more likely to live in damaging home environments. N. Zill et al., "The Life Circumstances and Development of Children in Welfare Families: A Profile Based on National Survey Data," in *Escape from Poverty: What Makes a Difference for Children?* Chase-Lansdale and Brooks-Gunn, eds. (New York: Cambridge University Press), 1995.

p. 25, children who grow up with uneducated parents are more likely to be in the bottom half of their class, etc. These conclusions are based on the regression in Zill et al., "Children in Welfare Families," appendix 1.

p. 26, Tillie Olsen quote. Tillie Olsen, "I Stand Here Ironing," in *Tell Me a Riddle* (New York: Delta), 1961.

p. 27, for a discussion of the benefits of opportunities for accomplishment, see Sherman, *Wasting America's Future*, p. 47–48. There is also evidence that extracurricular activities have positive effects on academic performance. See Doris Entwisle, "Schools and the Adolescent," in *At the Threshold: The Developing Adolescent*, Feldman and Elliot, eds. (Cambridge, MA: Harvard University Press), 1990, pp. 197–224.

p. 28, research on children who escape long-term poverty. Janis Long and George Vaillant, "Escape from the Underclass," in *The Child in Our Times: Studies in the Development of Resiliency*, Timothy Dugan and Roberts Coles, eds. (New York: Brunner/Mazel), 1989, pp. 200–213.

p. 28, the importance of friendships for development. Jeffrey Parker and Steven Asher, "Peer Relations and Later Personal Adjustment: Are Low-Accepted Children at Risk?" *Psychological Bulletin*, vol. 102, no. 3, p. 357.

Chapter 2

p. 31, Rutter's work. Michael Rutter, "Protective Factors in Children's Responses to Stress and Disadvantage," *Primary Prevention of Psychopathology*, vol. 3, *Social Competence in Children*, M. W. Kent and J. E. Rolf., eds. (Hanover, N.H.: University Press of New England), 1979, pp. 49–74.

p. 32, problems with risk-factor instruments in child protective services. Thomas McDonald and Jill Marks, "A Review of Risk Factors Assessed in Child Protective Services," *Social Service Review*, March 1991, pp. 112–132.

p. 33, Jerome Kagan quote, *New Republic*, September 5, 1994, p. 45.

p. 35, kids who are critical thinkers often drop out. Michelle Fine, *Framing Dropouts: Notes on the Politics of an Urban Public High School* (Albany: State University of New York Press), 1991, pp. 103–130.

p. 35, research shows that intellectually advanced black children tend to perform far below their capacity in school. See, for example, Ronald Ferguson and Mary Jackson, "Black Male Youth and Drugs: How Racial Prejudice, Parents and Peers

Affect Vulnerability," working paper, Malcolm Wiener Center for Social Policy, John F. Kennedy School of Government, Harvard University, September 1992.

p. 35, Negative parenting undermines children with peers. Steven Asher et.al., "Peer Rejection and Loneliness in Childhood," in *Notes on Peer Rejection in Childhood*, Steven Asher and John Coie, eds. (New York: Cambridge University Press), 1990.

pp. 35–36, for a discussion of the clash between peer values and parent values in Asian communities, M. B. Spencer and S. Dornbusch, "Challenges in Studying Minority Youth," in *At the Threshold,* Feldman and Elliot, eds., pp. 123-146.

p. 36, Earls's work on factors related to violence. Personal communication with Felton Earls, May 1994. See also Earls's article, "Violence and Today's Youth," *The Future of Children: Critical Health Issues for Children and Youth*, vol. 4, no. 3., Packard Foundation, Winter 1994.

p. 36, Prothrow-Stith quote. D. Prothrow-Stith with Michaele Weissman, *Deadly Consequences*, p. 70.

pp. 36–37, ties between early experiences of shame and humiliation and violence. James Gilligan, "Shame and Humiliation: The Emotions of Individual and Collective Violence," lecture sponsored by the Erik and Joan Erikson Center, Cambridge, MA, May 23, 1991.

p. 37, ties between poor communication skills, etc., and propensity for violence. American Psychological Association, *Violence and Youth Report*, Washington, D.C., 1993.

p. 37, Greenspan quote. Stanley Greenspan, "The Kids Who Would Be Killers: Violence—and Its Prevention—Begins in the Playpen," *Washington Post*, July 25, 1993, p. C1.

p. 37, For a discussion of how children's interpretation of violence is correlated with violent behavior, see B. S. Centerwall, "Television and Violence: The Scale of the Problem and Where to Go From Here," *Journal of the American Medical Association*, 267, June 1992. Cited in *The Future of Children*, Packard Foundation, p. 18.

p. 37, among middle-class children especially, anxiety can result in overeating and hence obesity. Personal communication with Thomas Wadden, University of Pennsylvania Medical School, August, 1995.

p. 37, vignette of new mother and child. Steven Parker, Steven Greer, and Barry Zuckerman, "Double Jeopardy: The Impact of Poverty on Early Child Development," *Pediatric Clinics of North America*, vol. 35, no. 6, December 1988, pp. 1227–1237.

p. 39, *The Bell Curve*. R. Herrnstein and C. Murray, *The Bell Curve: Intelligence and Class Structure in American Life* (New York: Free Press), 1994.

p. 39, *The Stress Proof Child*. A. Saunders and B. Remsberg, *The Stress Proof Child* (New York: Holt, Rinehart, & Winston), 1985.

pp. 39–40, For a discussion of attributes of resilient children, see, for example, E. Werner, "Resilient Children," in *Contemporary Readings in Child Psychology*, 3d ed., E. Hetherington and R. Parke, eds. (New York: McGraw-Hill, 1987), pp. 51–57; E. Virginia Demos, "Resiliency in Infancy," in *The Child in Our Times: Studies in the Development of Resiliency*, Timothy Dugan and Robert Coles, eds. (New York: Brunner/Mazel), 1989, p. 3–22; David A. Hamburg, *Today's Children: Creating a Future for a Generation in Crisis* (New York: Times Books), 1992; and Lois Barclay Murphy and Alice Moriarty, *Vulnerability, Coping, and Growth: From Infancy to Adolescence* (New Haven, CT: Yale University Press), 1976

p. 41, description of Susan. Murphy and Moriarty, *Vulnerability, Coping, and Growth*, p. 186.

pp. 41–42, study following adolescents into adulthood. J. W. McFarlane, "Perspectives on Personality Consistency and Change from the Guidance Study," *Vita Humana*, vol. 7, 1964, pp. 115–126.

p. 42, violence in boys between the ages of 3 and 7 not highly correlated with adolescent violence. Personal communication with Felton Earls, Harvard School of Public Health, June 1994.

p. 42, changing effects of divorce on teen girls. Judith Wallerstein and Shauna Corbin, "Daughters of Divorce: Report from a Ten-Year Follow-Up." *American Journal of Orthopsychiatry*, vol. 59, no. 4, October 1989, pp. 593–603.

p. 42, Texas community that revolves around high school football team. H. G. Bissinger, *Friday Night Lights* (Reading, MA: Addison-Wesley), 1990.

p. 44, Brent Staples, *Parallel Time* (New York: Avon Books), 1994, p. 259.

p. 45, Ibid., Brent Staples.

Chapter 3

p. 47, *Atlantic Monthly* reference. Barbara Dafoe Whitehead, "Dan Quayle Was Right," *The Atlantic Monthly*, April 1993, pp. 47–84.

p. 48, *Time* reference on the future of families. Claudia Wallis, "The Nuclear Family Goes Boom!" *Time*, special issue, Fall 1992, p. 42.

p. 48, 60 percent of children will spend part of their childhood in a single-parent home. *Divided Families: What Happens to Children When Parents Part?* Frank Furstenberg and Andrew Cherlin, eds. (Cambridge, MA: Harvard University Press), 1991, p. 11.

p. 48, children in single-parent homes in 1900. Furstenberg and Cherlin, *Divided Families*, p. 10.

p. 48, more children grow up with at least one parent today than 50 years ago. Stephanie Coontz, *The Way We Never Were: American Families and the Nostalgia Trap* (New York: Basic Books), 1992, p. 15.

p. 48, exaggeration of changes in extended families. M. J. Bane, *Here to Stay: American Families in the Twentieth Century* (New York: Basic Books), 1976, pp. 69-70.

p. 52, divorce rate tripled between 1960 and 1982. Coontz, ibid., p. 3.

p. 52, perhaps half of all children born in the early 1980s will suffer their parents' divorce. Hetherington et al., "Marital Transitions: A Child's Perspective," *American Psychologist*, February 1989, p. 303.

p. 52, divorced families are not "atypical or pathogenic." Hetherington, et al., "Marital Transitions," *American Psychologist*, p. 310.

p. 53, J. Wallerstein and S. Blakeslee, *Second Chances: Men, Women, and Children a Decade After Divorce* (New York: Tichnor & Fields), 1989.

p. 53, about 90 percent of children reside with a custodial mother after divorce. Hetherington et al., "Marital Transitions: A Child's Perspective," *American Psychologist*, p. 305.

p. 53, statistics on children's contact with fathers. ("No contact" means that these children have not seen their fathers in the last year.) Furstenberg and Cherlin, *Divided Families*, p. 35.

p. 53, 41 percent of men walk away from divorce without a child support agreement, and nearly half who have agreements in place renege on the full amount. U.S. Census Bureau, *Child Support and Alimony: 1989*, Current Population Report, Consumer Income Series P-60, no. 173, pp. 7-8.

p. 53, average child support payments are about $3,000 a year. *Child Support and Alimony: 1989*, ibid., pp. 7–8.

p. 53, children are almost twice as likely to be living in poverty after divorce. Census Bureau study by Susan Bianchi, cited in William Galston, "Home Alone: What Policy Makers Should Know about Our Children," *New Republic*, December 2, 1991, p. 42.

pp. 53–54, This analysis of the effects of divorce on children is drawn in part from Hetherington et al., "Marital Transitions," pp. 303–312; and Judith Wallerstein and Sandra Blakeslee, *Second Chances*.

p. 54, young children often fear desertion by both parents in wake of divorce. See Hetherington et al., "Marital Transitions," p. 305.

p. 54, children lose ideals and idealized images of themselves. Daniel B. Frank, "How the School Can Support Children of Divorce: Psychoanalytic Perspectives on the School Experience," a public forum sponsored by the Institute for Psychoanalysis at the University of Chicago, May 20, 1992.

p. 54, need to err and test. Whitehead, "Dan Quayle Was Right," p. 82.

p. 54, problems which erupt after divorce. Material on conflicts with friends from Vonnie C. McLoyd, "The Impact of Economic Hardship on Black Families and Children: Psychological Distress, Parenting, and Socioemotional Development," *Child Development*, 61, 1990, p. 330. Material on delinquency from a personal communication with Sara McLanahan, Princeton University. Material on school troubles from a study by Peterson and Zill, cited in Furstenberg and Cherlin, *Divided Families*, p. 69.

p. 55, children of divorced families are more likely to be poor as adults, to earn less as adults, and to have marriages that end in divorce. Sara McLanahan and Gary Sandefur, *Growing Up With a Single Parent* (Cambridge, MA: Harvard University Press), 1994. Sara McLanahan and Larry Bumpass, "Intergenerational Consequences of Marital Disruption," *American Journal of Sociology*, 93 (July): pp. 130–152, 1988.

p. 55, divorce does damage to trust. Data computed by Harold Pollack from the General Social Survey, conducted by the National Opinion Research Center.

p. 55, long-term effects of divorce. Judith Wallerstein, "The Long-Term Effects of Divorce on Children: A Review." *Journal of the American Academy of Child and Adolescent Psychiatry*, vol. 30, no. 3, pp. 349–360.

p. 55, divorced mothers have more self-respect and are less likely to abuse alcohol. Studies cited by Coontz in *The Way We Never Were*, p. 224.

p. 56, 1968 Berkeley study. Block, Block, and Gjerde, "The Personality of Children Prior to Divorce," 57 (1986) pp. 827–840. Cited in Furstenberg and Cherlin, *Divided Families*, pp. 64–65.

p. 56, depression in children from high-conflict homes versus children in single-parent homes. J. Peterson and N. Zill, "Marital Disruption, Parent-Child Relationships, and Behavior Problems in Children," *Journal of Marriage and the Family*, vol. 48, May 1986, p. 303.

p. 56, data comparing dropouts in single-parent and two-parent families, and single parenthood not the root cause of troubles. Sara McLanahan, "The Consequences of Single Motherhood," *The American Prospect*, Summer 1994, p. 49.

p. 56, 78 percent of white children from single-parent homes do not drop out. Furstenberg and Cherlin citing Sara McLanahan in *Divided Families*, pp. 69–70.

p. 57, a large majority of families do not suffer long-term poverty after divorce. If only 8 percent of children suffer long-term poverty (see p. 10), then a large majority of children do not suffer protracted poverty after a divorce.

p. 58, 75 percent of custodial mothers and 80 percent of fathers remarry, and divorce rate is higher in second marriages than in first marriages. Hetherington et al., "Marital Transitions," p. 303.

p. 58, 25 percent to 33 percent of custodial mothers elect to live with a relative after divorce. See D. J. Hernandez, "Demographics and the Living Arrangements of Children." in *Impact of Divorce, Single-parenting, and Stepparenting on Children*, E. M. Hetherington and J. D. Arasteh, eds. (Hillsdale, N.J.: Erlbaum), 1988, pp. 3–22.

p 58–59, data on adults per family household. William C. Apgar, George Masnick, and Nancy McArdle, *Housing in America: 1970–2000. The Nation's Housing Needs for the Balance of the 20th Century*. Joint Center for Housing Studies, Harvard University, 1991, p. 43.

p. 59, effects of dislocation vs. the effects of divorce per se. See studies cited by Coontz, *The Way We Never Were*, p. 223.

p. 60, David Elkind, *The Hurried Child* (Reading, MA: Addison-Wesley), 1988, p. 112.

p. 60, over 25 percent of children are now born to single mothers. "Vital Statistics of the United States, 1990," vol. 1, Natality, table 1-46, p. 89, U.S. Department of Health and Human Services, Public Health Services, Centers for Disease Control and Prevention, National Center for Health Statistics, Hyattsville, MD, 1994.

p. 61, movies about children who lose mothers. Melinda Beck, "Movies without Mothers," *Newsweek*, August 29, 1994, p. 56.

p. 61, children born to unmarried mothers more likely to be poor than children of divorce because parents are more likely to be young, uneducated, and on welfare. Irwin Garfinkel and Sara McLanahan, "Single-Mother Families, Economic Insecurity, and Government Policy." *Confronting Poverty*. S. Danziger, G. Sandefur, and D. Weinberg, eds. (Cambridge: Harvard University Press), 1994. And Sara McLanahan and Lynne Casper, "Growing Diversity and Inequality in the American Family." *State of the Union*, R. Farley, ed. (New York: Russell Sage), 1995.

p. 61, about 25 percent of children born out of wedlock are born to unmarried, biological parents who are cohabiting. Larry Bumpass and James A. Sweet, "Children's Experience in Single-Parent Families: Implications of Cohabitation and Marital Transitions." *Family Planning Perspectives,* 21, 6 (Nov./Dec.) 1989: pp. 256–260. Almost half of all unwed mothers eventually marry and a smaller minority of African American unwed mothers marry. Personal communication with Sara McLanahan.

p. 61, children born out of wedlock are as likely to see their absent fathers on a weekly basis as are children of divorce. Sara McLanahan and Gary Sandefur, *Growing Up with a Single Parent.*

p. 61, one third of nonmarital births are to teenagers. "Vital Statistics of the United States, 1990," vol. 1, Natality, table 1-46, p. 89, U.S. Department of Health and Human Services, Public Health Services, Centers for Disease Control and Prevention, National Center for Health Statistics, Hyattsville, MD, 1994.

p. 61, school and pregnancy outcomes for children born to unwed mothers compared to those of children of divorce. Sara McLanahan, "Consequences of Single Motherhood," p. 51.

p. 62, children from single-parent families are not more likely to drop out of school when there are supportive community networks. James Coleman, "Families and Schools," *Educational Researcher*, vol. 16, 1987, pp. 32–38.

p. 63, mentoring. M. Freedman, *The Kindness of Strangers: Adult Mentors, Urban Youth, and the New Volunteerism* (San Francisco: Jossey-Bass), 1993.

p. 63, researchers have identified certain reachable moments in fatherhood. Personal communication with father-researcher James Levine, Work and Families Institute, New York, July 1995.

p. 65–66, goat study on bonding and history of bonding concept. Laura Shapiro, "It Doesn't Come Naturally," *New York Times Book Review*, May 2, 1993, p. 12. Review is of Diane E. Eyer, *Mother-Infant Bonding: A Scientific Fiction* (New Haven: Yale University Press), 1993.

p. 66, 67 percent of mothers with children under 18 work at least part-time. Sylvia Ann Hewlett, *When the Bough Breaks*, p. 91. Half of mothers with children under 5 work. Naomi Goldstein, "Are Changes in Work and Family Harming Children?" prepared for the Task Force on Meeting the Needs of Young Children, Carnegie Corporation of New York, January 11, 1993, p. 14.

p. 66, of children living in single-parent homes, 70 percent live with a parent who works. *The Challenge of Change: What the 1990 Census Tells Us about Children*, Center for the Study of Social Policy, Washington, D.C., September, 1992, p. 37.

pp. 66–67, for a discussion of the effects of maternal employment on children, see L. Wladis Hoffman, "Effects of Maternal Employment in the Two-Parent Family," *American Psychologist*, vol. 44, no. 2, pp. 283–292. See also J. Wilson and D. Ellwood, "Welfare to Work Through the Eyes of Children: The Impact on Children of Parental Movement from AFDC to Employment," working paper H-93-5, Malcolm Wiener Center for Social Policy, John F. Kennedy School of Government, September 1993; and Coontz, *The Way We Never Were*, pp. 150-179.

p. 67, when mothers work, children's intellectual achievement is enhanced when fathers contribute to child-rearing. H. Mischel and R. Fuhr, "Maternal Employment: Its Psychological Effects on Children and Their Families," in Dornbusch and Strober, eds., *Feminism, Children, and the New Families* (New York: Guilford Press), 1988. Cited in Coontz, *The Way We Never Were*, p. 217.

p. 68, study of latchkey children and substance abuse. J. L. Richardson et al., "Substance Use among Eighth Grade Students Who Take Care of Themselves after School,"

Pediatrics, vol. 84, no. 3, September 1989, pp. 556–566. For an analysis of this study and others negating it, see Coontz, *The Way We Never Were*, pp. 220–221.

p. 68, many teens long for more parental involvement. "Speaking of Kids: A National Survey of Children and Parents," National Commission on Children, Washington, D.C., 1991. See in particular figure 4, p. 13.

p. 69, children of working mothers who receive muddled messages. Richard Louv, *Childhood's Future* (Boston: Houghton Mifflin), 1990, p. 87.

p. 69, Coontz quote. Stephanie Coontz, *The Way We Never Were*, pp. 215–216.

Chapter 4

p. 71, Newt Gingrich quote. Charles Sennott, "Kin Have Misgivings about Death Penalty," *The Boston Globe*, November 8, 1994, p. 10.

p. 72, Vermont bumper sticker. Whitehead, "Dan Quayle Was Right," p. 55.

p. 72, 96 percent of all American families are dysfunctional. John Bradshaw, *Homecoming: Reclaiming and Championing Your Inner Child* (New York: Bantam Books), 1990; and David Gelman, "Making It All Feel Better," *Newsweek*, November 26, 1990, pp. 66–67, cited in Stephanie Coontz, *The Way We Never Were*, p. 208. "Wounded, neglected child within" also from Bradshaw, ibid. Cited in Coontz, p. 207.

p. 72, For a discussion of history of neglect and abuse in this country, see *The Future of Children: The Sexual Abuse of Children*, vol. 4, no. 2, Packard Foundation, Summer/Fall 1994, and Coontz, *The Way We Never Were*.

p. 73, 12 percent of mothers of young children are clinically depressed, and 52 percent report depressive symptoms. Studies cited by Steven Parker, Steven Greer, and Barry Zuckerman, "Double Jeopardy: The Impact of Poverty on Early Child Development," *Pediatric Clinics of North America*, vol. 35, no. 6, December 1988, p. 1233.

p. 73, For a discussion of depressed mothers' relationships with infants, see Barry Zuckerman and William Beardslee, "Maternal Depression: A Concern for Pediatricians," *Pediatrics*, vol. 79, no. 1, January 1987; and Barry Zuckerman et al., "Maternal Depressive Symptoms during Pregnancy and Newborn Irritability," *Journal of Developmental and Behavioral Pediatrics*, vol. 11, no. 4, August 1990. Both cited in Naomi Goldstein, "Are Changes in Work and Family Harming Children?" prepared for the Task Force on Meeting the Needs of Young Children, Carnegie Corporation of New York, January 11, 1993. Goldstein also discusses the difficulties depressed mothers have entering the world of infants.

p. 73, quote from Sheila. Quoted by Felicia Lee in "Where Parents Are Learning to Be Parents," *New York Times*, March 14, 1993, section 1, p. 33.

pp. 73–74, depressed parents' methods of resolving conflict and discipline styles. Vonnie C. McLoyd, "The Impact of Economic Hardship on Black Families and Children: Psychological Distress, Parenting, and Socioemotional Development," *Child Development*, 61, 1990, p. 328.

p. 74, McLoyd quote. Ibid., p. 322.

p. 74, For a discussion of problems that befall children with depressed mothers, see Goldstein, "Changes in Work and Family," and Zuckerman and Beardslee, "Maternal Depression."

p. 74, depressed parents are aware of their impatience. McLoyd, "Impact of Economic Hardship," p. 328.

p. 74, study of unemployed fathers. Ibid, p. 328.

p. 75, crises in poor families often come in rapid succession. D. Belle, "Inequality and Mental Health: Low-Income and Minority Women" in *Women and Mental Health Policy*, L. Walker, ed. (Beverly Hills, CA: Sage), 1984, pp. 135–150. Cited in McLoyd, "Impact of Economic Hardship."

p. 75, Importance of parenting skills in allaying negative effects of maternal depression on children. Karlen Lyons-Ruth, David B. Connell, and Henry Grunebaum, "Infants at Social Risk: Maternal Depression and Family Support Services as Mediators of Infant Development and Security of Attachment," *Child Development*, vol. 61, 1990, pp. 85–98. Expanded analysis presented by Karlen Lyons-Ruth at a poverty seminar at the John F. Kennedy School of Government, Harvard University, 1993.

p. 75, overestimating children study. R. Galdston, "Observations on Children Who Have Been Physically Abused and Their Parents," *American Journal of Psychiatry*, vol. 122, 1965, pp. 440–443.

p. 75, benefits of newsletter. See D. Riley, "Experimental Field Trial of the Parenting the First Year Newsletter Series: Probable Effects upon Prevention of Child Abuse and Increase in Child IQ," University of Wisconsin, Madison, 1992.

p. 78, the greater the number of young children, the more likely the mother is to be depressed. See G. Brown and T. Harris, "The Social Origins of Depression," London, Tavistock Publications, 1978. Cited in Parker, Greer, and Zuckerman, "Double Jeopardy," p. 1233.

p. 78, birth of the family therapy movement. J. Malcolm, *The Purloined Clinic* (New York: Knopf), 1991, pp. 177-230. See especially p 181.

p. 79, influence of institutions on family patterns. Drawn in part from personal communication with family therapist Roger Friedman, January 1994.

Chapter 5

p. 84, Brown quote. B. Bradford Brown, "Peer Groups and Peer Cultures," in *At the Threshold: The Developing Adolescent*, Feldman and Elliott, eds. (Cambridge, MA: Harvard University Press), 1990, p. 172.

pp. 84–85, high school students spend twice as much time with peers. *Being Adolescent*, M. Czikszentmihalyi and R. Larson (New York: Basic Books), 1974, cited in Feldman and Elliot, *At the Threshold*, p. 179.

p. 85, U.S. teenagers versus those of Japan and Soviet Union. Ritch Savin-Williams and Thomas J. Berndt, "Friendship and Peer Relations," in Feldman and Elliott, *At the Threshold*, p. 278.

p. 85, studies show that peer groups often counteract children's destructive tendencies. Pressure to stay in school. B. Brown, in Feldman and Elliot, *At the Threshold*, p. 192. Pressure to avoid smoking. R. Savin-Williams and T. Berndt, ibid, p. 297.

p. 85, benefits of cliques. S. Hansell, "Adolescent Friendship Networks and Distress in School," *Social Forces*, vol. 63, pp. 698–715. Cited in Feldman and Elliott, *At the Threshold*, p. 180.

p. 87, shame and disrespect and their connection to violence. Elijah Anderson, "The Code of the Streets," *Atlantic Monthly*, May 1994, p. 82.

p. 87, relationship between shame and violence. James Gilligan, "Shame and Humiliation: The Emotions of Individual and Collective Violence," lecture sponsored by the Erik and Joan Erikson Center, Cambridge, MA, May 23, 1991.

p. 87, teens just want people to know their name. Deborah Prothrow-Stith with Michaele Weissmann, *Deadly Consequences* (New York: HarperCollins Publishers), 1991, p. 106.

p. 88, June Jordan quote. June Jordan, "Requiem for the Champ," originally published in *The Progressive*, Madison, WI, Progressive, Inc., February, 1992.

p. 89, discussion of Spur Posse. Joan Didion, "Trouble in Lakewood," *The New Yorker*, July 26, 1993, pp. 46–65.

p. 89, quote from Robert Scheer of the *Los Angeles Times*. Cited in Didion, "Trouble in Lakewood," p. 65.

p. 90, boys corrupted by poor economic prospects. Elijah Anderson, "Sex Codes and Family Life among Poor Inner-City Youths," *Annals of the American Academy of Political and Social Science*, vol. 501, 1989, pp. 60–77.

p. 90, Comer on black children's sense of marginality. Appears in William Finnegan, "A Reporter at Large: Out There—II," *The New Yorker,* September 17, 1993, p. 66.

p. 90, Nathan McCall quote. In Nathan McCall, *Makes Me Wanna Holler: A Young Black Man in America* (New York: Random House), 1994, p. 402.

p. 91, twelve-year-old James. Alex Kotlowitz, *There Are No Children Here: The Story of Two Boys Growing Up in the Other America* (New York: Doubleday), 1991, p. 31.

p. 91, For a discussion of the experiences of Asian refugee children see M. B. Spencer, S. Dornbusch in Feldman and Elliott, *At the Threshold*, pp. 123–146.

pp. 91–92, correlation between prolonged isolation and rejection and juvenile delinquency and dropping out. See J. G. Parker and Steven Asher, "Peer Relations and Later Personal Adjustment: Are Low-Accepted Children at Risk?" *Psychological Bulletin*, vol. 102, 1987, pp. 357–389. See also M. Rutter et al., *Fifteen Thousand Hours: Secondary Schools and Their Effects on Children* (Cambridge, MA: Harvard University Press), 1979.

p. 92, "then what's the whole point of playing?" Vivian Paley, *You Can't Say You Can't Play* (Cambridge, MA: Harvard University Press), 1992, p. 4.

p. 92, girls sensitive to being "dissed" and girl cliques. E. Anderson, "The Code of the Streets," p. 92.

p. 92, Lyn Brown discussion of sports and girls. See Lyn Mikel Brown, "Hope Is a Muscle," *New Moon Parenting*, vol. 1, no. 5, May/June 1994.

p. 92, girls' participation in sports half that of boys'. Ibid.

p. 92, pressure girls feel to "dumb down." Peggy Orenstein, *Schoolgirls: Young Women, Self-Esteem, and the Confidence Gap* (New York: Doubleday), 1994.

p. 93, Lyn Mikel Brown and Carol Gilligan, *Meeting at the Crossroads: Women's Psychology and Girls' Development*. See especially pp. 104–105.

p. 93, Valerie Polakow, *Lives on the Edge* (Chicago: University of Chicago Press), 1993, p. 145.

p. 93, Vivian Paley quote. Vivian Paley, *You Can't Say You Can't Play*, p. 22.

p. 93, children look to parents on key decisions and are affected by parents' values. Studies cited by B. Bradford Brown, "Peer Groups and Peer Culture," Feldman and Elliott, *At the Threshold*, p. 174.

p. 94, Resolving Conflict Creatively Program and the Violence Prevention Project. For a discussion of both programs, see Felton J. Earls, "Violence and Today's Youth," *The Future of Children: Critical Health Issues for Children and Youth*, vol. 4, no. 3, Packard Foundation, Winter 1994, pp. 15–16.

p. 94, study on the value of teaching social interaction skills. S. Oden and S. R. Asher, "Coaching Children in Social Skills and Friendship Making," *Child Development*, vol. 48, pp. 495–506.

p. 94, teacher's grid. *Educational Leadership*, vol. 52, no. 4, December 1994/January 1995, p. 66.

p. 95, parents can help with peer troubles. James Youniss and Jacqueline Smollar, *Adolescent Relations with Mothers, Fathers, and Friends* (Chicago, University of Chicago Press), 1985.

p. 96, New York couple creating activities for kids. Michael Norman, "One Cop, Eight Square Blocks," *New York Times Magazine*, December 12, 1993, p. 63.

Chapter 6

p. 97, Keniston quote. Kenneth Keniston, *The Uncommitted: Alienated Youth in American Society* (New York: Harcourt, Brace & World), 1960, p. 252.

p. 98, history of geographic mobility. Mary Jo Bane, *Here to Stay: American Families in the Twentieth Century* (New York: Basic Books), 1976, pp. 59–62. Study comparing geographic mobility in Boston. Steven Thernstrom, *The Other Bostonians*. (Cambridge, MA: Harvard University Press), 1973. Cited in Bane, ibid.

p. 98, Melville and uprootedness. Keniston, *The Uncommitted,* p. 252.

p. 98, exodus from small towns. Susan Cohen, "Missing Links," *Washington Post Magazine*, July 31, 1994, p. 11.

p. 98, Kai Erikson description. Kai Erikson, *Everything in Its Path: Destruction of Community in the Buffalo Creek Flood* (New York: Simon & Schuster), 1976.

p. 99, Lisa Sullivan quote. William Finnegan, "A Reporter at Large: Out There— I," *The New Yorker*, September 10, 1990, p. 56.

p. 101, effects of parental isolation. Studies cited by S. Parker, et al., "Double Jeopardy," p. 1232.

pp. 100–101, Deborah Belle study. Deborah Belle, "Social Ties and Social Support," in *Lives in Stress: Women and Depression*, D. Belle, ed. (Beverly Hills, CA: Sage Publishers), 1982, pp. 133–144.

p. 101, work of Carol Stack. C. Stack, *All Our Kin: Strategies for Survival in a Black Community* (New York: Harper & Row), 1974. Cited in D. Belle, ibid., p. 142.

p. 101, Granovetter on isolated communities. Mark S. Granovetter, "The Strength of Weak Ties," *American Journal of Sociology*, vol. 78, no. 6, pp. 1360–1379.

p. 102, many friendships among low-income parents are not burdened. See, for example, H. Weiss, "Families and Neighborhoods," unpublished paper, Cornell University, Ithaca, NY, p. 6.72.

p. 102, harmonious ties in middle-class communities. Weiss, "Families and Neighborhoods," pp. 6.63–6.69.

p. 102, study of steel mill town. Personal communication with Dan Frank. Research was conducted for his dissertation, "The Work of Unemployment," Human Development, Department of Psychology, University of Chicago, 1988.

p. 103, 58 percent of Americans describe themselves as "very private." Robert Wuthnow, *Sharing the Journey: Support Groups and America's New Quest for Community* (New York: The Free Press), 1994, p. 192.

p. 103, Don's story. Ibid., p. 214.

p. 103, the presence of one significant source of social support. S. Cohen and T. Wills, "Stress, Social Support, and the Buffering Hypothesis," *Psychological Bulletin*, vol. 98, pp. 310–357. Cited in Feldman and Elliott, *At the Threshold*.

p. 104, 40 percent of Americans now opt for support groups. Wuthnow, *Sharing the Journey*, p. 47. Wuthnow on support groups. Wuthnow, ibid.

p. 105, "trying on" various identities. Erik Erikson, *Identity, Youth, and Crisis,* (New York: Norton), 1968. Cited in Feldman and Elliot, *At the Threshold*.

p. 105, research suggesting that this exploration is critical to identity development. Studies cited by David A. Kinney, "From Nerds to Normal: The Recovery of Identity among Adolescents from Middle School to High School," *Sociology of Education,* vol. 66, January 1993, p. 22.

p. 105, Kinney study, ibid., pp. 21-40.

p. 105, benefits for unpopular children of nonclassroom friends. R. Schmuck, "Some Aspects of Classroom School Climate," *Psychology in the Schools*, vol. 3, 59–65. Cited in Jeffrey Parker and Steven Asher, "Peer Relations and Later Personal Adjustment," *Psychology Bulletin*, vol. 102, no. 3.

p. 106, excerpt from Lorenzo's diary. *The Me Nobody Knows: Children's Voices from the Ghetto*, S. Joseph, ed. (New York: Avon Books), 1969, p. 21.

p. 106, nearly 20 percent of families change residence each year. "Geographical Mobility: March 1992 to March 1993," U.S. Census Bureau, Current Population Reports, Series P-20-481, table E, p. xv. The overall moving rate for family householders with children under 18 is 18.9 percent.

p. 106, poor children are twice as likely as nonpoor children to move. Sherman, *Wasting America's Future*, p. 19. 1989 American Housing Survey tabulations by the Children's Defense Fund.

p. 107, Coles's description of Peter. Robert Coles, *Children of Crisis*, vol. 2, *Migrants, Sharecroppers, Mountaineers* (Boston: Little, Brown & Co.), 1967, p. 73.

p. 107, each move reduces a child's chance of finishing school by 2.6 percent. Naomi Goldstein, "Why Poverty Is Bad for Children," Ph.D. Dissertation, John F. Kennedy School of Government, Harvard University, 1991, p. 120.

p. 108, families in the early 1900s moved to join relatives. Tamara Hareven, "Historical Changes in the Family and the Life Course: Implications for Child Development" in *Children's Social Networks and Social Supports*, Deborah Belle, ed. (New York: John Wiley & Sons, Inc.), 1989, chap. 1.

p. 108, the average center-based early education and care program has 25 percent teacher turnover. See Kisker et al., "A Profile of Child Care Settings: Early Education and Care in 1990," prepared under contract for the U.S. Department of Education by Mathematica Policy Research, Inc., Princeton, NJ, p. 146, table iv.14.

Chapter 7

p. 111, ways neighborhoods are unresponsive to parents with young children. *Starting Points: Meeting the Needs of Our Youngest Children*, a report of the Carnegie Corporation of New York, 1994, p. 85.

p. 111, distribution of single-parent families. For Census tract breakdown see tabulations by Paul Jargowsky, University of Texas, Dallas, based on U.S. Census Summary Tape File 3A.

p. 112, *Time* magazine cover story. J.D. Hull, "A Boy and His Gun," *Time* magazine, August 2, 1993, cover and p. 20.

p. 112, *Newsweek* cover story. B. Kantrowitz, "Wild in the Streets," *Newsweek*, August 2, 1993, cover and p. 40.

p. 112, National Commission on Children survey, "Speaking of Kids," report of the National Opinion Research Project, submitted June 24, 1991, p. 27.

p. 113, it appears that violence has not risen in the great majority of American neighborhoods. This assertion is based on the fact that national violent crime rates were at the same level in 1992 as they were in 1973. "Criminal Victimization in the U.S., 1973–1992 Trends," Bureau of Justice Statistics, July 1994. While violent crime data is not broken down by ghetto neighborhood, lethal violence has increased, according to data from the National Vital Statistics System, in large metropolitan counties. Families and professionals working in ghetto neighborhoods also frequently report an increase in lethal violence among children.

p. 113, The prediction that an increasing number of children will reside in ghettos is based on the steady increase in the number of ghetto neighborhoods in the past two decades. For data on this increase in past decades, see Paul Jargowsky, *Ghettos, Barrios, and the Concentration of Poverty* (New York: Russell Sage Foundation), forthcoming.

p. 113, effects of violence on children. Much of this discussion is drawn from J. Garbarino et al., *Children in Danger: Coping with the Consequences of Community Violence* (San Francisco: Jossey-Bass), 1992. See also Deborah Prothrow-Stith with Michaele Weissman, *Deadly Consequences* (New York: HarperCollins Publishers), 1991; Joy Osofsky "The Effects of Violence in the Lives of Young Children," background paper for the Task Force on Meeting the Needs of Young Children, Carnegie Corporation, New York, May 7, 1993; and D. Cicchetti and M. Lynch, "Toward an Ecological/Transactional Model of Community Violence and Child Maltreatment: Consequences for Children's Development," *Psychiatry*, 1993.

p. 113, wooden corral. Tom Mashberg, "Parents Act in a Season of Violence: Boys' Shootings a Spur," *The Boston Globe*, July 14, 1993, p. 1.

p. 113, McDonald's steel hamburger. Isabel Wilkerson, *The New York Times*, April 4, 1993, p. 20.

p. 113, descriptions of Chicago schools. T. Wiltz and S. Johnson, "Once Safe Havens, Schools Now in the Line of Fire," *Chicago Tribune*, September 26, 1991, sec. 1, p. 19. Cited in Garbarino et al., *Children in Danger*, p. 61.

p. 113–114, children feel helpless. D. Cohen and S. Marans, "Children and Inner City Violence: Strategies for Intervention," in *Psychological Effects of War and Violence on Children*, in press.

p. 114, Ricky. A. Kotlowitz, *There Are No Children Here*, p. 73.

p. 114, Diante. Kotlowitz, *Wall Street Journal*, October 27, 1987. Cited in Prothrow-Stith, *Deadly Consequences*, p. 64.

p. 114, study of Israeli kibbitzum. A. Ziv and R. Israel, "Effects of Bombardment on the Manifest Anxiety Level of Children Living in Kibbutzim," *Journal of Clinical Psychology*, vol. 40. 1973, pp. 287–291. Cited in Garbarino, *Children in Danger*, p. 55. See Garbarino, ibid., pp. 54–55, for other studies on same topic.

p. 115, community violence "last straw." Garbarino et al., *Children in Danger*, p. 2.

p. 115, children are less likely to be scarred when they can talk to an adult soon after exposure to violence. Personal communication with psychologist Michael Vickers, November 1994.

p. 116. For a discussion of the importance of religion in helping families cope with stress, see Lois Barclay Murphy and Alice Moriarty, *Vulnerability, Coping, and Growth* (New Haven, CT: Yale University Press), 1976; also, Garbarino et al., p. 111.

p. 116, description of support services for those exposed to violence in Philadelphia suburb. Charisse Jones, "An Act of Youthful Savagery Stuns a Suburb," *New York Times*, November 19, 1994.

p. 116, reaction to Winnetka shooting versus reaction to shooting in the Henry Horner Homes. A. Kotlowitz, *There Are No Children Here*, p. 105.

p. 116, young children suffer neurological impairment. B. A. van der Kolk, "Psychological Trauma," *American Psychiatric Press*, Washington, D.C., 1987. Cited in Garbarino et al. *Children in Danger,* p. 10.

p. 116, three times more likely that exposure to violence will lead to PTSD if a child is under twelve. J. Davidson and R. Smith, "Traumatic Experiences in Psychiatric Outpatients," I, July 1990, vol. 3, no. 3, pp. 459-475. Cited in Garbarino et al., *Children in Danger*, p. 13.

p. 117, for a discussion of the importance of parents' activism, see Garbarino et al., *Children in Danger*, p. 109.

p. 118, taxis will not enter the area and stores will not deliver. Adam Walinsky, "What It's Like to Be in Hell," *New York Times*, December 4, 1987.

p. 118, Kotlowitz quote on aging of adults. A. Kotlowitz, *There Are No Children Here*, p. 10.

p. 119, children in ghettos more vulnerable to emotional and learning difficulties. See Sherman, *Wasting America's Future*, 1994, p. 34.

p. 119, head injuries. Natalie Angier, "Elementary, Dr. Watson: The Neurotransmitters Did It," *New York Times*, January 23, 1993, "The Week in Review."

p. 119, ghetto children more likely to be exposed to toxic pollutants. Sherman, *Wasting America's Future*, p. 12.

p. 119–20, problems with child care in ghettos. Sherman, *Wasting America's Future*, p. 24.

p. 120, "We are our own police." Michael Marriott, "Provider, Protector, and Felon: Freddie, 17," *New York Times*, April 18, 1993, p. A1.

p. 120, Lafayette quote. A. Kotlowitz, *There Are No Children Here*, p. 55.

pp. 120–21, effects of hearing loss. Lisbeth Schorr, *Within Our Reach*, p. 30.

p. 121, Putnam study. R. Putnam, "The Prosperous Community: Social Capital and Public Life," *The American Prospect*, Spring 1993, no. 13. Benefits of social capital for inner-city youth. Studies cited by Putnam, ibid, 39.

p. 122, description of Sandtown-Winchester project. Drawn from materials produced by Community Building in Partnership. [For further information, contact Community Building in Partnership, 1137 North Gilmor Street, Baltimore, MD, 21217, (410) 728-8607.] See also David Kennedy, "Showcase and Sandtown: In Search of Neighborhood Revitalization," Issues and Practices Report, National Institute of Justice through Abt Associates, September 9, 1994.

p. 123, for more information on the Shorebank Initiative, see R. Giloth, "Social Investment in Jobs: Foundation Perspectives on Targeted Economic Development During the 1990s," *Economic Development Quarterly*, col. 9, no. 3, August 1995, pp. 279–289.

Chapter 8

p. 125, Portions of this chapter are derived from R. Weissbourd, *Making the System Work for Poor Children*, working paper, Malcolm Wiener Center for Social Policy, John F. Kennedy School of Government, May 1991. The paper evolved from discussions of the Executive Session on Making the System Work for Poor Children, convened with funding from the Carnegie Corporation of New York. A group of two dozen practitioners, scholars, and policy makers met at the Wiener Center six times over the course of three years from 1988 to 1990. Opinions are the author's alone.

p. 129, For a strong analysis of problems with the system and constraints on frontline workers, see *Case Management and System Reform: Issues in Examining the Skills and Training Needed by New Front-Line Workers*, Internal paper for the Center for the Study of Social Policy, Washington, D.C., 1990.

p. 133, high-risk children lose Medicaid. Bella English, "Aging Out," *The Boston Globe Magazine*, October 16, 1994, p. 37.

p. 134, many parents have difficulty tracking down services. Findings of studies in San Diego and Cambridge. For further description see "New Beginnings in San Diego: Developing a Strategy for Interagency Collaboration," *Phi Delta Kappan*, October 1992, p. 143. For Cambridge survey data, see City of Cambridge, *Human Service Resident Needs Summary*, Center for Survey Research, University of Massachusetts, Boston, February 1992.

p. 136, for a useful discussion of the constraints on caregivers and of caregivers' coping capacities, see Margot Adler Welch, "Thrivers: A Study of Job Satisfaction and Success in Multi-Problem Human Service Agencies," a thesis prepared for the Graduate School of Education, Harvard University, 1990. Available through UMI Dissertation Information Service, (800) 521-0600, #9032470.

p. 139, most important element of prenatal care is "friendly support." Lisbeth Schorr, "What Works: Applying What We Already Know About Successful Social Policy," *The American Prospect*, no. 13, Spring 1993, p.47.

p. 141–42, Richard Newman quote and California report on violence against social workers. Reported by Sam Dillon in "Social Workers: Targets in a Violent Society," *New York Times*, November 18, 1992.

PART II

p. 145, Theodore Roethke quote. T. Roethke, "In a Dark Time," *Theodore Roethke: Selected Poem,* (London: Faber & Faber), 1969.

Chapter 9

p. 149, the effects of low birth weight. L. Schorr, *Within Our Reach*, pp. 66-67.

p. 149, Mothers seek medical attention for their children even when they don't seek help for themselves. Barry Zuckerman, "Health Care for Children Living in Poverty: Problems, Programs, and Policy," *The Urban Institute*, January, 1993, p. 6.

p. 149, for information on American prenatal care compared to other countries, see David Hamburg, *Today's Children,* (New York: Times Books), 1992.

p. 149, close to 900,000 mothers do not receive prenatal care during the first trimester. "Advanced Report of Natality Statistics, 1992," *Vital Statistics of the United States*, vol. 43, no. 5, supplement, October 25, 1994.

p. 150, for more information about the South End Clinic, see Linda Lewis, "Neighborhood Health Care: An American Dream?" *The Boston Globe Magazine*, March 21, 1982.

p. 155, A report by Boston's Trustees of Health and Hospitals indicated a reduction of hospitalizations in Boston communities served by community health centers. Lewis, ibid., p. 23.

p. 155, lack of good physician-patient relationships leads to less information about preventive measures. Sherman, *Wasting America's Future*, pp. 43-44.

p. 158, history and successes of community health-care centers. Schorr, *Within Our Reach,* pp. 130–134. Personal communication with Dr. Jack Geiger, August 1995.

p. 160, "Reach Out and Read" and other programs at Boston City Hospital. See Anita Diamant, "Zuckerman Unbound," *The Boston Globe Magazine*, December 25, 1994.

p. 160, Hawaii's experiment with Healthy Start. Much of this description of Healthy Start is based on research conducted by Teresa Eckrich Sommer. For a report, see Teresa Eckrich Sommer and Megan Berryill, "Healthy Start: Hawaii's Response to Family Stress and Child Health," in C. Bruner, ed., *Improving Infant and Child Health: Case Studies of Exemplary State Initiatives,* Child and Family Policy Center, Des Moines, Iowa, May 1993.

p. 164, home visiting outcomes. For a review of these outcomes see Martha Minow and Richard Weissbourd, "Final Report on Home Visiting Research and Initiatives," presented to the Pew Charitable Trusts by the American Academy of Arts and Sciences Initiatives for Children, 1994.

p. 164, Resource Mothers. This description of Resource Mothers is based on research by Lisa Hicks and also draws from Schorr, *Within Our Reach*, pp. 79–84.

p. 167, David Hamburg quote. David Hamburg, *Today's Children*, p. 60.

p. 168, For further discussion of redesigning funding, see Barry Zuckerman, "Health Care for Children Living in Poverty."

Chapter 10

p. 170, percent of children in public school. Preliminary estimates of Fall 1993 school enrollment for children grades K–12, prepared by the U.S. Department of Education, National Center for Educational Statistics, based upon the Common Core of Data survey collected each year.

p. 171, Data on dropping out. Defined as proportion of 25–29 year olds failing to complete high school. U.S. Bureau of the Census, Current Population Reports, Series P-20, *Educational Attainment in the United States* (various years), Washington, DC. For more dropout statistics and for Fernandez quotes, see Tony Hiss, "The End of the Rainbow," *The New Yorker*, April 12, 1993, p. 43.

p. 171, schools have reinforced race and class barriers despite individual success stories. See Lisbeth Schorr, *Within Our Reach*, p. 217.

p. 171, correlation between teacher pay and student achievement. Ron Ferguson and Helen Ladd, "Additional Evidence on How and Why Money Matters: A Production Function Analysis of Alabama Schools," paper prepared for Performance Based Approaches to School Reform, conference at the Brookings Institution, April 6, 1995. See also Ronald Ferguson, "Paying for Public Education: New Evidence on How and Why Money Matters," *Harvard Journal on Legislation*, vol. 28, no. 467, pp. 465–498.

p. 172, Comer schools. Information on Lincoln-Basset Elementary School is based on research conducted in 1991. Since then, the school principal has left. For further description of the Comer schools, see J. Comer, "Educating Poor Minority Children," *Scientific American*, vol. 259, no. 5, 1988, pp. 42–48. Also, J. Comer and N. Haynes, "Summary of School Development Effects," Yale Child Study Center.

p. 173, Kim Marshall quote. Kim Marshall, "Teachers and Schools—What Makes a Difference?" *Daedalus*, Journal of the American Academy of Arts and Sciences, Cambridge, Winter 1993, p. 223.

p. 174, research on parent involvement in schools. See, for example, S. Black, "The Parent Factor," *The Executive Educator*, April 1993.

p. 175, evaluation of Comer schools. Comer and Haynes, "Summary of School Development Effects," Yale Child Study Center.

p. 175, Accelerated Schools. For further description of the Accelerated Schools, see Wendy Hopfenberg, "The Accelerated Middle School: Moving from Concept to Reality," Stanford University School of Education, April 1991.

p. 176, evaluations of Accelerated Schools. Pia Wong, "Accomplishments of Accelerated Schools," available through The National Center for the Accelerated Schools Project, School of Education, CERAS 109, Stanford University, (415) 725-1676. See also Henry Levin, "Accelerated Schools After Eight Years," in L. Schauble and R. Glaser, eds., *Innovations in Learning: New Environments for Education* (Hillsdale, NJ: Erlbaum); and unpublished paper by C. Ferguson, "Accelerated Schools," for HCP-204, Kennedy School of Government, April 1994.

p. 177, For further description of the Success-for-All schools, see Robert E. Slavin et al., *Whenever and Wherever We Choose...The Replication of Success-for-All*, Center for Research on Effective Schooling for Disadvantaged Students, Johns Hopkins University, Baltimore, MD.

p. 178, evaluation of Success-for-All. For a summary of the evaluation data, see Robert Slavin et al., "Success-For-All: A Summary of Research," presented at the annual conference of the American Educational Research Association, San Francisco, April 1995.

p. 178, early results from 21st Century Schools. Personal communication with Edward Zigler, Bush Center in Child Development and Social Policy, Yale University, July 1995.

p. 181, principles of effective schools. These were drawn in part from Kim Marshall, "Teachers and Schools." See also R. Edmonds, "Effective Schools for the Urban Poor," *Educational Leadership*, 1979.

p. 184, innovative models tend to evaporate over time. Personal communication with Richard Elmore, Harvard University Graduate School of Education, November 1984.

p. 185, burdensome bureaucracratic regulations. Claudia Wallis, "A Class of Their Own," *Time*, October 31, 1994, p. 54.

p. 185, teacher training doesn't typically include parent involvement. Heather Weiss, "We Must Move beyond Finger Pointing," *Education Week*, October 5, 1994.

p.186, Michael Timpane quote. "Voices from the Field: Thirty Expert Opinions on 'America 2000,' the Bush Administration's Strategy to 'Reinvent' America's Schools." William T. Grant Foundation Commission on Work, Family, and Citizenship, and Institute for Educational Leadership. Washington, DC, 1991.

Chapter 11

p. 197, Homebuilders model. For information on family preservation and the Homebuilders model, see Joan Barthel, *For Children's Sake: The Promise of Family Preservation*, The Edna McConnell Clark Foundation, 1992. See also Lisbeth Schorr, "What Works," *The American Prospect*, no. 13, Spring, 1993, pp. 49–52. See also *Strategy Statement of Program for Children*, The Edna McConnell Clark Foundation, February 1992.

p. 198, quote about respecting families. Barthel, *For Children's Sake*, p. 20. "Trouble has no timetable," ibid., p. 30.

p. 198, results of family preservation evaluations. See, for example, B. Blythe, M. P. Salley, and S. Jayaratne, "A Review of Intensive Family Preservation Services Research," paper supported by the Edna McConnell Clark Foundation and the Annie Casey Foundation.

p. 198, one-half million children today are living outside their homes. The Edna McConnell Clark Foundation, *Strategy Statement of Program for Children*, p. 2.

Chapter 12

p. 201, This discussion of community policing is based on conversations with George Kelling, David Kennedy, and Frank Hartmann at the Kennedy School of Government, Harvard University, and on Susan Michaelson, George Kelling, and Robert Wasserman, "Toward a Working Definition of Community Policing," working paper, John F. Kennedy School of Government, Harvard University, Program in Criminal

Justice Policy and Management, January 1988. Information was also drawn from Michael Norman, "One Cop, Eight Square Blocks," *New York Times Magazine*, December 12, 1993; and from Mark Harrison Moore, "What Is Community Policing?" John F. Kennedy School of Government, Harvard University, December 12, 1991.

p. 203, "just the facts, Ma'am." William Bratton, "Neighborhood Policing: The Challenge of Managing Change," lecture given at the Boston University School of Management, November 10, 1993.

p. 203, "Broken Windows." J. Q. Wilson and George Kelling, "Broken Windows," *Atlantic Monthly*, March 1992, pp. 29–38.

p. 210, description of Bratton. J. Lardner, "The CEO Cop," *The New Yorker,* vol. 70, no. 48, February 6, 1995, p. 46.

p. 211, North Camden police. Richard G. Malloy, "Look at Who the Camden Kids Are Looking Up to These Days," *Philadelphia Inquirer*, November 6, 1993.

p. 214–15, Difficulties police have sharing emotional frailties with family, colleagues, and supervisors, and 52 police suicides in NY between 1985 and 1994, editorial, *New York Times*, December 1, 1993, p. A22.

p. 217, New Haven program. Information about this program was drawn from the "Program Description of the Yale University Child Study Center–New Haven Police Department Child Development Community Policing Program" and from conversations with Dr. Steven Marans at the Yale Child Study Center.

p. 221, Norfolk, VA. City of Norfolk's Police Assisted Community Enforcement (PACE) program brochure, City of Norfolk, October 1992.

Chapter 13

p. 226, family support. For further information on family support, see S. Kagan and B. Weissbourd, eds., *Putting Families First* (San Francisco: Jossey-Bass), 1994.

p. 228. For further discussion of the importance of the transition to high school, see M. Roderick, "The Path to Dropping Out Among Public School Youth," Malcolm Wiener Center for Social Policy Dissertation Series, #D-91-2, May 1991.

p. 231, Royer quote and innovations. Speech given at the John F. Kennedy School of Government, Harvard University, Summer 1994.

p. 232, Norman Rice initiatives. Norman Rice, "Local Initiatives in Support of Families," in Kagan and Weissbourd, *Putting Families First*, pp. 321–337.

p. 232, Seattle planning department promoting community. Don Fraser, "HUD's Role in Strengthening Families," unpublished report for the Department of Housing and Urban Development, November 1, 1994, p. 13.

p. 233, promoting a child-friendly climate in cities. See "Children and Families in Cities: Services and Resources for Local Government Officials," and "Your City's Kids," publications of the National League of Cities Institute, 1301 Pennsylvania Avenue, NW, Washington, DC, 20004-1763.

p. 233, San Francisco ballot initiative. P. Taylor, "Nonprofits Boost Advocacy in the Interests of Children," *Washington Post*, January 13, 1992.

p. 234, for a discussion of parent and child demographic trends, see Julie Boatright Wilson, "The Future of America's Families and Children—Who Will

Support Them?" Malcolm Wiener Center for Social Policy, John F. Kennedy School of Government, Harvard University, March 21, 1992.

p. 234, demographic trends resulting in shrinking constituency for public education. For further analysis of the effects of these trends on schools, see Michael J. Barrett, "The Newest Minority," *Atlantic Monthly*, July 1993, p. 22.

p. 235. For a useful discussion of the importance of this kind of public accountability, see Mary Jo Bane, "Paying Attention to Children: Services, Settings and Systems," working paper for the Executive Session on Making the System Work for Poor Children, Malcolm Wiener Center for Social Policy, John F. Kennedy School of Government, Harvard University, April 1991.

BIBLIOGRAPHY

SELECTED BIBLIOGRAPHY

Coontz, Stephanie, *The Way We Never Were: American Families and the Nostalgia Trap*. New York: Basic Books, 1992.

Feldman, S. Shirley and Glen R. Elliot, *At the Threshold: The Developing Adolescent*. Cambridge, MA: Harvard University Press, 1990.

Freedman, Marc, *The Kindness of Strangers: Adult Mentors, Urban Youth, and the New Volunteerism*. San Francisco: Jossey-Bass, 1993.

Furstenberg, Frank and Andrew Cherlin, eds., *Divided Families: What Happens to Children When Parents Part?* Cambridge, MA: Harvard University Press, 1991.

Garbarino, James, Nancy Dubrow, Kathleen Kostelny, and Carolyn Pardo, *Children in Danger*. San Francisco: Jossey-Bass, 1992

Hamburg, David A., *Today's Children: Creating a Future for a Generation in Crisis*. New York: Times Books, 1992.

Hewlett, Sylvia Ann, *When the Bough Breaks: The Cost of Neglecting Our Children*. New York: HarperCollins Publishers, 1991.

Jencks, Christopher, *Rethinking Social Policy: Race, Poverty, and the American Underclass*. Cambridge, MA. Harvard University Press, 1992.

Kotlowitz, Alex, *There Are No Children Here: The Story of Two Boys Growing Up in the Other America*. New York: Doubleday, 1991.

McLanahan, Sara and Gary Sandefur, *Growing Up with a Single Parent*. Cambridge, MA: Harvard University Press, 1994.

Newman, Katherine S., *Falling from Grace: The Experience of Downward Mobility in the American Middle Class*. New York: The Free Press, 1988.

Olsen, Tillie, *Tell Me a Riddle*. New York: Delta, 1961.

Paley, Vivian G., *You Can't Say You Can't Play*. Cambridge, MA: Harvard University Press, 1992.

Polakow, Valerie, *Lives on the Edge: Single Mothers and Their Children in the Other America*. Chicago: University of Chicago Press, 1993.

Prothrow-Stith, Deborah and Michaele Weissman, *Deadly Consequences: How Violence is Destroying Our Teenage Population and a Plan to Begin Solving the Problem*. New York: HarperCollins Publishers, 1991.

Schorr, Lisbeth, *Within Our Reach: Breaking the Cycle of Disadvantage*. New York: Doubleday, 1988.

Sherman, Arloc, *Wasting America's Future: The Children's Defense Fund Report on the Costs of Child Poverty*. Boston: Beacon Press, 1994.

Wuthnow, Robert, *Sharing the Journey: Support Groups and America's New Quest for Community*. New York: The Free Press, 1994.

PERMISSION ACKNOWLEDGMENTS

The excerpts from "In a Dark Time," copyright © 1960 by Beatrice Roethke, Administratrix of the Estate of Theodore Roethke, from *The Collected Poems of Theodore Roethke* by Theodore Roethke are used by permission of Doubleday, a division of Bantam Doubleday Dell Publishing Group, Inc.

The lines from Tillie Olsen, "I Stand Here Ironing," in *Tell Me a Riddle*, copyright © 1961 by Doubleday & Co., New York, are reprinted with permission.

Material from Rick Weissbourd, "Divided Families, Whole Children," *The American Prospect 18* (Summer 1994): 66–73 is reprinted with the permission of *The American Prospect* © by New Prospect, Inc.

Material from Marc Freedman, *The Kindness of Strangers: Adult Mentors, Urban Youth, and the New Voluntarism*, copyright © 1993 by Jossey-Bass, Inc., Publishers is reprinted with permission.

The excerpt from "Lorenzo's Diary," from *The Me Nobody Knows: Children's Voices from the Ghetto* edited by Stephen M. Joseph, copyright © 1969 by Avon Books is reprinted with permission.

Material from Alex Kotlowitz, *There Are No Children Here*, copyright © 1991 by Alex Kotlowitz is used with permission of Doubleday, a division of Bantam Doubleday Dell Publishing Group, Inc.

Material is reprinted with permission from James Garabino et al., *Children in Danger: Coping with the Consequences of Community Violence*. Copyright © 1992 by Jossey-Bass Inc., Publishers.

INDEX